Drawing Down the Spirits

Drawing Down the Spirits

The Traditions and Techniques of Spirit Possession

Kenaz Filan
and
Raven Kaldera

Destiny Books
Rochester, Vermont

Destiny Books
One Park Street
Rochester, Vermont 05767
www.DestinyBooks.com

Destiny Books is a division of Inner Traditions International

Library of Congress Cataloging-in-Publication Data
Filan, Kenaz.
Drawing down the spirits : the traditions and techniques of spirit possession / Kenaz Filan and Raven Kaldera.
p. cm.
Includes index.
Summary: "An insider's view of the inner workings and prevalence of spirit possession in our modern world"—Provided by publisher.
ISBN 978-1-59477-269-6
1. Spirit possession. 2. Witchcraft. I. Kaldera, Raven. II. Title.
BL482.F56 2009
133.4'26—dc22

2008052637

Printed and bound in the United States by Lake Book Manufacturing

10 9 8 7 6 5 4 3 2 1

Text design and layout by Virginia Scott Bowman
This book was typeset in Garamond Premiere Pro with Legacy Sans, Gil Sans, Delphin, and Mason Alternate as display typefaces

To send correspondence to the authors of this book, mail a first-class letter to the authors c/o Inner Traditions • Bear & Company, One Park Street, Rochester, VT 05767, and we will forward the communication.

Contents

PART THREE

The Spirits

PART FOUR

Possession

PART FIVE

The Community

PART SIX

The Future

Prologue
Wild Horses

Kenaz's Story
July 1994

He sits atop the garbage can, his skin dingy dust-gray as the shirt he's been wearing for the past four weeks. He chuckles to himself. If you saw only the bottom of his face, you might think he was laughing at some private joke or celebrating whatever passes for good fortune in his world. The eyes give him away; nobody could mistake them for human.

Nobody who was watching, that is. In New York City you turn away from homeless people; you pretend they're not there and hope they'll return the favor. Those of us who have lived on the streets know better; we know the angels and devils who live in the subways and alleys, the sad and the mad and those who have been touched by . . . something else.

People like him. People like me.

This is what demonic possession looks like. The smile becomes a rictus, something you might see in the final stages of lockjaw or rabies. The motions are jerky as the new host tries to acclimate itself to a meat body with all its quirks and shortcomings. First the gaze goes dark and hollow; the aura feels like a husk, like a paralyzed wasp waiting for the larva to break through. Then comes the cold light in the eyes as the parasite takes control.

Is this how it ends for me? I wonder.

Don't worry, child, Legba whispers in his velvety baritone.

The chuckling turns to muttering obscenities. The demon takes a long swig from the half-pint of vodka at his side, then stares at me. For a couple of seconds I catch his eye; tendrils slither around me. The air smells of reptiles and rot with a sweet undertone, like crack smoke in the dragon's den. I turn my head away.

I told you, don't worry, Legba says. *Remember what I told you? Legba's going to show you everything.*

The demoniac's muttering turns to high, shrieking laughter. I walk away, afraid of what I might see reflected in his eyes.

Legba's going to show you everything.

I nod to the voice in my head and try to believe his promises of sanity. Because I have no other choice, I succeed.

Raven's Tale

1981–1988

At sixteen, it began, and I didn't know what to call it.

I had no history of mental illness, including dissociation—no repressed sexual abuse, no repressed anything, really—so I didn't understand it when my vision would blur, I would feel as if I was falling, and then I would hear through a fog a distant voice speaking to the friend next to me. It was my voice, or at least it came through my vocal cords, but it didn't sound like me. When I would come back into myself a minute later, they would be staring at me as if I'd grown horns. Once a friend asked me, "How did you know that?"

I didn't know anything, and I told her. She informed me that I had called her by a name that was known only to herself. I had to come up with some kind of explanation, so I said, "Well, maybe I picked it up from your thoughts. Don't worry, whatever it was, it's gone. I don't remember it. It went right through me." Apparently I also told her to do something, but she didn't say what, and I didn't ask. Even then, I knew that hearing these things was not for me.

But I also knew that I hadn't picked up anything from her thoughts. That was a hastily crafted lie, spoken for both our comfort. That hadn't been me who had said those things, and I had no idea what had been spoken. Another presence had moved into my body and shoved me aside, and I could only flounder as it used me and moved on. It occurred about every four to six months, just often enough to make me doubt my sanity.

I wondered if I'd somehow developed multiple personalities, and I searched my head for them—and found nothing. I wrote notes to myself, pleading with myself, telling whoever was in there to at least write something back, but there didn't seem to be anyone in my head but me. After a while, I decided that this had to be external, because it felt so very . . . inhuman. It felt bigger than me, much bigger. I was like a cowering child next to these Presences—and yes, there was more than one of them, which seemed even more worrisome.

I started watching them, observing in the moment before I "went away," psychically "sniffing" the scent when I came back—and I figured out that one of them, anyway, was the goddess who had been talking to me off and on since my childhood. I didn't know Her name at the time, but I knew that She was a Death, and that She had some kind of a strong connection to me. Nailing down this fact was both a relief and a greater terror—my body was being borrowed by deities, but why? How? And what would this entail?

I joined a local Wiccan coven, but the high priestess was young and unsure of what to do about my situation. At first she told me that it was just "drawing down," although she'd never heard of it happening spontaneously, not in a circle via a trained high priestess. The other possibility, she said ominously, was that I was being possessed by "lesser creatures." I was pretty sure this wasn't the case, although I had no way to prove it. I witnessed her "drawing down" the generic Wiccan goddess soon afterward, and since I have always been able to see auras, I noticed the way that her aura changed . . . its colors became brighter, more glittery, with a hint of another Presence. Is that what it looks like when it happens to me? I wondered. But I was young and untrained, and they told me that I couldn't do "high priestess stuff" until I was older and more experienced, so I resigned myself to waiting.

Then a visiting Pagan from another group mentioned Vodou folk, and that they do spirit-possession as a matter of course. My head jerked up, and I felt my high priestess's eyes on me from across the room. I didn't know where to go in order to find any Vodou people, and I wasn't sure that they would even let white folks in, so the information didn't seem all that useful. However, a week later that visiting Pagan called me up and gave me the contact for an Umbanda house (an Afro-Brazilian group) about an hour away from me. They had a lot of white folks, or so he'd heard; maybe they could do something for me.

At seventeen, I ran away from my parents' house and began to live on my own, but it was still years before I was able to follow up on that contact and hesitantly introduce myself. How do you say to a group of colorfully dressed strangers, "I think that gods are borrowing my body, and how do I make it stop?" Because it hadn't stopped; in fact, it had become more frequent. It felt like a violation, and control freak that I was, it frightened and shamed me. To my surprise, the House Mama was entirely sympathetic—this was hardly the first time that someone had come to her with this problem—and she turned me over to her assistants, to be taught the practicalities of god-possession. Drinking salt water, putting cold water on the back of the neck, and non-rhythmic activities could put off possessions for a while. The real issue, though, she cautioned me, was that I had to make proper alliances with the spirits who wanted to ride me. It was the first time that I heard the terms *horse* and *ridden* . . . and discovered that this gift/curse that had chosen me could not be unchosen.

Later that month, I went to a *bembe* (an Umbanda ceremony) and stood with my back to the wall, shaking, as three people became possessed. I watched their auras, and it was not like what I'd seen happen to my former high priestess—or perhaps it was along the same lines, but far more intense. Their auras simply shrank away to almost nothing, and Something Else blossomed in their place—something with an aura that reached out across the room, bright and powerful like nothing I'd seen in a body before. Although it seemed to center on their dancing, stalking, screaming, or prone forms, it looked more like an anchoring point than anything else. The Presence spun around the centerpoint of their bodies, and looking at it made me shake and twitch even more.

One of them came straight for me: Ogoun, the Hunter. He grabbed me by the arm and spun me out of the crowd, but it wasn't just as a dance partner. His grip flung me to the floor in front of one of the altars—purple-draped, copper-crowned, set with old-fashioned fans. My forehead touched the edge of the small coffee table, and I was gone. Oya moved into me like a whirlwind, and then there was nothing except flashes of my vision spinning around like a dervish. She taught me something in passing, did Oya, the Lady of storm and wind and the cemetery. *This is part of what you are for,* she said as she left me.

I learned what I could from the Umbanda house, but while they helped me to understand the phenomenon, and at least no longer doubt my sanity, they could not tell me who the Presences were who moved through me. It would be years before I discovered their names and their motives. In the meantime, the Umbandistas gently shooed me out the door, and I went back to the Neo-Pagan community—or what passed for it at the time—armed with new knowledge explained in no popular Pagan books of the day.

Introduction

THIS IS THE WAY THAT THE STORY GOES, according to a friend who claims to have seen it happen: It was the mid-1980s, and they were part of a traditional Wiccan coven. There was going to be a Drawing Down the Moon, that rite in which the Goddess speaks through the female leader of the group. Lately, instead of merely calling the Goddess by her many names, the coven had been calling specific goddesses . . . Aphrodite for love, Demeter for healing of the Earth. Tonight they were calling Athena to bless them with clear minds and knowledge. As usual for a Gardnerian-style coven, they were skyclad—nude except for their sacred jewelry.

On this night, however, something happened that they did not expect during the chanting of the rite. The priestess suddenly jerked, and then her head came up with a glare that they had never seen in her eyes before. Chills ran down the spines of every man and woman present. The figure in the center of the circle stared down at her body, lifted her head again, and demanded in a compelling and resonant voice, *"Why am I naked?!"*

She proceeded to tell them what incompetent fools they all were, and how they were completely unworthy of her blessings. Then the priestess collapsed, and the Presence was gone, leaving the coven frozen and unable to speak. Later, some blamed the priestess for deliberately ruining the circle in order to get attention. Others were more certain that the voice that chastised them didn't belong to her at all. Someone bothered to look up Athena and discover more about her than the brief paragraph that the coven members who had suggested invoking her had absorbed from their high school ancient history class. She found that Athena was never shown in the nude; it would be a great sacrilege to do so. In fact, her statue was regularly dressed in many changes of fine robes, and a new cloak was ritually crafted for her every year by local weavers. A Jungian-archetype Athena—the Cliffs Notes version of a real deity—might not have cared, but the actual Athena had let the coven know exactly how wrong they were.

This situation never happened a second time with this particular coven, as the priestess was fairly traumatized by the event and refused to draw down any more goddesses for some time. The coven broke up soon afterward for other reasons. The incident became something of a legend among the local Wiccan groups, and eventually found its way into the greater Pagan community. Most Pagans didn't know what to think about the idea of being possessed by a deity, just like that, but for the most part it made them uncomfortable. Possession was something done by evil spirits, like in *The Exorcist,* right? If they had some knowledge of Afro-Caribbean religious practices, they might associate it with those traditions, but even that seemed rather far-fetched and alien to a modern Western spiritual tradition. There was also the fear of being seen as foolish, or delusional, or manipulative. After all, how could one defend it to the skeptics? It all had the air of the madhouse to Pagans, who prided themselves on being rational people. The actual deliberate practice of spirit-possession for ritual purposes veered between being discouraged and being disbelieved entirely. And so it was pushed aside into oblivion . . . except that people kept getting possessed, sometimes by entities who claimed to be the gods whom those people claimed to be worshipping.

In the last ten years, spirit-possession as a phenomenon has gained new ground in many places. People are becoming more knowledgeable and informed about the traditional faiths that practice it, such as the African-diaspora religions. Interest in shamanic traditions from all over the world is growing, and seekers find that spirit-possession is an integral part of many (although not all) of those practices. New Age channelers are letting spirits who claim to be ascended spiritual masters speak through their mouths to give general advice to ordinary people. In Neo-Pagan communities—the demographic where educated white Westerners are most likely to be in close quarters with polytheism and animism—possession of willing and unwilling people by ancient gods and goddesses is growing slowly but steadily, sometimes to the dismay of community leaders who are not sure how to handle the phenomenon safely and sensitively.

Roll forward in time, to a Neo-Pagan gathering held in 2004. The drum circle, a regular festival event that consists of a bonfire around which drummers and dancers go at it all night, is in full swing. An attendee who practices Vodou and who is a horse (the Afro-Caribbean term that we will use throughout this book to describe someone whose body regularly hosts gods and/or spirits) comes down to see what this drum circle is all about. She lands next to someone of an entirely different tradition, beating on a shaman-drum. A door is opened, and one of the *lwa* spirits—Ogou, hunter and warrior and smith—takes her body with a mighty cry. That body goes leaping around the circle, yelling, as Ogou is known to do, until he seizes a woman by the hand and pulls her forcibly into the circle to dance.

The woman is also a Vodou practitioner, although she is from a different part of the country and has never met the dancer whose body Ogou holds. She knows Ogou, though, just as he recognizes her, and smiles with delight. After a minute, the possession ends, and the horse stumbles out of the circle. She is promptly surrounded by a team of well-meaning festival first-aiders who think that they have a bad drug trip, some sort of seizure, or a psychotic break on their hands. They crowd the horse, trying to get her to respond, and generally make her state worse. Other well-meaning people come up after she manages to reassure them, telling her that she really needs therapy, or to get all her dark stuff out by dancing more. The next day, rumors fly that the horse flipped out and attacked a woman in the crowd. The shaman whose drum brought the spirit through her feels vaguely responsible for the turmoil of misunderstanding, but also feels strongly that Ogou wanted to come through, wanted his dance and his moment around the fire. It would have gone much better if there had been a cultural context for such things, not to mention a safety net of people who knew what to do before, during, and after the event.

That's why we wrote this book. We are both veterans of multiple spiritual communities and religious views, and have both researched the phenomenon independently. Kenaz Filan is a long-term practitioner of Vodou with a ten-year membership in Société la Belle Venus #2, a Vodou temple in Brooklyn, and also has links to the Neo-Pagan community. Raven Kaldera is a Northern Tradition Pagan shaman who spent six months in an Umbanda house many years ago. We are also the horse and the shaman in the story above. The next day we met, talked, and both decided that people need more useful and practical education about possession, rather than more typical stories told from the anthropologist's distancing eye, watching the "superstitious strangers go through their strange gyrations."

We are also both horses, and have experienced spirit-possession from both sides, in entirely different cultural contexts, and found many similarities and a few differences. This gives us an admitted bias, for which we will not apologize. This book is written from the perspective of fully and actually believing in the gods and spirits whom we love, respect, serve, and occasionally host in our flesh. While we will try, in these pages, to be as objective as possible, we are unashamed believers in the reality—and sacredness—of ritual possession. This attitude permeates our writing and our lives, and gives us the insider's view of these happenings. If you're looking for something in a more skeptical, material-rationalist, isn't-this-quaint-and-sociologically-interesting vein, this is not the book for you . . . because that attitude will never give any aid or useful information to people who are really dealing with real spirit-possession in their real lives.

For the purposes of this book, a *possession experience* is one in which the subject's identity is subsumed into that of Someone or Something Else. She or he loses all control over speech and actions for a period of time, during which the other entity takes control of her or him. This can be, but is not always, accompanied by a fugue state where the subject has little or no memory of what transpired during the possession. There may also be physical manifestations of various sorts.

In the pages of this book, we interviewed many people in and out of the Neo-Pagan community who had seen or experienced ritual possession, often as part of planned events. Unless there was good reason to think otherwise, we have assumed that the people quoted herein were being truthful to the best of their ability. If they said "I was possessed," we've generally credited their report as a possession experience. There are times when we suggest that certain passages from poems, legends, or the like describe possession. However, we have tried to avoid redefining the experience of others to fit our theories. Accordingly, we've distinguished between primary testimony and speculations thereon.

Allowing spiritual horses to define their possession states would seem to be reasonable enough, yet this definition also comes with its problems. There are innumerable reasons why an individual might falsely claim that she or he was possessed. "Demoniacs" can shriek obscenities at authority figures, discuss the most taboo sexual topics at length, and even physically attack others without being held responsible for their misbehavior. False "channelers" can make large sums of money for dispensing wisdom as Atlantean Masters or Lemurian Priest-Kings. Aspiring religious leaders can gain great power over their devotees by convincing them "it is not I who commands you, it is our deity who commands you through me." As long as someone receives some form of positive reinforcement, he or she has motivation to fake a possession.

On the other hand, there are many reasons why someone might want to write off genuine possession experiences as fraud. In cultures where spirit-possession is widely accepted, there is frequently keen economic competition between spiritual practitioners. When asked about Priest X's qualifications, Priestess Y may well say, "He runs around acting like he has the spirits, but he's just pretending so that he can take your money. You should talk to *my* spirit instead . . ." Established religions frequently go to great lengths in order to silence "heretics" and "false prophets." Their income and power is based largely on their role as intercessors between humanity and the Divine; hence, they have every incentive to discredit those who might usurp that role.

Distinguishing possession from a trance journey, or from an attempt to feign possession for the horse's own purposes, requires knowledge of the horse's interior state—and knowing what is going on in someone else's mind is, of course, a very difficult task indeed. We can examine the behavior of a person who is purportedly possessed, but we cannot know conclusively the motivation for that behavior. Even a horse who believes sincerely that she is possessed could be experiencing a medical crisis, not a spiritual one.

Assuming that we can establish that something is a genuine possession and not playacting or a mental illness, we are then faced with another difficult question: possession by who or what? A dervish *sema* (whirling ceremony) leads to a loss of identity and a feeling of union with Allah. At a Pentecostal revival, you might see members of the congregation "slain in the spirit" or "filled with my Lord Jesus." A Yogi in Mumbai or Sonoma might practice Yoga for years until at last they attain Nirvikalpa Samadhi, or absorption into the Atman or Oversoul. Are they experiencing the same thing? Is the St. Philomena who is honored at Our Lady of Grace Church in Mugnano, Italy, the same St. Philomena who possesses devotees at ceremonies in Haiti and Trinidad? And what if two devotees, one in Havana and one in Brooklyn, are simultaneously possessed by an entity that identifies Herself as Oshun?

And, of course, there is the most central question of all: What does the average person who has not been raised in a culture that accepts spirit-possession do when they find themselves suddenly getting regularly possessed . . . and not by something that acts like a "typical" evil spirit? What does the leader of a Pagan religious group do when one of its members becomes possessed by one of the deities that revere the group?

As you can see, even though we now know *what* we are talking about, we still need to address the questions of *how* the possession experience happens, *why* it occurs, and what to do about it when it happens to you, or to someone around you.

PART ONE

The Past

I

Metaphysics and History

A Long View of Spirit-Possession

THE MEANINGS OF "POSSESSION"

When writing a book on possession, one might begin by asking, "What does the word *possession* mean?" And so we start by consulting the dictionary—or, more precisely, by checking dictionary.com, where we find:

> 1: the act of having and controlling property [syn: ownership] 2: anything owned or possessed 3: being controlled by passion or the supernatural 4: a mania restricted to one thing or idea [syn: monomania] 5: a territory that is controlled by a ruling state 6: the trait of resolutely controlling your own behavior [syn: self-control, self-possession, willpower, self-command, self-will] 7: (sport) the act of controlling the ball (or puck); "they took possession of the ball on their own goal line"[1]

You may think that only the third definition meets our purposes. However, the others also deserve careful consideration. They reinforce that *to possess* is *to have ownership and/or control of something.* Possession may last for an instant (as when a football team gains possession of the ball) or it may last for generations ("Our family has held possession of this land since the Revolutionary War" or "Puerto Rico and Guam are United States possessions"). It can involve a thing ("Among my most cherished possessions are my LP collection and my great-aunt's credenza") or an emotional state ("Possessed by gambling fever, I lost my life savings at the blackjack table").

POSSESSION AND THE LAW

Of course, questions of control and ownership can be quite difficult and emotionally charged: as a result, a long tradition of laws and customs connected with possession has risen. Today the law recognizes several varieties of possession. *Actual possession,* for example, is the direct occupancy, use, or control of real property. If you rent an apartment or lease a car, you have actual possession even though you do not hold the title to the property. The person who owns something is frequently not the person who controls it. Warring parties may argue over the division of property and things in an estate, and possessing stolen items does not make one their rightful owner. If you are delinquent in your obligations to the leaseholder, they can seek to regain control of their property by *repossessing* it. But if you hold control over the property for an extended period of time and the owner makes no effort to assert his rights, you may be able to assert "squatter's rights," or *adverse possession.* Something may be owned and/or controlled by one person (*sole possession*) or shared by any number of people (*joint possession*).

A similar dynamic comes into play when we are discussing the possession experience. The *horse's* property—his or her body—is controlled by Something Else. This loss of control can be involuntary—she or he may even call on higher authorities (otherwise known as "exorcists") to settle the dispute—or it may be a voluntary loss of ego for the benefit of one's clients or congregation. The possession may be partial: the horse may retain some memory of the proceedings, or she or he may be shunted off to the Cosmic Waiting Room and remember nothing of the trance. In some traditions, an initiation ceremony may prepare the candidate to become a horse.* The spirit is "mounted" or placed *within* the prospective medium; from that moment onward, it shares ownership of the medium's body and can use it to speak, move, and work magic.

In other traditions, spirits can be passed on through a genetic or spiritual lineage. After the death of a *houngan* or *mambo* (priest or priestess of Vodou, respectively), some or all of the lwa who possessed them may later possess other members of the congregation. (Indeed, one of the reasons for joining a Vodou *société* is access to its *rasin lwa,* or "root spirits.") A Vodouisant (follower of Vodou) who angers or offends his lwa may find that they no longer wish to possess him. To restore their working relationship, she or he will throw *fets* (parties) on their behalf or make other offerings or sacrifices. Similarly, a lwa who troubles its horse through overly violent possessions or unreasonable demands may be "bound" with new restrictions through the intervention of a skilled priest or priestess.

METAPHYSICS AND DANGERS

Although many agree that possession is dangerous (or, at the very least, something to be avoided), there is considerable disagreement as to just *why* this is. Some warn solemnly of "demonic oppression" as "Satanic" entities feast on your soul as on a cosmic pizza. Others explain that experimenting with possession will exacerbate your neuroses and lead to full-blown schizophrenia. ("You'll put out somebody's EGO with that thing!") Still others will inform you that possession doesn't exist, and your experiments will lead only to wasted time and self-delusion.

All these people are using the word *possession,* but they are defining it quite differently. To understand their objections, we must first

*In Vodou a person possessed by a lwa is said to be a *chwal* (Kreyol for "horse," from the French *cheval*). In Lukumi and other forms of Afro-Cuban spirituality, the person who is being "ridden" by an orisha is called a *caballo* (horse). Today many spirit-workers in other traditions use the word *horse* to describe a possessed person.

determine what they are talking about. In order to make practical use of their data, we must turn to something that may at first appear singularly impractical—metaphysics.

Speculation about our essential nature and the nature of the world around us evokes smoky French cafés, or maybe cannabis-scented dorm rooms. Navel gazing and contemplation about "reality" is useful only as an amusing diversion, you may think; surely it has little bearing on our daily lives. But when dealing with possession, we should first take some time to determine just *what* is going to be stepping into our heads and taking control of our bodies. One of the best ways to do that is to explore how others have explained—or failed to explain—this phenomenon.

POSSESSION AS A TOOL OF THE DEVIL

> . . . there was an old Indian who answered them according to their expectations or in accordance with a consultation addressed to him whose evil image was standing there; and it is to be thought that the Devil entered into him and spoke through him as through his minister.
>
> **—Gonzalo Fernández de Oviedo, describing the medicine men of Hispaniola, 1535**[2]

The first Europeans to encounter possession among "primitive" peoples believed in a personal devil, and in witches and sorcerers who paid homage to him and to his minions. They also believed that sometimes these devils would possess people. When they saw tribesmen going to the village healer for potions and fetish items, they assumed the healer was acting as a "sorcerer." When they saw the healer writhing on the ground or acting in a bizarre fashion, they considered this the inevitable consequence of "devil worship."

Today this sounds like the worst sort of bigotry, but at the time it was a perfectly logical conclusion. The phenomena these explorers were witnessing could easily be explained within their belief structure. If they had not seen "demoniacs" up close and personal, they were certainly familiar with the symptoms of this condition. The accoutrements that often accompany shamanic practices—drums, wild dancing, genuflecting before idols—would have evoked old wives' tales of the Witches' Sabbath. They had no reason to question their conclusions; the evidence in favor of their paradigm was (to them) overwhelming.

If you think that this biased view on possession is held solely by Christians, think again. Vedic Hindus look down on those who have incorporated possession experience into their service of the gods. (One swami has even blamed Kali Ma worship, which often involves possession by the Great Mother, for incest among Guyanese and Trinidadian devotees![3]) Greek authorities sought to stamp out the Maenads and their Dionsysian trances as a threat to the social order. In Java, centuries of Islamic rule has nearly wiped out the trance-possession culture that still flourishes on Bali.[4]

This is not entirely surprising. Leaders generally favor well-defined roles, preferably with themselves at or near the top. Books and sacred scriptures can be carved in stone, printed in authoritative editions, and subjected to Official Interpretation (accept no heretical substitutes). Official ceremonies can be choreographed and scripted: inconvenient or embarrassing beliefs can be deprecated, minimalized, or written out of existence. Religious leaders gain much of their power by acting as intercessors between their congregations and the divine. That office becomes far less important when the rabble can talk with their gods up close and personal.

The gods cannot be so easily censored or controlled. There is a difference between acting as the mouthpiece of the divine and actually being that mouthpiece. Like children, gods frequently blurt out uncomfortable truths. They may not offer unconditional support for the ruling party or the priests; in fact, they may call the leaders on the carpet and castigate them for insufficient devotion. They may not come bearing blessings and promises of future prosperity; indeed, they often come to deliver dire warnings.

This is not to say that there is nothing to claims of "demonic possession." Most cultures that encourage positive possessions also speak of negative spiritual entities. (See Harmful Possessions in chapter 11.) A great deal of the practical work connected with preparing a possession ritual involves purifications of the space and the participants (see chapter 9, Sacred Spaces). We should make allowances for the prejudices of these early reporters, but we should also make allowances for our own. Saying "not all possessions are harmful" is not at all the same thing as saying that none is.

POSSESSION AS FRAUD

> SHAMANS, noun, masc. plural is the name that the inhabitants of Siberia give to imposters who perform the functions of priests, jugglers, sorcerers, and doctors.
>
> **—Denis Diderot, Encyclopédie, 1765[5]**

Later, much of that parochial worldview would be jettisoned, as the Renaissance became the Enlightenment and the Age of Faith gave way to a new Age of Reason—and skepticism. Anticlerical feelings abounded, as people sought to break the shackles of superstition. Wracked by Catholic and Protestant wars as Reformation ran headlong into Counter-Reformation, many Enlightenment-era Europeans cast a jaded eye on all religious belief, so when they encountered possession, they assumed it was fraud, and that the horses were playacting to gain control over their gullible followers. Where earlier observers saw possession experiences as a sign that Non-Christian Religions Are Dangerous, the children of the Enlightenment saw it as evidence that You Can't Trust Priests.

Few scholars today would dismiss horses as mountebanks or imposters, but that does not mean that they take their claims at face value. They might not say that a shaman is a "con artist"—but they would discuss at length the "social functions" served by their "performance."

They might have once said the horse was faking possession for personal gain, but now they might say that the shaman fakes possession for sociological reasons. The language became less accusatory, but the end result is the same: the possession experience is reduced to an elaborate game of "let's pretend."

Attacking from this angle allows the scientist to explore the ways in which a society reacts to possession. It allows us to explore the theology that has developed around possession, or tensions between pro-possession and anti-possession factions in a society. It allows us to catalog the behaviors associated with the "possession performance." It also allows us to study possession without recourse to a spiritual realm. Many theorists believe that drama and theater began as possession rituals. There are certainly theatrical aspects to many possessions—and there are actors whose role-playing may at times border on an actual possession experience, and there certainly are people who fake possessions for one reason or another (see chapter 13, Recognizing Fakes and Frauds); even cultures that recognize possession generally recognize the possibility of fraud.

But this fails to address one major problem: In their own language and by their own account, possessed people are *not controlling the experience*. They do not claim to be "performing" or "play-acting." Rather, they claim that someone or something else is speaking through them. In reinterpreting their experience to suit our own theories and preconceptions, do we fall into the same trap as the missionaries who redefined other religions as "devil worship"?

Some scholars have been more willing to take their subjects at their word. They accepted claims that horses lost control of their bodies and that they were not consciously speaking or acting when in a possession trance. But because these scholars did not accept the existence of spiritual beings, they had to find some alternate explanation. Instead of accepting the shaman's belief system, they tried to explain away possession using the language of disease.

POSSESSION AS ILLNESS

> Cases of demoniacal possession correspond to the neurosis of the present day . . . What are thought to be evil spirits to us are evil wishes, the derivatives of impulses which have been rejected and repressed . . . We have abandoned the projection of them into the outer world, attributing their origin instead to the inner life of the patient in whom they manifest themselves.
>
> **—Sigmund Freud, 1923**[6]

Afterward, other scholars tried to explain away possession using the new language of medicine, especially mental health theories. They saw a shaman writhe and dance about madly and assumed that possession was a form of psychosis. They heard priests talking in "spirit language," which sounded like animal howls and gibberish, and decided possession was like schizophrenia. The explanations were different, but the overriding message remained the same: Possession was the hallmark of a "savage" culture, one that was morally and culturally inferior. As the psychologist T. K. Oesterreich wrote in 1921: "Possession begins to disappear among civilized races as soon as belief in spirits loses its power. From the moment that they cease to entertain seriously the possibility of being possessed, the necessary auto-suggestion is lacking."[7]

It is certainly easy to see how a clinician might be confused. Quite a few psychiatric conditions can mimic the symptoms of a possession experience. Schizophrenics will frequently feel as though their ego is shattering or dissolving. Often they will identify their own thoughts as voices coming from outside their bodies. "Word salad"—strings of words, phrases, and sounds thrown together via strange logical connections—can mark both a florid schizophrenic experience and trance possession. Other clinicians pointed to dissociative identity disorder and suggested that the various personalities that spoke through mediums were merely coping strategies.

Yet other observers looked for neurological explanations. When they saw shamans fall to the ground, they assumed that possession was a form of epilepsy. Still others noted the harsh living conditions found in many shamanic cultures, as well as the rigorous initiation and other ordeal rituals, and explained the possession experience as a chemical imbalance. (In northern Eurasia, with its long winter nights, the activities of Siberian shamans were put down to "arctic hysteria," a supposed mega-version of what modern doctors would call seasonal affective disorder.) Whether brought about by sleep deprivation, ingestion of mind-altering herbs, malnutrition or other stressors, the bizarre behavior associated with trance possession was considered a reasonable effect of natural causes.

There are definitely situations when a clinical and scientific approach can prove useful. Mistaking mental illness for possession (or vice versa) can have catastrophic consequences. Indeed, most possession cultures draw clear distinctions between insanity and possession, but these distinctions can be subtle. Learning the boundaries between acceptable and unacceptable behavior can be a Herculean task for any outsider seeking to understand a culture. To further complicate matters, many Victorian and Edwardian gentle scholars defined sanity and insanity by the rules of their own culture. Behavior that would be deviant in a London drawing room or Boston teaching auditorium was equally deviant in a Malaysian village or a Nigerian temple. By this standard, there was no reason to distinguish between possession and mental illness. Both were unacceptable in polite company and hence both were signs of insanity or disease.

Once again, "primitive" people were denied the right to define their own experiences. Their disconcerting alien behavior was placed within a safe and comfortable scientific paradigm for the benefit of scholars and curious onlookers. In defining possession as a disease, we added an unspoken assumption that it could be, and indeed needed to be, cured. Given the right drug, the right diet, or a few sessions with the right therapist, spirit-horses could be "fixed" and become sane, productive, and "normal" members of a proper and "civilized" society.

SPIRITUALISM: POSSESSION AS LABORATORY EXPERIMENT

In 1843 Dr. James Stanley Grimes, a professor of jurisprudence at Castleton Medical College, gave a lecture on mesmerism in Poughkeepsie, New York. Introduced by an Austrian doctor named Franz Mesmer (1733–1815), this technique of "magnetic healing" had been repeatedly debunked as fraud by scientific and medical societies in France and elsewhere in Europe. Because these commissions could not explain the trance states that Mesmer was able to invoke, they had declared the whole thing to be chicanery or autosuggestion. But while mesmerism had gone out of fashion on the Continent, it was still the height of fashion in a more rustic America. Still, attendees at Dr. Grimes's Poughkeepsie lecture might have recalled the skeptics as Grimes failed to mesmerize a seventeen-year-old named Andrew Jackson Davis.

Despite this failure, Davis continued experimenting with mesmerism. A short time later his interest paid off: A local tailor named William Livingston succeeded where Dr. Grimes had failed and successfully put Davis in a mesmeric trance. While so entranced, Davis displayed many of the symptoms and signs that had baffled those scientists. He was able to read from closed books; he was also able to detect illnesses and prescribe treatments. Davis claimed that when he was entranced, the human body became transparent to his spirit eyes; each organ stood out clearly and shone with a special luminosity of its own, this light being greatly diminished in cases of disease.

On the evening of March 6, 1844, Davis was suddenly thrown into a trance by some outside power. This led him to "fly" from his Poughkeepsie home in a semi-trance state: so entranced, he had a life-changing encounter with two spirits, who identified themselves as the Roman physician Galen (129–ca. 199) and the Swedish scientist, philosopher, and visionary Emanuel Swedenborg (1688–1772). Galen lectured, Davis on the many ways in which people were violating natural laws; Swedenborg told him, "Thou hast become an appropriate vessel for the influx and perception of truth and wisdom . . . By thee will a new light appear . . ."[8]

From this moment forward, Davis dedicated himself tirelessly to public lectures and classes on spiritualism. While entranced, Davis would offer erudite observations on scientific matters and ancient texts. In 1845 Davis began dictating from trance *The Principles of Nature: Her Divine Revelations and A Voice to Mankind*; upon its release in 1847, *Principles* would become one of the most popular works of the decade. Although he had little formal education, Davis would go on to write other bestsellers, such as *The Great Harmonia* (1852), *The Temple: On Diseases of the Brain and Nerves* (1871), and *Views of Our Heavenly Home* (1883), with the aid of spiritual inspiration.

Inspired by his example, and by the "spirit rappings" of the Fox sisters, a generation of Americans became obsessed with Spiritualism and various phenomena. In 1852 Boston trance medium Maria Hayden began an extended tour of Great Britain, and soon the craze that was sweeping America established roots in Europe as well. In France an academic named Hippolyte Léon Denizard Rivail (1804–1869) became fascinated with table-rappings and other phenomena associated with Spiritualist séances. Working with trance mediums and Spiritualists, he compiled (under the pseudonym Allan Kardec) a number of channeled works that discussed the spirit world. By the 1880s, millions had declared themselves Spiritualists, and suddenly events that had earlier been studied only by explorers or colonial officials were occurring in middle-class homes.

Spiritualism provided a means for Victorian women to achieve personal and financial independence; a skilled medium could earn a comfortable living—and many, perhaps most, of the most famous mediums were female. With the aid of her spirit guide "Demosthenes," Victoria C. Woodhull was able to launch a popular magazine (*Woodhull and Clafin's Weekly*), open her own brokerage firm (with some help from one of her admirers, Commodore Vanderbilt), and make an 1872 presidential run at a time when women could not vote. Another medium, the beautiful Cora L. V. Hatch, was toasted in an 1857 article as "the intellectual wonder of the age" for the flowery speeches she gave while in a mediumistic trance. Spiritualists also played important roles in other reform movements—Harriet Beecher Stowe, author of *Uncle Tom's Cabin,* was a devoted Spiritualist who in 1849 reminded skeptical clergymen that "the Bible distinctly says that there is a class of invisible spirits who minister to the children of men."[9]

A few intellectuals took these anomalous events seriously. In 1866 Alfred Russell Wallace, one of England's most famous naturalists, wrote *The Scientific Aspect of the Supernatural,* a book that discussed Spiritualism in a positive light. The noted physicist Sir Oliver Lodge discussed his experiences with Spiritualism and contacts with his deceased son in *Raymond: or, Life and Death* (1916). Other devoted Spiritualists were Sir Arthur Conan Doyle and New York Supreme Court Judge John Worth Edmonds, who resigned his position on account of the outcry raised against his beliefs and went on to write several tracts on Spiritualism. Spiritualist and ex-governor of Wisconsin Territory Nathaniel P. Tallmadge wrote that those who doubted Spiritualist claims were "far behind the intelligence of the age [in which] . . . mesmerism and clairvoyance . . . are considered by intelligent and scientific men as well established as electricity and magnetism."[10]

As time went on, the phenomena associated with Spiritualism became ever more spectacular. Sitting in darkened rooms, clients might feel the touch of "ectoplasmic hands" as the spirits descended; they might hear not rappings but the blowing of "spirit trumpets"; they might find the table at which they sat turning or even levitating. In Buffalo thirteen-year-old Ira Davenport and his fifteen-year-old brother, William, became famous for making musical instruments play while they were securely bound inside their "spirit cabinet." William Mumler, a Boston engraver married to a trance medium, attracted widespread attention with his 1868 exhibition of "spirit pictures"; other mediums used "direct writing," placing a pencil stub inside a closed writing slate and allowing the spirit to write without human assistance.

But while some scholars gave credence to Spiritualism's claims, many more were skeptical. In 1887 the Seybert Commission on Spiritualism (founded by wealthy Spiritualist Henry Seybert) presented a scathing report on Spiritualism. It found "that as soon as an investigation, worthy of the name begins, all manifestations of Spiritualist power cease" and that Spiritualism "presents the melancholy spectacle of gross fraud, perpetrated upon an uncritical portion of the community."[11] In 1888 the Fox sisters, now impoverished alcoholics, confessed that their séances were fraud and their "spirit knockings" caused by Margaret Fox's double-jointed big toe. Later, Harry Houdini would expose many other "mediums" as frauds: as a trained magician, he was able to spot sleights-of-hand and parlor tricks that mystified many observers. Soon science began following the lead of T. H. Huxley, who snarled, "If anybody would endow me with the faculty of listening to the chatter of old women and curates in the nearest cathedral town, I should decline the privilege, having better things to do. And if the folk in the spiritual world do not talk more wisely and sensibly than their friends report them to do, I put them in the same category. The only good that I can see in the demonstration of the truth of 'Spiritualism' is to furnish an additional argument against suicide. Better live a crossing-sweeper than die and be made to talk twaddle by a 'medium' hired at a guinea a séance."[12]

After a dismal series of debunkings, it became clear that the legitimate trance-possessions going on in Spiritualism had been outnumbered and overshadowed by overenthusiastic or avaricious frauds, motivated by the public's need for thrilling entertainment. The entire issue of otherworldly spirits and spirit-possession became stained with the disrepute of table-tappers and fake ectoplasm, and both researchers and the religious quickly distanced themselves from it. There were exceptions—Britain's Society for Psychical Research, founded in 1882 by a number of Cambridge scientists, is still in operation—but by and large the academic establishment dealt with these strange events by ignoring them . . . a nonresponse that continues to this day.

INTO CHANNELING: SPIRITUALISM MEETS THEOSOPHY

In 1874, a wealthy attorney named Henry S. Olcott arrived at a Chittenden, Vermont, guesthouse. He was hoping to debunk the innkeepers, two purported "mediums" named Horatio and William Eddy, and thereby discredit the burgeoning Spiritualist movement. Olcott spent ten weeks at their unkempt home, examining the place thoroughly and attending séances that featured as many as thirty visible manifestations and which included rappings; the disturbance of material objects from a state of rest; painting in oil and watercolors under influence; prophecy; the speaking of strange tongues; the healing gift, the discernment of spirits; levitation, or the floating of the body in free air; the phenomena of instrument playing and the show of hands; the writing of messages on paper flying in midair, by pencils held by detached hands; psychometry, or the reading of character and view of distant persons upon touching scaled letters; clairvoyance; clairaudience, or the hearing of spirit-voices; and, last, and most miraculous of all, the production of materialized phantom forms, which become visible, tangible, and often audible by all persons present.[13]

Olcott left disliking the house, the food, the Eddy brothers, and the state of Vermont but convinced that there was no trickery or fraud involved. He also became fast friends with another attendee at the Eddy séances, Madame Blavatsky. While Blavatsky agreed with Olcott that *something* had happened in Chittenden, and defended the brothers against accusations of fraud, she believed the manifestations were caused by lower astral entities. In 1884 Blavatsky proclaimed, "Occultists do not believe in any communication with the 'spirits of the deceased' in the ordinary acceptation of the term, for the simple reason that they know that the *spirits* of 'the deceased' cannot and do not come down and communicate with us."[14]

Whereas Spiritualists communicated with departed friends, relatives, and loved ones or with deceased "Spirit Guides" who had come to share their wisdom with those on this side of the veil, Blavatsky claimed her "Masters"—Koot Hoomi and Moorya—were alive and well and sending messages from their home base in Tibet. She scornfully rejected any claims that they were spirit guides, insisting "they are living men, born as we are born, and doomed to die like every other mortal."[15]

The confusion was understandable. The Masters spoke with her via telepathy and occasionally by materialized messages that appeared in a dedicated shrine that much resembled a Spiritualist "spirit cabinet." Critics noted that the handwriting on these materialized messages was nearly identical to Blavatsky's, and the books they "inspired" Blavatsky to write contained a great deal of plagiarized material. Those skeptics dismissed her as just another phony medium looking to profit from human gullibility; the fact that her fraud involved mind-reading swamis rather than someone's dearly departed uncle George was of no consequence to them.

Blavatsky's followers, for their part, had little trouble believing her claims. At the time, mountainous Tibet was accessible only to the hardiest explorers and known largely by rumor and legend. India, under British rule, was better known but hardly more understood than Tibet. While reports abounded of "Hindoo superstition," "fire walking," and "fakir marvels," little solid information about Hinduism or other religions of Asia was available; hence, many Europeans saw Asia as a land of powerful mystics and magicians whose inscrutable wisdom could bend the very fabric of reality and whose magic could traverse time and space.

Theosophy retained a distaste for most communications with the deceased. Two years after Blavatsky's 1891 death, Theosophist William Q. Judge expressed contempt for "the spook of the spiritualistic seance-rooms," which was nothing but the "astral shell of the deceased—wholly devoid of his or her spirit and conscience,"[16] and the mediums who promoted "Worship of the Dead, old-fashioned necromancy, in fact, which was always prohibited by spiritual teachers."[17] Theosophy distinguished itself from necromancy by concentrating not on mere dead spirits, but rather on the spirits of those who had "ascended" to a higher state of being. Unlike the Christian-influenced Spiritualism, Theosophy accepted the reality of reincarnation. They believed the Ascended Masters had spent many incarnations in human form and worked through their karma and physical limitations. They were concerned not with mere trickery like rappings and materializations, but in the global spiritual reawakening and transformation of mankind.

These Ascended Masters would inspire many spin-off movements. Alice Bailey (1880–1949) wrote twenty-four books that she claimed were channeled through her by a Tibetan master named Djwhal Khul. Khul identified himself as a representative of a hierarchy of advanced beings who sought to prepare the way for the "Reappearance of the Christ" and usher in the New Age of Aquarius. Khul-inspired works include *Initiation, Human and Solar* and *A Treatise on Cosmic Fire*; many consider them seminal works in the New Age movement. (Khul remains a prolific speaker and writer after Bailey's passing; some of his contemporary channels are Terri Newlon, Kathlyn Kingdon, Moriah Marston, and Violet Starre). Russian painter and explorer Nicholas Roerich (1874–1947) compiled the teachings of Theosophical Master Moorya as channeled by his wife, Helena (1879–1955), to form Agni Yoga, a movement that enjoys widespread popularity in Russia. Their message combined Bailey's emphasis on a new age of human evolution with an emphasis on a coming era when there would be no nations and the world would be ruled under the guidance of the masters of Shambhala, a kingdom existing simultaneously in Central Asia and in another dimension and ruled by masters of the Great White Lodge.

In 1930 a Theosophy student named Guy Ballard (1878–1939) encountered the entity Saint-Germain while hiking on California's Mt. Shasta. Under the pen name Godfré Ray King, Ballard would go on to publish several books detailing his encounters with Saint-Germain, which would serve as the cornerstone of the I AM Movement. Ballard claimed Saint-Germain had pulled gold from the air, tamed a panther, and taken Guy and his wife to a convention of Venusians in the Grand

Tetons.[18] He also taught the use of a Violet Flame meditation and visualization to transform imperfections into perfections until one attained unification with their "I AM," or inner Christ-consciousness.

Interest in the Saint-Germain teachings grew throughout the 1930s, but when Guy Ballard (along with his wife, Edna, and son, Donald) was convicted of mail fraud in 1939, the I AM Movement was nearly destroyed. Even after their conviction was overturned, in 1946, the movement never regained its early momentum. Undeterred, Saint-Germain followed Djwhal Khul's lead and began appearing to other scribes and channels. Among the most famous are Mark Prophet (1918–1973) and his wife, Elizabeth Clare Prophet (b. 1939); with the help of Saint-Germain and other Masters, including Buddha, Confucius, and Jesus, they founded the Summit Lighthouse, an umbrella organization covering groups like the Church Universal and Triumphant and Keepers of the Flame Fraternity. The Prophets would receive information from Saint-Germain about his previous incarnations as Merlin, Roger Bacon, Christopher Columbus, and a Roman soldier named Alban. But while the Ascended Masters were making their presence known, a photographer and aspiring insurance salesman in Hopkinsville, Kentucky, was seeking relief from his chronic laryngitis. He would find a cure—and much more—at the hands of a traveling mesmerist.

EDGAR CAYCE: THE SLEEPING PROPHET

In 1901 a hypnotist called Hart the Laugh Man hypnotized the young, virtually mute Edgar Cayce (1877–1945). While in a trance, Cayce was able to speak; unfortunately, he was once again near mute when he awakened. Hart tried a posthypnotic suggestion that Cayce's recovery would survive his return to normal consciousness, but this proved ineffective. Intrigued, Cayce sought help from a local hypnotist named Al Layne, who hypnotized Cayce and then asked him to describe the condition and the cure.

Cayce announced, "We have the body," then told the hypnotist that blood circulation was increasing to the affected area. Cayce's face became flushed with blood and his chest area turned bright red. After twenty minutes Cayce, still in trance, declared the treatment over; he then awakened and was able to speak normally. After a number of follow-up sessions, the cure turned out to be a permanent one. Layne asked the entranced Cayce to describe his health and any potential dangers; he found Cayce's diagnoses to be accurate and effective. Intrigued, Layne recommended he use his trance abilities to help others, but the deeply religious Cayce was reluctant to do so. Finally he agreed, on the condition that the readings would be free.

Cayce began his readings by lying on his couch with necktie and shoelaces loosened. Within a few minutes he would begin to mumble, then clear his throat and say "Yes, we have the body," then go into a half-hour discussion of the physical condition of the person who was ill. He soon became famous for the accuracy of his readings, particularly when in 1910 the *New York Times* Sunday magazine ran an article titled "Illiterate Man Becomes a Doctor When Hypnotized," and as a result he was sought out by people who wanted to use his psychic skills for worldly affairs like speculation and gambling. Although frequently short on funds, Cayce refused these requests.

Then in 1923, when he was working as a photographer in Selma, Alabama, Cayce accepted a request from a wealthy Ohio printer named Arthur Lammers. Lammers wanted answers to big questions like "What is the meaning of life? What is the real nature of man? What is the meaning of birth and death? Why are we here?"[19] Cayce obliged by giving him a life reading—and, while entranced, claimed Lammers had lived a previous life as the Trojan War hero Hector. In other readings he would report that the querent had previously lived in ancient Egypt, in biblical Israel, or in Atlantis before the deluge.[20] While entranced he would also speak of Atlantean and Lemurian society, of Christ's training in India and Tibet, and other things that scandalized the devoutly Christian Cayce upon awakening. (Ultimately, Cayce would decide that these observations were not unbiblical.) Moving to Virginia Beach in 1925, he set up the Association for Research and Enlightenment, where he would continue to dispense trance advice on health and other matters until his death in 1945.

To date many of Cayce's predictions have failed to come true. The Atlantean Library was not found in 1998, nor did California's coastline slide off into the ocean in that year, but nobody has yet been able to explain some of his remarkably accurate diagnoses. In one instance, a girl in a faraway city was described to him as being "mad." He explained that an impacted wisdom tooth was causing her problems; when it was removed, the girl made a swift, full recovery. At other times, he prescribed a long-forgotten or obsolete medicine and then told the patient where he would find it, often in a musty warehouse or in some neglected corner of an old pharmacy.[21] But despite their somewhat spotty record, his predictions of "Earth Changes" are what have established his fame and set the groundwork for others interested in the Harmonic Convergence of 1987 and the Mayan end-date of 2012.

JANE ROBERTS

Eighteen years after Cayce's death, the world would receive still more channeled literature, as a New York writer named Jane Roberts (1929–1984) discovered that her experiments with a Ouija board were more productive than she could ever have hoped. In late 1963, Roberts was working on a book on extrasensory phenomena. As part of that research, she and her husband experimented with a Ouija board. Within a few sessions they had encountered a male presence that identified itself as "Seth." Seth soon began speaking to Jane in her head, allowing her to dictate the messages instead of using the board. For the next twenty-one years, she would regularly go into a trance and channel Seth while her husband took dictation or recorded her.

Like Theosophy's Ascended Masters, Seth claimed that he had completed his incarnations on this plane and was currently speaking from a neighboring reality. He espoused many concepts that would become hallmarks of New Age thinking, among them, "When you think in terms, for example, of abundance and plenty, then those thoughts draw to you abundance and plenty as a magnet does."[22] While Roberts would channel other spirits, notably the Impressionist painter Paul Cézanne and the psychologist William James, her Seth books would eventually sell more than seven million copies.

JZ KNIGHT AND RAMTHA

One day in February 1977, a Tacoma, Washington, housewife named JZ Knight was experimenting with a cardboard pyramid in her kitchen. In her own words:

> So I put [the pyramid] on my head and started laughing. And I picked it up and there was this glitter at the end of my little kitchen—this glitter, like you would take a handful and turn it loose through a ray of sunshine—and there were these lights happening at the end of my kitchen, and I was just mesmerized. And there appeared this seven-foot-tall entity who was as big as life and the most beautiful thing I had ever seen in my life. And he had this big beautiful smile on his face. He had long fingers and long hands, black dancing eyes . . . And he looked at me and he said, "Beloved woman, I am Ramtha the Enlightened One, and I have come to help you over the ditch." And, well, what would you do? And I didn't understand that because I am a simple person, so I looked to see if the floor was still underneath the chair. And he said, "It is called the ditch of limitation." And he said, "I am here, and we are going to do grand work together."[23]

For the next two years Ramtha would instruct Knight in leaving her body so he could enter. The Ramtha School describes the process by which Ramtha speaks through Knight:

> The form in which he communicates his teachings is through the phenomenon called channeling. In fact, it was Ramtha who made

> the term known in the late 1970s. . . . A channel is different from a medium in that the channel is not the intermediary between the consciousness coming through her and the audience. The channel does not remain in a transfixed altered state while channeling; rather she leaves her body completely and allows the consciousness coming through to have full faculty over all her bodily movements and functions. Ramtha, while being channeled through JZ Knight, has the ability to open his eyes, walk, dance, eat and drink, laugh, speak, converse, and teach his students personally. JZ Knight is the only channel he has chosen and uses to deliver his message.[24]

All that work paid off: Ramtha attracted a number of famous devotees, notably Linda Evans of *Dynasty;* Shirley MacLaine discussed JZ Knight and Ramtha in her bestseller *Out on a Limb.* Ramtha books and tapes are still selling well. For her part, Knight has taken forceful steps to ensure her status as Ramtha's chosen channel; when another channeler, Judith Ravell of Berlin, began delivering messages from Ramtha, Knight called on the Austrian Supreme Court, and after a three-year battle, the court awarded copyright to Knight and ordered Ravell to drop her claim to be in contact with Ramtha and to pay eight hundred dollars in damages for leaving Knight "hanging in spiritual limbo."[25] Since that time, Ramtha has refrained from possessing anyone other than Knight.

AFTER RAMTHA AND SETH

Channeling has become an important part of the New Age movement. The magazine *Sedona Journal of Emergence* consists exclusively of channeled material. Lee Carroll and Jan Tobler, authors of the 1999 bestseller *The Indigo Children,* received the material from a channeled entity called Kryon. Extraterrestrials have joined the bandwagon as well; a group of extraterrestrials and "multidimensional spirit beings" from the Pleiades star cluster have contacted various channels. And Neale Donald Walsch had little problem visualizing abundance after channeling you-know-Who for his 1995 *Conversations with God,* a book that spent 137 weeks on the *New York Times* bestseller list.

Many skeptics note that most "channeled" literature consists of unverifiable claims, alongside "factual" claims that range from dubious to easily disproven. They also note that most of these channeled messages encourage a bourgeois audience to feel good about their prosperity and claim that the poor and sick have "chosen their own reality" (thereby conveniently relieving listeners of any obligation to help them). Others dismiss channeling as a goofy fad; *Doonesbury*'s Boopsie, a ditsy California blonde, was regularly possessed by Atlantean warrior Hunk-Ra in a none-too-subtle spoof on JZ Knight. But what if we took the channelers at their word? Let us grant them the same courtesy we give other horses and assume that at least some are possessed by spiritual entities who have some message to deliver, whether or not they are who they claim to be or are as wise as their PR suggests. The idea that prosperous people worship differently from poor, disempowered people might rub some the wrong way, but to be fair, to most ancient cultures it would have been obvious. Much of what we call "Greek mythology" is actually the beliefs and stories told by wealthy Athenians; we know far more about the gods of the pharaohs than those of Egyptian tradesmen, farmers, and laborers; and the Maenads became notorious largely because they enrolled rich men's wives in their ranks.

It is certain that there are charlatans within the channeling community. (It would be a rare spiritual group that didn't attract a few!) It is also clear that there are some flaky and insubstantial people whose spirit guides produce reams of dreck, but there are also a large and growing number of people who sincerely believe they are channeling *something* from beyond, and an even larger number who feel they have attained some benefit from those transmissions. This large audience suggests that some spiritual needs are being met by what some call modern-day oracles and others scorn as contemporary false prophets.

As a practical matter, we have some concern about the attitude many channelers have toward the spirit world. Although there are some beings that are happy to offer oracular advice and wisdom to anyone who asks, there are some that are not so benign. Allowing yourself to open up spiritually to anything that will enter your head and say things that sound enlightening may be a recipe for disaster if you are in a spiritually infected place or if you have some underlying issues. While many people have channeled without harming themselves, we'd advise treating channeling with the caution that should be exercised with any other possession ritual. There is also the issue that Swami Beyondananda, a New Age–spoofing comedian, has succinctly referred to as "just because they're dead doesn't mean they're smart!"

According to many channelers, anybody wanting to be possessed can be so. It's not a "wild talent" but rather an ability that everybody has and that we will all remember as we advance on the path of transhuman evolution. Like the Theosophists who believed that we all had the potential to be Mahatmas, they believe that we can all be channels. We note, of course, that only a few channelers attract the attention of a spirit guide who can write or speak well enough to garner public attention. Most people can attain some degree in aspecting or shadowing, but not everyone can do a full-on possession or move his or her subconscious out of the way enough to be of use to a supposed Ascended Master, or higher life-form.

ENTER MIRCEA ELIADE

In 1951 the Romanian scholar Mircea Eliade published a book titled *Le Chamanisme et les techniques archaïques de l'extase* (Shamanism and the Archaic Techniques of Ecstasy). This book described various forms of belief and ritual behavior found in animistic and "archaic" cultures around the world. Many of these bore a remarkable resemblance to the religious practices of Siberian shamans, the native spirit-workers closest to Eliade's region, and therefore Eliade described these practices as *shamanism,* a word that has become a generic term for spirit-workers everywhere. But where others had scorned these practices as superstition, fraud, or illness, Eliade made a radical suggestion: These shamans were *technicians of the sacred,* and their sometimes bizarre behaviors were *techniques for attaining ecstasy.*

Eliade did not see trance-possession as a shamanic tool, however. For him the truest shamanic experience was the *spirit journey*—something akin to what we have come to call guided visualization or pathworking. In spirit journeying, the shaman travels to the heavens, the underworld, or some other place by entering a trance state. Once there, he or she may do magical work on behalf of the client or tribe, or he or she may seek advice and counsel from spiritual beings encountered during the vision. For Eliade, possession represented "an aberrant shamanic tradition . . . he who does not succeed in mastering the 'spirits' will be 'possessed' by them, in which case the magical technique of ecstasy becomes a mere mediumistic automatism."[26] The early twentieth century was still too soon after the Spiritualism debacle for Westerners to be comfortable with the phenomenon again.

Still, Eliade's work opened the floodgates to a new generation of anthropologists who wished to research archaic cultures and their religious rites. As they traveled to various far-flung locations and recorded their findings, it became clear that the distinction between journeying and possession was often murky. And so whereas some scholars continued to uphold Eliade's distinction, others came to recognize possession as yet another tool in the shaman's tool kit.

The problem is that all this scholarship was still being done by outsiders. The people who were chronicling shamanic ceremonies were not doing so as believers or participants. Those who were debating the nature and causes of possession were not themselves experiencing it. While a few scholars would become initiates in possession traditions (Maya Deren, Karen McCarthy Brown, and Claudine Michel are the most notable examples in Vodou), most continued to write as academics. Though they did a more or less fair job of compiling data and subjecting it to various forms of scholarly analysis, their observations generally suffered from one fatal flaw: They didn't believe in the spirits who possessed their subjects.

POSSESSION AS SIMPLY . . . POSSESSION

The metaphysical preconceptions underlying this book are quite simple. The authors believe that possession is a real phenomenon; we also see the spirit world(s) as a real place, and that at least some instances of possession involve the displacement of the horse's ego by an outside entity. We acknowledge the scientific method as a useful tool, but we do not limit ourselves to this method, nor do we believe it can explain all possessions.

For our purposes, a *possession experience* is one in which the subject's identity is subsumed into Something Else; the person loses control over speech and actions for a greater or lesser period of time. This can be, but is not always, accompanied by a fugue state in which the subject has little or no memory of what transpired during the possession. There may also be physical manifestations of this possession: a horse may show spectacular strength, consume toxic quantities of alcohol with no ill effect, or evidence knowledge to which the possessed person had no access. However, there are also many very real and powerful possessions where these manifestations do not occur. What is most important to us is the possession itself, rather than the fireworks that may accompany it.

This may appear to be a radical approach, but in our experience it is the only way one can truly understand this phenomenon. Much as we could not understand evolution if we refused to accept the existence of dinosaurs, we cannot hope to explain possession until we acknowledge the reality of the beings who are stepping in and taking control. Nor can we have any understanding of the very real risks that are attendant upon possession work—or any other kind of religious experience.

REAL GODS, REAL DANGERS

According to many Neo-Pagan and New Age folks, the spiritual world is a peaceful, benevolent place filled with light, love, healing, and positive energy. The creatures therein have your best interests at heart: they are there to lead you, and the rest of the universe, to enlightenment. They know your intentions: if your heart is pure, they will accept your blunders and anything you do will work out for the best. Should you encounter something threatening, you need only visualize white light surrounding you and affirm your connection to the God or Goddess.

This idea of deity as one part indulgent parent, one part private tutor, and one part amusement park ride is of very recent provenance. When dealing with the gods, our ancestors approached them with a good deal of caution. They told stories of angered deities inflicting horrible punishments on the disrespectful—and on their neighbors. Plagues, natural disasters, and invading armies could bring down a kingdom if a god was displeased. Just as They could be kind beyond all human understanding, so too were They capable of inhuman cruelty if provoked.

Approaching our gods with fear may seem strange to us. It has a whiff of servility about it, an air of groveling superstition. Modern people are uncomfortable with supplication; we'd much rather relate to our gods in a less threatening fashion. Today we honor (even if we don't always observe) ideas of "equality" and "fair play." We claim that everyone is entitled to justice, that everyone's opinion counts, that everyone has certain inalienable rights. These expectations carry over into our spiritual lives, and we find it hard to imagine that a deity might ask us for anything that wasn't safe, sane, and consensual. We assume that, once contacted, our gods will be fair and just and that they will care about our needs.

Our ancestors had a very different set of expectations. In their world, raw power had raw privilege. Kings and nobles took what they wanted and had no qualms about stepping on those who were in the way. Those in charge were entitled to treat their underlings as chattel, and often did. Even the most benevolent and beloved kings expected due deference and were entitled, nay, expected, to punish disobedience or disrespect. To our ancestors, the idea that the gods had a cosmic obligation to treat humans nicely would have been seen not as blasphemy but as utterly ridiculous.

> *I would encourage people who are observing god-possession to treat the deity as you would imagine royalty being treated in a historical film. You can't be too courteous to the gods.*
>
> **—Wintersong Tashlin, Pagan spirit-worker**

But then, the same could be said of the question "Do the gods exist?" For our ancestors, the gods were as real as the mountains and sky, as accessible as their next-door neighbor or the local temple. People who don't fear the gods often don't believe in them either. They see the gods as "symbols" or "archetypes" or "vibrations"—words that add up to "this is all a great game of psychologically empowering make-believe." The Morrigan becomes "a symbol of feminine rage," Mercury is presented as "a metaphor for human thinking," and poor Aphrodite gets reduced to a tingling sensation in the worshipper's genital region.

Those who work with trance possession know better—and if they don't, they learn very quickly. Once you begin to work with gods and spirits who are real and not just mental constructs, you soon realize that They are dangerous. They can turn your life upside down on a whim. They can have you dressing in sackcloth and ashes, or decide you need to spend the rest of your life living a different gender. They can break up your relationships, cost you your health, home, and job, or drive you bug-fuck nutty insane. And that includes *all* the gods, not just the ones you've heard described as "evil."

This isn't to say that you shouldn't work with possession (assuming you've been given a choice in the matter, of course). Yes, possession is dangerous—but so are many other things you take for granted. Consider your automobile. Millions of people have died or been maimed in automobile accidents. Cars have been used as tools of suicide and homicide; they've been indispensable tools for smugglers, murderers, kidnappers, and other heinous criminals. You are far, far more likely to die or seriously injure yourself in an automobile than in a possession ritual.

We don't ban automobiles, but nor do we tell student drivers that their good intentions will protect them if they miss a STOP sign. We don't explain that automobiles are there for our convenience and that their unconditional love ensures that they will never bring harm to us or others; instead, we recognize the dangers of driving and teach people how to use their automobiles in a responsible manner. We provide financial and legal incentives to drive carefully and punish those who endanger themselves and others by carelessness, malice, or ignorance. As a result, we reap the benefits of driving automobiles while keeping fatalities and injuries to a minimum.

If you give a possession ritual the same respect you give to your daily commute, you will be able to avoid any injuries. Part of that respect involves recognizing that they are just as real as that eighteen-wheeler crossing in front of you and just as capable of smearing you on the pavement. If you came to this book looking for new mind-altering mental exercises—or if you cannot accept that the beings that possess you are real, and that this is not some elaborate dramatic game—then you should no work with trance possession. If you are not ready to treat this as a serious undertaking, with serious consequences, you need to put down this book and experiment with other techniques. We are not posturing; we are deadly serious.

First, it must be recognized that the gods are *individuals,* and like any individual, They have good days and bad days. They can be stubborn, capricious, ill-tempered, and at times downright unlikable. The guest of honor at your possession party may arrive in a pissy mood—and if they do, the burden will be on you to make things right, if you can make them right. She or he might say some things you really don't want to hear, and that you really didn't want the crowd hearing either. When the gods show up, you are not in control of the experience: They are.

If you find this discomfiting, you should. The spirit world has never been a comfortable place, even if it is a place of power and mystery and magic. The act of possession brings that world, in all its glory and terror, into this realm. Understanding that will help to ensure that your possession ritual becomes a powerful transformative experience, not a silly and potentially dangerous travesty.

2

The Geography of Spirit-Possession

WHEN WE BEGAN THIS PROJECT, Kenaz expressed some concern that it might be difficult to find examples of possession outside of African and African-diaspora traditions. Possession has become a hallmark of these spiritual paths; many anthropologists, academics, and journalists have dedicated time and resources to studying them in an effort to sort, quantify, and explain this strange phenomenon. The quality of research has varied widely, and many far-fetched explanations have been proposed as the "True Solution to the Problem of Possession among Africans and Their Descendants"—but these efforts still provided us with a great deal of data on possession among this subset of people and traditions.

Kenaz suspected strongly that possession was more widespread than many believed, and knew that possession rituals are not confined to Africa, but feared that Eliade's prejudice against possession as a "failed" form of shamanism (combined with the idea that possession is something "primitive," something that higher cultures just don't do) would result in a "whitewashing" of the available records. Things that a horse or spirit-worker would find obvious signs of possession might go over the head of a scholar who had already decided possession was mere play-acting, willful fraud, or mental illness. Those worries proved to be unfounded, as we gathered numerous examples of possession and possession rituals among a wide range of time periods and peoples, ranging from hunter-gatherer tribes to highly organized and advanced urban cultures.

We have referenced a number of trance possession cultures in this book; what follows is a small sampling of other historical and contemporary accounts of trance possession and possession ritual around the world. Although this is by no means even remotely exhaustive (indeed, books could be and have been written on each of the phenomena covered), it should provide evidence of just how important possession is, and show that this "anomalous behavior" is far less unusual than you might have supposed.

AFRICA

Probably the most studied of African possession traditions are the rituals of the Yoruba peoples of modern-day Nigeria. These spirits and rituals helped form the New World's Candomblé and Lukumi, as well as Trinidad's Orisha Baptist (a.k.a. Shouter Baptist) movement. The rituals of various Kongo nations have received some study as well; a large number of African-Americans are descended from Kongo peoples brought to the New World as slaves. But other, equally vibrant and complex possession traditions can be found in Africa.

Northern Africa

In southern Egypt and throughout much of northeast Africa, there are few opportunities for women. Female circumcision (more accurately called female genital mutilation) is widespread; one's worth as a female is measured largely by one's success at attaining a husband and bearing children. Yet despite these obstacles, many women have preserved their power—and paid tribute to spirits that the village's men had long forgotten—through trance possession experiences that have become famous as Zar (or Zaar) Dancing.

According to some practitioners, Zar originated in Ethiopia and southern Egypt; trade routes through northeast Africa carried Ethiopian slave women who spread the Zar cult and its attendant dance ritual. The Zar cult believes that people at some point in their lives are possessed by at least two *jinn* (known as *asyad,* or "masters of the spirit"). These guardians are generally helpful and beneficial, but when they are offended or when the person is cursed by the evil eye or malevolent sorcery, they may inflict injury or illness.[1]

Some devotees keep a special room in their house for the Zar; others rent a house specifically for this purpose. In Egypt, the Zar is usually held in a large room. In the center is a tall stool on which is placed a large tray; this is covered with a white cloth and piled high with nuts and dried fruits. The officiant for this ritual is called the Kodia in Egypt, the Shaykha in northern Sudan, and an Umiya in northern Sudan. She has experienced Zar possession and has a working relationship with her spirits. Usually this position is hereditary, passed from mother to daughter or through female members of the family. (Men cannot inherit possession, but may claim to have been "called to it.")

The Kodia owns *al-ilba* (the box), a large trunk containing the paraphernalia of her profession. In this she keeps items for her spirit and for other spirits who might arrive. The Kodia is also a trained singer who knows the drumbeats and rhythms for each particular spirit. (According to Somali Diriye Abdullahi, two of the major spirits are Azuzar and Ausiti or Aysitu—spirits who are known in the West as Osiris and Isis, respectively.[2]) The Kodia or Shaykha is aided by between three and six "helpers," musicians who provide rhythmic accompaniment on a *tar* (tambourine) and tabla. During the ceremony, they provide the distinctive drumbeats (or "threads") that summon the spirits.

The woman for whom the Zar is prepared usually wears white, often a man's *jalabiya,* or shirt. She wears henna on hands and body, and kohl around her eyes, and may also be heavily perfumed, as are the guests. (Frankincense and perfumes are some of the favored offerings to the Zar spirits.) The Kodia and her musicians occupy one side, while the participants (who are expected to contribute an amount of money appropriate to their station) claim the rest of the room.[3]

As the Kodia sings, the women will begin a dance that consists of a head toss, forward and back, while the dancer walks in a circle around the central altar. When the musicians play a rhythm associated with a woman's possessing spirit, she will begin dancing faster, convulsing and bobbing as she does. As the spirit comes into full possession, the horse rises from the prone or a seated position to a kneeling position, ultimately to full-standing height. At this point, the Zar leader will communicate with the spirit and try to negotiate an amicable settlement. An animal may be sacrificed: depending on the wealth of the person throwing the Zar, chicken, pigeons, a sheep, or even a camel may be sacrificed. Coffee and sweet cola will be provided for Ethiopian and Moslem spirits, whereas non-Moslem spirits may demand (and receive) alcohol. When the spirit is pacified, it leaves the same way it came in, with the horse collapsing to the floor.

In Sudan, this is almost exclusively a women's cult. Men may participate in the animal sacrifice (or may be required to make offerings to one or more of the spirits who arrive), and may assist in drumming—but the vast majority of Kodias and Jinn-horses are female. Gnaoua or Gnawa, a practice found farther west in Morocco and Mauritania, features male or mixed groups and involves salutes to Allah, the Prophet and his family, and various Jinns, but is similarly focused on possession by spirits called by particular songs and rhythms. In Tunisia practitioners of *stambeli* pay homage to sub-Saharan "Black Spirits" as well as Islamic "White Saints."[4]

Uganda

On May 25, 1985, a twenty-nine-year-old Achioli woman named Alice Auma was possessed by a spirit who struck her deaf and mute. Her concerned father took her to eleven witches, but none could help.

Finally Alice wandered into the Paraa National Park, returning forty days later as a trance medium whose spirit, Lakwena ("the Messenger"), soon gained a reputation as a skilled healer and diviner. In 1986 the peace, always fragile in Uganda, was shattered as the country collapsed once again into civil war; Lakwena, who claimed to be the spirit of an Italian commander killed in Africa during the colonial era, informed Alice that she was to cease her work as a healer and diviner and instead create a "Holy Spirit Movement," which would uproot evil and create a paradise on earth. Now known as Alice Lakwena, the medium provided her followers with blessed palm oil and amulets that would protect them against bullets "if their hearts were pure." They went into battle in cross formations, singing hymns as they marched. According to Alice Lakwena, they were destined to take Uganda and bring about a new kingdom based on the Ten Commandments and the wisdom of Lakwena and her other spirit guides. Alas, government troops had other ideas, and in 1987 slaughtered thousands of HSM fighters in a battle outside Kampala, the country's capital. Betrayed by Lakwena, Alice moved to a refugee camp in Kenya, where she died in January 2007.

But though Lakwena was done with Alice, he was not done with Uganda. Alice's cousin, a young man named Joseph Kony, reorganized his followers into a Lord's Resistance Army. Under Lakwena's guidance, the LRA began expanding its ranks by kidnapping Achioli children and training them as guerrilla soldiers or as sex slaves. Today more than two million people have been displaced in the conflict between the LRA and the Ugandan government; many who survived the vicious machete attacks and shootings have had their lips cut off or suffered other mutilations.[5] As of April 2007, peace talks between the LRA and the Ugandan government are being held in southern Uganda, but the results are inconclusive. Kony, meanwhile, continues to act as a medium for Lawkena and other spirits: "I don't know the number but they speak to me. They load through me. They will tell us what is going to happen. They say 'you, Mr. Joseph, tell your people that the enemy is planning to come and attack.'"[6]

ASIA

India

The Bhils, a tribal people living in central India, observe an annual ceremony during which young initiates climb a bamboo pole in a state of trance after performing self-injury acts such as fire tests and flagellation. The pole probably represents Bhavani Mata, a form of the Hindu Great Goddess, who possesses these apprentice shamans in the course of this ceremony. The *panda,* a Gond shaman who horses Marai Mata, the goddess of epidemics, ascends a ladder whose pegs are often formed by swords and knives; once he gets to the top, he starts scourging himself publicly. Meanwhile, other pandas drive swords through their cheeks, dance on nail-covered planks, or walk on hot coals.[7] In the Narbada and Tapti valleys of central India, the Holi Festival is celebrated with a pole of wood that represents the god Khandera, women who approach this pole are sometimes possessed by Him.[8]

Although many Hindu paths focus on attaining "oneness" with the Divine and overcoming the ego, high-ranking Brahmins and Vedic scholars generally look askance on trance possession. They have little difficulty with the idea that a god (or goddess) might incarnate in a fitting avatar or *guru:* the concept that she or he might temporarily appear in a low-caste body and offer help to the crowd is much more difficult to grasp.

As with African traditions, Indian possession rituals have also been carried into the Indian diaspora. In Trinidad, the goddess Lakshmi sometimes appears in possession at Orisha Baptist ceremonies; in Guyana, Kali Mai often arrives at Kali Ma churches that combine Christian and African religious practices with veneration of the Dark Mother. At Thaipusam, a Hindu festival celebrated by Malaysians of Indian descent, devotees celebrate by bearing *kavadis* (sacred burdens); these range from pots of milk carried on the head to heavy racks fitted with spikes that pierce the flesh. While carrying their burdens or fulfilling their vows through body mortification, many are possessed by the gods and awaken from the ritual with little or no memory of the pain they have endured.[9] The *kavadi* ritual has been recently rediscovered as a spiritual ordeal by Western aficionados of what is coming to be known as "hook-sports"—people who pull or suspend from hooks in their flesh, similar to the Lakota Sun Dance ritual. Hook-sports workers who use the practices for spiritual rather than recreational purposes have reported that walking with the Kavadi spear-altar on the body is quite useful for getting into the open state of trance that is necessary for possession.

Japan

On February 3, 1892, an impoverished widow named Deguchi Nao was first possessed by Ushitora no Konjin, a spirit who later identified himself as "the god who will reconstruct the world." Nao described the experience of possession. First she felt extraordinarily heavy, then she felt a great force in her abdomen. At this time all fatigue left her and her body became rigid. She would then begin rocking backward and forward, her chin drawn in and her eyes glittering until the pressure in her stomach forced itself out of her as a gruff, masculine voice. While so possessed, Nao was able to heal the sick and prophesy. Although Nao was illiterate, Ushitora no Konjin would produce, through automatic writing, approximately two hundred thousand pages of text, none of which Nao could read.

Today Deguchi Nao is revered as the founder of Oomoto, a Shinto-inspired religious movement in which *kamigakari* (spirit-possession) continues to play a prominent role. Practitioners believe that most possessions are "obsessions" caused by lower animal spirits, and evil and malicious spirits try to control mentally debilitated or ethically challenged humans. However, they also recognize that possession by angels and gods (they see all gods as part of the Great Divine) can occur, albeit rarely. They continue to revere the writings of Deguchi Nao and other founders of the religion, but they officially discourage spirit-possession because of the danger of excessive curiosity leading to a person "becoming the plaything of a malicious spirit and deviating from correct faith." Rather, they recommend that their approximately 170,000 followers "pleasurably serve in the holy work, receiving inflow of Divine nature through correct faith, that is, through heart and deeds full of longing for Divine love and wisdom."[10]

Shintoism has retained many traditional Japanese customs, including shamanic practices and trance possession. Ono Satsuki, an *ogamisama* (trance medium) from northeastern Japan, fasted and performed cold-water ablutions for twenty-eight days before her initiation. There she knelt while other adepts sang and chanted until her guardian spirit possessed her. As Ono says: "Someone who was quick would continue for about three hours or so. But if the divine possession didn't take, it might go on all day and still continue. And they'd keep it up until the possession occurred. Because the individual herself had to declare who the possessing spirit (tsukigamisama) was."[11]

Nepal

Before the coming of Buddhism and Hinduism, Nepal's people practiced shamanic religions. Today many of these shamanic rituals, including trance possession, exist alongside Vedic Hinduism, Tibetan Bon Buddhism, and contemporary biomedical practitioners. The *dhami, bijuwa,* or *jhankri* (shamans) work with ancestors and local genii to heal the sick and appease angered spirits. A *janne manche* (person who knows) will call his or her guardian spirits down in possession; other shamans use the technique of shamanic journeying, with drums or brass singing bowls providing the stimulus for trance.[12] Out of a population of approximately 28 million, there are presently thought to be between 400,000 and 800,000 shamans in Nepal.

The Chepangs in Nepal, a nomadic forest tribe, honor a family god in the Tokolong Festival at the end of winter. The god is represented by a stone placed in the trunk of a tree or in a temple; a member of the family is chosen to be possessed by the god, who, after being summoned by beating the *dhyangro* (drum), speaks through his mouth. Possession causes the shaman to leap about, and the people ask questions and warn him not to let other jealous gods steal the offerings. Among other ethnic groups, the shaman is possessed by a Masta (god) that first appears in a dream or in some other form, then takes possession of the dhami and speaks through his mouth. The dhami is momentarily the incarnated god and may act like a god; he has all divine powers and the right to sit on the god's seat and under the god's parasol. The villagers ask him about their problems, illnesses, accidents, their futures, or those of ones close to them. Literally translated, the trance state is called "carrying the god on his back." While in this state the shaman can perform miracles (oracular or spectacular), which can go as far as the recitation of the Vedas without having ever learned them.[13]

The dance of Nava Durga (Nine Forms of the Goddess Durga) begins each year during the holiday of Dashain. The Nava Durga, together with four attendant gods, dances traditional steps; often the goddess comes down to inhabit the body of a dancer to be worshipped and to grant blessings. For the festival of Ghantakarna (a grotesque demon who wards away evil), dancers engage in extensive ritual preparations, including the production of ritual masks made of mud taken from a sacred spot. There are thirteen dancers altogether: Bhairava (always in blue), Simhini, Vyaghrini, Ganesha, Kumar, Camunda (Ajima), Varahi, Indrayani, Vaishnavi, Kaumari, Mahalakshmi, Brahmayani, and Rudrayani. The dancer who incarnates Bhairava becomes the guru of the dancers at the next twelve-year festival.[14]

Nepal's reigning Shah Dynasty has institutionalized the Newar Dhāmi into the religious guarantor of Nepalese royalty. Prithivi Narayan Shah, the founder of modern Nepal, attributed his conquest to the divine intervention of the Bhairavī of Nuwakot. The Newar Dhāmi is possessed by Bhairava, then offers oracles to representatives of the king. The Dhāmi, a farmer, wears royal emblems that he receives personally from the king in Kathmandu, and is assisted by Vajrācārya priests, who come all the way from Katmandu to direct the festival on the king's behalf and administer the bath that qualifies the Dhāmī to assume his divine role. It is after this "royal consecration" (*rājābhisheka*) that the Dhāmī dons the dark blue costume of Bhairava, bearing the auspicious emblems that he wears only during this festival and when he visits the king once every twelve years in Kathmandu.[15]

Tibet

In the eighth and ninth centuries, efforts were made by Tibet's Buddhist ruling class to root out the influences of Bön-Pö, the indigenous shamanic practices. The practitioners of Bön-Pö were presented as uncivilized and their practices as a dubious collection of sorcery, black magic, and blood sacrifice. The Bön practitioners, for their part, were happy to incorporate Buddhist lore and legend in their practices and to be ridden by Buddhist holy spirits as well as the sky and soil gods they had worshipped since prehistoric times. Today the two practices have become intimately entwined, as the Dalai Lama consults a Bön oracle and Bön-Pö shamanism absorbs influences from Buddhist holy men.

Tibetan oracle-spirits frequently arrive with a show of strength, wearing an oversized helmet or twisting swords into spirals, or *rdo rje mdud pa* (knotted thunderbolt). Oracle-carriers may thrust their own sword so deep into their chest that the point emerges at the back, and withdraw it without suffering harm. Sick people are brought into the presence of a possessed oracle, who will beat them with his sword to drive the evil out of them. When a Tibetan manifests mediumistic powers, he usually begins to fall into spontaneous trances at about the time of puberty. This is not epilepsy, as Tibetans distinguish clearly between epileptic fits and oracular trances.[16]

In Hangjia, a small Tibetan village, the mountain gods regularly participate in the Laru Festival through their medium, the *lhawa* (godman). Unlike the Buddhas, who are concerned primarily with spiritual matters, the mountain gods are seen as capable of protecting the general welfare of the village, of families, and of individuals in this life and in this place. While the lhawa is dancing during his possession, his god may speak through him or punish people. The village's Living Buddha (a high-ranking monk who is considered a reincarnation of another monk) composes and writes out a scripture that he gives to the villagers for the purpose of calling the mountain god, while a different scripture is prepared for the lhawa to ease the process of possession.[17]

The Chinese government considers Tibet the Tibetan Autonomous Region (TAR), and has persecuted Buddhist monks and Bön shamans alike. As a result, many Tibetans have moved through the rugged Himalayas into neighboring India and Nepal; others have made their way to the United States and Europe, where they have established monasteries and initiated various students into Bön and Tibetan Buddhist teachings. At the time of this writing (2007), most practitioners interested in possession are still concentrating on the African and African-diaspora faiths, but we suspect Tibetan Bön will become an increasing subject of interest as material on and initiations into the traditions become more widely available.

Korea

In Korea, Buddhism floats in a layer over the enduring indigenous shamanic tradition, of which the main shaman-officiants are the *mudang*—nearly all female except for occasional effeminate men. There are two types of mudang—hereditary and possessed; the latter type is seized by a spirit (or several) and learns to make it her ally and harness its powers, while the former type generally inherits the title from a mudang mother or foster mother. The hereditary type of mudang does not generally do possession, although a few are accepted by the spirits and end up being possessed. As part of learning to control the relationship with the spirits, as well as teaching, healing, and doing public religious ceremonies, a mudang will learn hundreds of sacred songs that function as history, magic spells, ceremonial performance, and trance-cues for possession.[18]

When a mudang is officially initiated—usually a large, grueling affair lasting days and attended by sacred people to witness it—she is required to horse several spirits as part of the ritual. Racks of sacred costumes are brought in, each dedicated to a particular entity—elemental spirits, gods, deified mortals, and the more ordinary dead (and the lines between these groups are vague and permeable)—and she will be ritually dressed in every one of them by turn. Those spirits that have claimed her will show themselves by possessing her when she wears their clothing; she must be genuinely possessed by more than one spirit over the course of the initiation, and the veracity of the possessions are attested to by the experienced onlookers. Some spirits may have the new mudang going through such ordeals as standing on the edge of a sword blade, and cutting herself with knives, ostensibly without damage. The lack of wounds proves that the spirits are present, and then the mudang is considered ready to work in the world.

EUROPE

The Ancient World

Unlike modern indigenous societies, the traditions of ancient Europe are mostly lost. Some left few or no written records before their tradition went down to Christianity; others left extensive records that were burned and purged during medieval times. This means that finding a historical trail of spirit-possession in these times and places is like trying to track a lost child via trail signs left several miles apart in an untouched forest that has gone up in flames at least once since the beginning of the search.

Greece

One of the classic examples of possession in ancient Greece is the Pythia of Delphi, who became possessed on a regular basis by the god Apollo and uttered prophecies for clients. Although the mechanism by which she achieved her altered states is argued, the fact that it was indeed possession is agreed upon by many scholars, and very convincingly argued by L. Maurizio in his article "Anthropology and Spirit Possession: A Reconsideration of the Pythia's Role at Delphi."[19] The behavior of various Pythias was observed and recorded over the centuries, and ranged from sedate muttering to wildly thrashing about, calling out often cryptic answers to questions. Another example of possession among the ancient Greeks was the phenomenon of the Dionysian Maenads, who formed a great traveling procession of wildly dancing women in the wake of the god Dionysos. Some would become possessed by the spirits of wild animals and tear apart livestock, eating it raw; the occasional intruding human being was said to meet the same fate.

Scandinavia

In the Norse *Heidrek's Saga,* the god Odin comes to the hall of the evil king Heidrek in the flesh, after a local chieftain who considers himself wronged by Heidrek has made offerings to him. Odin supposedly shows up wearing the visage of the chieftain Gest, but he is able to ask clever riddles that Heidrek cannot answer, and prophesies Heidrek's later murder by his own thralls. In another saga—*Gautrek's Saga*—the father of the main character Gautrek, Grani Horsehair, takes his son to a strange ritual where he speaks as (and claims to be) the god Odin and another man claims to be the god Thor, and the two bestow various curses and blessings on the youth. Both these tales have been suggested as lingering remnants of the memory of deity-possession, as have similar ones in other ancient myths in which the gods appear in the forms or bodies of known human beings.

The Age of Enlightenment

France and England

In 1685 King Louis IV revoked the Edict of Nantes and with it tolerance of France's Huguenot (Protestant) minority. The Huguenots found themselves once again faced with intolerance from their neighbors. More than half a million left the country; thousands who were not so fortunate faced martyrdom or forced conversion to Catholicism. Then, in 1688, Isabeau Vincent, a young shepherdess in Dauphiné, began to speak in the voice of the Holy Spirit. In her mundane life, Isabeau spoke a patois of Occitan (Provençal) and French, but when the spirit was on her, she declaimed in perfect French and told her listeners, "Repent! . . . Those who will persevere unto the end and receive eternal life must suffer for His word . . . The evildoers will perish with their evil and be consumed like dry grass before the scythe!"[20] Isabeau attracted the attention of experts like the Protestant theologian Pierre Jurieu and the Catholic bishop Esprit Fléchier, who debated the issue of her prophetism. Ultimately, however, the young girl was sent to one of the era's newest inventions—a hospital where the insane could be safely cared for. From there the prophetess was sent to a convent, and she disappears from history.

But although Isabeau Vincent might be taken away, the spirit of prophecy remained strong in France. Among the Huguenots who had taken a last desperate stand in the Cévennes Mountains, a new movement arose. Prophets and prophetesses would fall to the ground violently; contemporary witnesses described them as "shaking their heads, crawling on the floor, quaking and trembling, drumming, trumpeting, thundering, snuffling, blowing as with a horn, panting, sighing, groaning, hissing, laughing, pointing, shaking, threshing, using childish repetition, howling like a dog and generally acting in a disorderly fashion."[21] Then the convulsions would suddenly end as the spirit came on them, and the horse would now speak in a calm, ethereal voice as listeners gathered to hear their words. Illiterate women and children as young as five or six spoke French rather than Occitan . . . and by 1700 these spirits were telling the Huguenots to arm themselves against Babylon and Egypt, meaning the Catholic clergy and government. The Camisards (so named because of their white shirts) took up a desperate stand against the royal armies, but by 1702 their steadfast faith was overcome by superior numbers and control of the roads.

Many of the Camisards came to France's old enemy, England. There they at first encountered a warm reception as soldiers against "Popish tyranny," but their spectacular possession rituals (what they called Sacred Theatre) proved too much for staid and steadfast England. Noted theologians like John Wesley and John Knox took pains to distance themselves from the "French Prophets" and their extravagances, and only a few Englishmen would try to incorporate these practices into their spiritual life. One of them, a middle-aged laborer's wife named Ann Lee, would soon discover her facility for allowing the Holy Ghost to speak through her. Using the intense prayers and meditation favored by the French prophets, she and others were able to experience the convulsions followed by channeling that would give them the name Shakers after they emigrated to America.

THE LEVANT AND THE MIDDLE EAST

While we have some familiarity with the frenzy-possessions of Levantine gods like Dionysus and Cybele, many have forgotten (or seek to downplay) evidence of possession in the Abrahamic faiths, but the prophets can be seen as utilizing both trance-journeying and divine possession to bring the message of YHVH to their people. There are many cases of prophets being "taken up into heaven" and experiencing visions; there are also many cases that suggest the prophets worked as oracles and that they were used as mouthpieces.

In the Old Testament the prophet Samuel poured oil over Saul's head and said, "Has not the Lord anointed you prince over his people Israel?" (1 Samuel 10:1). Later, when Saul left Samuel and arrived at Gibeah, he met a group of prophets, whereupon the spirit of God came violently over Saul and he prophesied among them (10:9–11). After the spirit of God had descended upon him, Saul overcame all enemies he met in his path and became a mighty king. When the King of Israel needed counsel, the prophet Elisha used a common trance technique—music—to call down the Spirit of the Lord. He requested a minstrel; when that minstrel played, "the power of the LORD came upon Elisha" and prophesied victory over the Moabite army (2 Kings 3:15–20).

The Hebrew prophets were not the only ones possessed by the Spirit of the Lord, who spoke through them; in Arabia a mystic named Mohammed acted as a channel for the archangel Gabriel. When Gabriel took control of his body, he would begin chanting in a sophisticated poetic style that belied his earlier life as an illiterate camel merchant. The compiled results of Mohammed's various trances would become famous throughout the world as Al-Q'uran (the "recitation"). Centuries later, Mevlevi Sufis would use trance techniques like drumming and whirling dance to still their egos and allow themselves to be filled with the knowledge of Allah's presence. These "whirling dervishes" can still be found in Turkey, Albania, Iran, and many other parts of the Islamic world.

We should note here that it is impossible to establish whether or not any of the prophets were possessed when fulfilling their sacred office. In all these religions, historical facts lie buried beneath millennia of legend and spiritual truths; often they have been reinterpreted to suit one political cause or another. In attempting to explore them, we cannot avoid speculation, reconstruction, and educated guessing; nor can we avoid dealing with images and legends that are an intimate part of many people's lives. Our speculations are done in a spirit of reverence, as we consider prophecy not an ancient curiosity but a living and vital practice, but we also recognize that many might consider our theories blasphemous. Possession has long inspired controversy in Christian culture, as can be seen by the story of a horse named Montanus.

Phrygia (Northeastern Turkey)

The first Christians might have accepted Jesus as the one true way to heaven—after all, every other mystery cult that proselytized in the streets of the Roman Empire claimed a unique pathway to eternal life and power—but accepting a religion without an oracle was another matter altogether, especially when that religion had not yet established an official gospel and ruling body. Today official doctrine holds that the Church's apostolic age ended with the death of St. John soon after the writing of his Apocalypse, but for centuries afterward, various prophets arose claiming new dispensations and divine revelations, and three Phrygians claimed that they *were* the Holy Spirit and the Paraclete prophesied by John, starting a movement that lasted for centuries and led to one of the first great conflicts within the faith.

In 170 CE, Montanus, a recent convert to Christianity, began prophesying in a small village in Phrygia (northeastern Turkey). Soon two wealthy women, Prisca (also known as Priscilla) and Maxilla, left their husbands to join Montanus and prophesy by his side. According to one of his detractors, St. Jerome, before joining the church Montanus had been a *gallus* (castrated priest) of Cybele. While other authorities dispute this, later jokes accused Montanus of tinting his hair and wearing makeup, things that were certainly associated with the gallae. But whatever their connection to the Great Mother, it was clear that Montanus and his followers sought the same kind of direct ecstatic connection to the Divine. Almost immediately after his baptism, he had begun speaking under the influence of the Holy Spirit, stating that as the Dispensation of the Father had given way to the Dispensation of the Son, so had the dispensation of the Son given way to the dispensation of the Holy Spirit, for Christ's promise of the Paraclete (the Holy Spirit as intercessor, comforter, and spiritual adviser[22]) had now been fulfilled in the person of Montanus.

An opponent of the Montanists described a Montanist ritual as follows: The prophet first evidenced symptoms of agitation and fear, but as they gained control of their terror, they became still, and then was seized by an uncontrollable madness (*akousios mania psyches*). When so possessed, the prophet spoke not as a messenger but as God himself. On one occasion Montanus was quoted as saying "I am the Father, the Word and the Paraclete"; on another, "I am the Lord God omnipotent, who have descended into man," and "neither an angel, nor an ambassador, but I, the Lord, the Father am Come." Maxilla, when possessed, enjoined her listeners to "hear not me, but hear Christ" and "I am speech, and spirit, and power." To further distinguish between Montanus and the Person who spoke through him, the spirit explained: "Behold the man is like a lyre, and I dart like the plectrum. The man sleeps, and I am awake."[23]

The spirits that spoke through Montanus and the other prophets did not urge their followers to abandon the Church—indeed, the ruling orthodoxy condemned them for the severity of their rule. Whereas bishops were willing to remarry a widow, the Montanists held that second marriages were sinful. Whereas the bishops proscribed meat for just two weeks of the Liturgical Year, the Paraclete regularly ordered the faithful to fast and to abstain from meat and wine. The bishops allowed members threatened with persecution to flee to safer areas; the Montanists gleefully welcomed martyrdom and condemned anybody who paid off a judge or sought to escape the arenas. This fervor gained an increasing number of converts, most notably the famous Church scholar Tertullian.

But as this prophetic fervor attracted some, so too did it alienate others. Bishops tried to exorcise Maxilla of the "demons" that spoke through her, but were prevented from doing so by loyal Montanists. There were rumors that Montanist prophets and prophetesses took gifts (under the guise of "offerings") for their services and were paid for their preaching. Over and over again, polemics condemned the possession trances that were the heart of Montanist worship. A Catholic writer, Miltiades, wrote a (now lost) book called *How a Prophet Ought Not to Speak in Ecstasy,* which distinguished between possession and Old Testament prophecy. According to Miltiades, the true prophets had spoken "in the Spirit," as mouthpieces of the Spirit, but retained their free will. Total possession was condemned as inappropriate—and, when a priest spoke in the first person as the Father or Paraclete, blasphemous.

There were others within the Church who disagreed with him; in 176 CE the Church leader Athenagoras, in his *Apology to Aurelius and Commodus,* described the inspiration of the prophets as follows: "Moses, or Isaiah, or Jeremiah, or the other prophets who, lifted in ecstasy above the natural operation of their minds by the impulses of the Divine Spirit, offered the things with which they were inspired, the Spirit making use of them as a flute player breathes into a flute." The Christian apologist Justin Martyr (100–165 CE) also claimed that the prophets prophesied in a state of ecstasy. But by the fifth century, official doctrine identified trance possession with demonic infestation and witchcraft—a worldview that would persist for centuries and claim the lives of innumerable shamans and horses.

OCEANIA

Bali

Like Tibetan Buddhism, Balinese Hinduism combines traditional Hindu beliefs and rituals with local animist customs (what the Balinese call *adat*). Their ceremonies incorporate Hindu *pujas* (offerings) with dancing, storytelling, and dramatizations of folk songs, legends, and historical events. Often these performances culminate in the dancers experiencing *taksu,* the possession of their body by a divinity during the sacred dances that are designed to call Their presence. These dances also feature sacred and specially prepared masks that come not from Hinduism but from indigenous tradition. When used as decoration, these masks are reputed to frighten off evil spirits and disease and discourage floods; when worn in the proper context, they can quickly induce possession.

Possessions are important not just in folk practices but also in official Balinese Hinduism. Whenever there is an important *odalan* (a ceremony celebrating the annual anniversary of the temple), the priest will become possessed so the appropriate divinity can say whether the ceremony was correct or something was done poorly or left out, or whether further responsibilities must be carried out. Other people too may be possessed by gods or demons. Entranced people frequently display unusual behavior. When dancing the *colongarang,* a ritual dance displaying the conflict between evil (represented by the *rangda* spirit) and the forces of good (represented by the *barong*), the latter will sometimes turn their knives on themselves; but though rangda's magic may force them to place the point of the knife on their breast, head, or face and writhe and fall on the ground, the forces of good protect them so that they do not hurt themselves.[24]

Micronesia

Micronesia, a collection of hundreds of small islands located in the Pacific Ocean, remains relatively isolated on account of its remote location. Still, the evidence suggests that even limited contact has caused problems for the indigenous culture. Early explorers brought back numerous reports of priests offering counsel and healing while possessed by tribal and ancestral spirits. The possession rituals were stimulated by the rapid chewing and spitting of betel nut, and were responses to petitions from the chiefs or from community individuals, accompanied by offerings of money or more betel nut. The spirit medium responded, with legs and arms trembling and face distorted, speaking in the voice of a *chelid* (spirit), often for hours at a time.[25]

Similar reports were found on islands that were separated by language, by culture, and by thousands of miles of ocean, making it clear that there has long been a possession tradition in these islands. However, by the 1970s and 1980s, anthropologists working in this region noted a great decline in the number of official mediums and traditional priests. Those who remained were mostly old; younger Micronesians scorned the practices as old-fashioned and uncivilized. Anthropologists also noticed a great increase in the number of involuntary possessions. They have also noticed a troubling increase in the number of Micronesians suffering from schizophrenia and other psychoses and thought disorders. On the island of Palau over 2 percent of the male population shows severe symptoms of schizophrenia; on Kosrae and Yap this is well over 1 percent.[26] Western scholars have interpreted this as a response to modernization and colonial pressures. Spirit-workers, however, might note that gods and spirits can wreak a horrible revenge if they are ignored too long. From a spirit-worker's perspective, the schizophrenia and involuntary possessions could be the vengeance of the ignored spirits.

Vanuatu

The first missionaries to set foot in Vanuatu in 1839 were promptly killed and eaten, leading to some consternation among the mission societies. By the 1860s they had overcome these immediate obstacles and various denominations had set up shop in these islands they called the New Hebrides, and soon British and French people became an intimate (if minority) part of the local scene. But in early 1940, as more soldiers landed and war became imminent, these white settlers faced unexpected unrest.

In meetings from which whites and women were excluded, a little man named John Frum, with "bleached hair, a high-pitched voice, and clad in a coat with shining buttons," was enjoining people to take *kava* (a root with mild hallucinogenic and sedative properties), engage in communal gardening, and resist idleness. Soon John Frum was promising his followers a new age in which they would enjoy the material wealth that the White people enjoyed; he also promised that every White person on the island, including the missionaries, would leave. To gain this paradise, John Frum ordered his followers to return to *kastom* (tribal customs) and to reject Western education, money, and Christianity. In 1941, they rid themselves of their money in a frenzy of spending, left the missionary churches, schools, villages, and plantations, and moved farther inland to celebrate traditional custom through feasts, dances, and rituals. Authorities hoped the craze would be over when they arrested "John Frum" in the person of an illiterate native named Manehivi. The authorities sentenced Manehivi and several of his followers to imprisonment, and tied Manehivi to a tree for a day as an imposter, but soon thereafter another "John Frum," a young man named Joe Nalpin, arose to spread the word.[27]

At this time Vanuatu was an important refueling point as war loomed in the Pacific; by the end of the 1940s, over 300,000 American soldiers and sailors would pass through. The idea of a native uprising unnerved many military leaders, but the islanders were impressed by both the wealth and power of Americans and their generosity. Soon John Frum took on aspects of other mythical American heroes, like Uncle Sam and Santa Claus, and his followers built symbolic landing strips to encourage American airplanes to alight and bring them gifts.

Anthropologists of the time wrote off these bizarre rituals as "cargo cults." Today we can see them as an expression of NiVanuatu beliefs in a spirit world that brings blessings to those who pay it proper homage, and which speaks to its followers through trance possession.

Today the John Frum Movement has its own political party, led by Song Keaspai. On John Frum Day (February 15) 2007, the John Frum Movement celebrated its 50th anniversary. Chief Isaac Wan, its leader, remains strong in his belief in John Frum and was quoted by the BBC as saying that John Frum was "our God, our Jesus," and would eventually return. Since 1957 the "Tanna Army" has organized nonviolent, military-style parades, their faces painted in ritual colors, and wearing white T-shirts with the letters "T-A USA" (Tanna Army USA). This parade still takes place every year on February 15, and attracts many tourists, who bring some of the wealth that John Frum promised.

PART TWO

The Present

Kenaz's Story

March 2003

I'm stumbling about blindfolded, still dizzy from the endless prostrations and turns that mark the Kanzo's opening. The person behind me steadies my step as I stumble, then spins me around again. I reach out my hands as unseen persons break my fall. I try to regain my balance and almost succeed before the unseen persons push me forward again.

Someone shakes a *chacha*: the hissing rattle coils through my head. I'm close to the wall now, near the saint images that help make this unfinished Brooklyn basement a temple of the lwa. The plaster feels cold against my skin; I feel a sharp pain as my shin strikes a bench, then someone jostles me back toward the center of the room.

I'm moving toward the drums now, everything is pearly luminescence behind the cotton scarf that covers my eyes. The rhythm shakes me; I'm gasping for breath, the air tastes like sweat and tobacco and Florida Water. A woman curses in Kreyol as I step on her foot; the heat is oppressive as a crowded elevator stalls between floors.

"DE! DE! DE DE DEDEDEDE DE!!!"

Someone has Danto, I think as I whirl in the luminescent blindness. Behind my shoulder I can feel the scarred warrior mother staring at me, her eyes shining bright red as her heart, bright red as the wounds on her face, bright red as the edge of her knife. The dizziness is gone now; there's nobody standing in my way, my guide is taking me exactly where I want to go. I move forward toward the doorway that leads into the *djevo,* the place where I will be secluded until my baptism on Sunday.

"DE! DE! DE! DE! DE!" I hear again before falling into silence and darkness.

The next day I ask, "Who got ridden by Danto?" Mambo Edeline says it was I.

Raven's Tale

September 1991

When I rejoined the Neo-Pagan community and began to help design and create ritual, one of the first things I discovered was this: If I were to take on the part of a deity, there would always be the chance that I would get pushed aside and They would take the floor. This first came home to me when some Pagans created a Wild Hunt ritual for Mabon and asked me to be the Hunter. Herne, they called him, and so did I, but he was far older than that British name. He was the deer-headed, wolf-pawed god on the ancient cave walls, the Keeper of Predator and Prey. As long as animals have hunted and eaten each other, he has been present. At that time I knew little about him, but I made a horned mask and came to the ritual.

The moment I put the mask on my head—just minutes before the start of the rite—he moved into me, incredibly huge, old, inhuman. For once I did not lose consciousness. *Do you want to watch?* He asked. *If you set the boundaries, I will abide by them, as long as I get the hunt that I want. I understand boundaries, and the marking of territory.* So I watched from the backseat, seeing my body move about. He was honorable with me, was the Hunter; he kept his word—but then, after it was over, he said: *I will be back again next year.*

Next year? My breath caught in the throat that had just been given back to me. Yes, every year, every Mabon or thereabouts, I would be expected to provide my body and run the Wild Hunt, until I was too old and could no longer do it. It was a lesson in expectations: sometimes the gods see our deeds as promises before we do. At any rate, the effect of the actual presence of the Hunter on the group of ritual-goers was electric. All who surrounded him—those who had chosen to be hounds and those who had chosen to be prey—found themselves in a kind of altered state. They all became, at least partially, those roles in a way that was far more intense than mere method acting. Afterward, they spoke about it in wonder. "What happened? That felt so real . . . it was so powerful!" It was my first experience with the reason why god-possession is done at all. It is a valuable thing for both the gods and the community to touch each other.

3
Cosmologies

PAGAN PERSPECTIVES ON GODS AND SPIRITS

Modern Western Neo-Paganism is less a coherent faith than a collection of vaguely similar faiths all trying to fit under one umbrella, and there is an enormously variable conception of what a god or a spirit might be when it comes to different places on that spectrum. For various demographic and social reasons, coherent theological study of Paganism has lagged behind that of other modern religions, but it is finally being tackled in small pieces by brave souls. The first major step forward in discussing Pagan theologies could be said to be the definitional division of belief into three major camps: polytheism, pantheism, and archetypism.

Polytheism is the belief that there are many deities, some personal and "human," some impersonal and "not very human." Polytheism is distinct from pantheism in the sense that in polytheism, deities are highly distinct, and sometimes at odds with each other. Although a deity may appear under different names, all love goddesses are not one goddess, and so forth. Some Pagans refer to themselves as "hard polytheists," meaning that they don't indulge in even occasional pantheism by conflating minor deities; in this belief, every single deity is separate from every other, and deserves to be treated in this manner. There is an underlying assumption in polytheist belief that to do otherwise will insult the deity or spirit, who will not fully manifest to speak to them if one is not fully believing in them as a separate entity and addressing them appropriately. The metaphor that is often used by polytheists to explain their stance is: "If I owe you ten bucks, and I say that humanity is all one anyway and I give the ten bucks to Bob over there, you're not going to be pleased."

Some Pagan theologians and sociologists divide the "traditions" (what other faiths might call "sects") of Neo-Paganism into five basic varieties: Traditional British Wicca, Modern Wicca, Wiccan-derived traditions, reconstructionists, and reconstructionist-derived traditions. Of the lot, reconstructionists (groups who are attempting to reconstruct the ancient religions of specific cultures, e.g., Norse/Germanic traditions such as Asatru and Heathenry; Roman groups such as Religio Romana; Hellenic groups such as Hellenion; and Egyptian traditions such as Kemet) tend to be the most polytheistic, in order to re-create the strong polytheism of the ancients. Reconstructionist-derived groups range from extremely polytheistic to somewhere between polytheism and pantheism, but generally work with more than one culture or pantheon of deities.

There are several very few good resources available to fully explore and understand the theology of polytheism. One decent book on the subject is John Michael Greer's *A World Full of Gods.* The descriptions of how polytheism compares with other versions of the religion are excellent, but the book becomes rather self-righteous toward the end. Polytheism, in general, has been so slandered by centuries of monotheistic monopoly that many folk still see it as somehow superstitious or ignorant. Polytheists sometimes defend their faith by pointing out that it was the faith of thousands of years of human history, and that to assume our forefathers were all stupid is to do them a great disservice.

Pantheism is the belief that although there may be more than one manifestation of deity, they are all part of one larger Godhead. Some versions of pantheism posit that all living things are also part of this Godhead, that we are as integral to it as any deity, and that any personalized "human-type" deity is merely a specific mask on the larger force of Divine Power. The simile often used to describe pantheism is that the Godhead is like a many-faceted jewel: the kind of divine being that approaches you is based on which facet is turned to the light.

Much Eastern religion is pantheist; most modern educated and urbanized Hindus will hastily explain away the apparent polytheism of their faith in pantheist terms. Among Neo-Pagans, it may well be that the majority of people and traditions are pantheist, although no one has done any surveys. Pantheism tends to be more comfortable intellectually to modern Westerners, raised as we were in a culture that sees polytheism as superstitious and personalized deities, often, as "too humanlike" to be divine. It is a way to get one step closer to monotheism; claiming that all gods are part of one Godhead is a way to bridge the seeming gulf between polytheism and the monotheist or non-deist beliefs of others. It fits reasonably well with animism (the belief that not only all living things but also all natural things, and some man-made things, have an indwelling spirit and soul of their own), which was inherited originally from polytheistic worldviews, but can be theoretically adapted to the concept of an indwelling universal Soul or Consciousness.

The third point of this triangle we refer to as archetypism. This is a form of atheism (or, perhaps in some cases, agnosticism) that believes that divine archetypes are either psychologically rich internal structures that are spiritually useful for self-improvement or specific flavors of universal energy that can be "worked with" or even "commanded" in order to gain personal power. Archetypists may discuss a god or a spirit as a "being-ness," a mythical way of being rather than a specific entity (such as the average Jungian psychologist talks about), or as a "god-form," a sort of energy that can be invoked into one's presence or one's self for one's own gain (such as the average ceremonial magician practices). Some archetypists, while not exactly believing in the gods and spirits as actual entities, will acknowledge that many people find suspending their belief and "acting as if" they believe in them to be spiritually useful; the "child self" or unconscious still believes in miracles and wonders and "make-believe" people and will respond emotionally to a ritual that invokes them. Nearly all ceremonial magic practices are archetypist in nature, and while we do not know of any hard-line archetypist Neo-Pagan groups, archetypists tend to be scattered throughout the Pagan community in all but the most polytheistic traditions. Archetypism also tends to be found where Neo-Paganism borders with demographics interested in psychology, self-help, and New Age spirituality, although the last group also tends to be high in pantheism.

To be fair, one should point out that these three divisions are by no means cleanly separated. Even hard polytheists admit to a certain amount of pantheism at a high level, the "we are all one if you move high enough" level, but generally feel that this level is useless to human beings on a daily basis because it makes everything impersonal and there is no personal contact from the undifferentiated All That Is. Some pantheists will acknowledge that while they may believe that all gods are part of One Higher Being, one gets much more personal satisfaction—and results—out of "acting as if" there were highly separated gods and calling on them.

In their article "Pagan Deism: Three Views,"[1] Margarian Bridger and Stephen Hergest posit (albeit only in a Wiccan paradigm) the three divisions as points on a triangle, with a spectrum of belief between each point. In this view, some Pagans fall on the continuum between polytheism and pantheism (the gods are sometimes separate and sometimes not, to varying extents) or between pantheism and archetypism (the gods may be creations of our minds, but there is also sometimes a divine force behind those thoughtforms). The line between polytheism and archetypism is a bigger and more mind-boggling stretch, as these seem like the "most theist" and "most atheist" points. Bridger and Hergest suggest only that this continuum might belong to people who have deep and personal relationships with thought-form deities that they don't actually believe in; others have commented that it might belong to people who believe in the gods, but don't believe that the aspect that appears to them is actually one of Them.

Of the three "corners," polytheism obviously poses the least theological difficulty with the practice of god-possession. If there are a lot of different gods, just as there are a lot of different "spirits," and they are all People in the same sense that we are individual people, then of course they might want to come share our world in the best way that they can. To be realistic about the nature of god-possession and how it actually occurs, one could make the statement that for the most part the gods tend to act, when possession is involved, as if polytheism was the truth of their nature. They appear as separate individuals with separate likes and dislikes, and those likes and dislikes tend to stay consistent when dealing with vastly different groups and horses. They recognize people whom they have seen before, or who have been involved in long-term devotional activity toward them.

It has also been noticed that when different people manage to successfully horse the same nonspecific pantheistic-style deity (e.g., "the Mother Goddess" or "the Love Goddess"), they usually get deity-presences that have those attributes but are very different in other ways. Occasionally the preferences of those deities are noted and looked up, and have been identified as different specific polytheistic deities who "work in the same building," as some people have put it with affectionate irreverence. This has given rise to speculations that "calling up" a nonspecific greater "category" of deity simply opens the door for any one god or goddess who falls under that category to enter, e.g., calling on "the Mother Goddess" might have an equal chance of getting you Gaea, Mawu, Jord, Demeter, and so forth.

To pantheists, divine possession is the overarching god or goddess choosing to show one aspect of his- or herself to the audience, manifesting through one single human being. Since most pantheists are comfortable, in ritual practice, with "acting as if" the various deities are separate beings, there usually isn't much trouble on the practical end of dealing with the actual entities, as long as they keep "acting as if." When pantheists (or archetypists) have addressed horsing gods and goddesses in ways that conflated them with other specific deities, the responses we've seen have been mixed, ranging from flat, offended denial ("I am neither Kali nor Hecate, I am Hel, and you are a fool if you think otherwise!"), to tolerance ("The name you give Me is not so important; it is that you know Me and My essence, and recognize Me when I call you; your ancestors called Me by different names, but knew Me"), to acceptance ("Love is Love, regardless of its manifestation"). There is also the issue that different deities and spirits are higher or lower on the personal/impersonal axis, a problem that will be tackled in chapter 6, On the Nature of Spirits. In theological terms, however, while pantheists may argue with polytheists over the exact nature of the possessing deity(ies), they usually agree that some spiritual force with its own mind and will is present.

Archetypism is the real difficulty in the triangle. Modern Neo-Paganism may be in a corner accompanied only by Buddhism when it comes to religions with a serious percentage of followers who are technically atheists. Many Neo-Pagans come to this demographic for reasons far removed from being called by the gods. Some are searching for a faith that supports individualism, or ecology, or sustainable living, or equal human rights, or feminism, or sexual freedom, or other values less supported in other faiths. Some are seeking to re-create the traditions of their ancestors, some are fascinated by historical re-creation, and others are drawn aesthetically to the panoply and theater of the various rites and rituals. Some come to it through magical practice, via the Pagan and non-Pagan mystery traditions, and are drawn in by the trappings. Some are recruited by their spouses and partners. Some have had psychic experiences and are looking for validation. Some are attracted to it as a "subculture," with its own fashions and rules, rather than as a religion. Some are attempting to rebel against majority religions, and find Neo-Paganism sufficiently shocking to their family members. Some merely find Paganism spiritually moving as a practice, without feeling obligated to believe in the entities that are invoked in its rituals. Whatever the reason, at any given Pagan gathering, a not insignificant percentage of the people attending any ritual or workshop will not be convinced of the external reality of the gods that others may be worshipping.

The reaction of Pagan trendsetters to this situation varies. Some are careful not to use language that will sound as if they are trying to force the reader or listener into believing in the gods, especially since proselytizing is a social sin among most modern Pagan groups, and anything that reeks of it will be generally condemned. Others are more hardline, using terms that assume a belief in gods and spirits, and feel that to do otherwise would be as unthinkable as using a Christian liturgy that discounted the existence of both Jesus and Jehovah. However, it is the archetypist percentage of the Neo-Pagan demographic that has the hardest time coping with the literal reality of deity-possession, in or out of ritual, and it will be this "faction" that a Pagan group running a possession rite will have to decide, one way or another, how to deal with.

One writer referred to experiencing the sacred archetypes of deities as "standing in their shadow," which makes a good deal of sense. Standing in their shadow, however, is not the same as touching them. Archetypists, especially those who are basically atheists, will tend to assume that what is actually "possessing" the horse is some deeply held and perhaps unconscious bundle of needs and motivations, or perhaps even a personal delusion. Those who lean toward agnosticism may see them as drawing down "god-forms"—energy constructs that can theoretically be controlled and used. This can cause strife and difficulties within a group, especially when the possessing deity or spirit does something that can be blamed on the horse. If those members of the audience—be it in a private group or a large open gathering—simply do not believe in the literal existence of those entities, the resulting clash of theology is going to create problems.

However, one can't force anyone to believe, and arguing with those from that place will likely only make things worse. Trying to convince someone of the existence of a spiritual reality for which they have only your word is not only ineffective but discourteous as well. As we discuss in the chapter on Neo-Pagan group ritual, the leader of a group openly practicing ritual god-possession, whether within the group or in a larger forum, must make careful decisions as to how to tread with the percentage of Pagans who will inevitably see spirit-possession as metaphorical acting at best and self-delusion or mental illness at worst.

To date, the Neo-Pagan demographic has only occasionally come to strife and argument over the differing points of belief listed above. Part of this is due to the social ethic of religious tolerance prevalent in Neo-Paganism today (which, admittedly, varies from group to group), but part of it is due to the fact that serious Pagan theological study and comparative writing is still in its infancy within our own faiths, and not yet taken seriously enough by outside faiths to be worthy of comparative study by reputable interfaith theologians. This situation will inevitably change as more deep writing and discussion is created and discussed across religious lines (a maturation of faith that is already occurring), and as Neo-Paganism continues to grow in numbers. It is not impossible to see the phenomenon of god-possession as a touchstone in this oncoming argument, being as it is the point at which our worlds and the worlds of Spirit touch most closely. Frankly, we suggest that you all hold on for an interesting ride. So to speak.

THE AFRICAN-DIASPORA WORLD

Most Haitian Vodouisants spend little time contemplating the cosmology behind their practices. They don't need elaborate philosophical justifications to prove that the lwa exist: they can talk to them—or horse them—at any *fet*. Since the majority of Haitian Vodouisants are illiterate, there is little call for tomes of metaphysical speculations. They care more about results than rationale: As long as their magic works, they are not particularly concerned with the whys and wherefores.

In practice, Vodou's cosmology is (like Vodou) a mélange of African traditional beliefs and folk Catholicism. The world was created by Bondye ("Bon Dieu" or "Good God"); after completing the universe, he withdrew from creation and left day-to-day maintenance in the hands of the *misté* (mysteries, a blanket term that comprises the lwa, saints, angels, *djabs* or wild spirits, and other spiritual entities). While Bondye is recognized as the Supreme Ruler, he figures little in the everyday lives of Vodouisants.

Some have tried to paint this as a "European corruption" of the original African traditions, a way by which African gods were reduced to mere servants of YHVH. In fact, it is quite in keeping with religious beliefs throughout the African continent. The Zulu of South Africa call God uZivelele (He who is of Himself, the Self-existent One), while the Masai of Kenya and Tanzania speak of Engai (the Unseen One) and the Tenda of Guinea speak of Hounounga (the Unknown). Alongside this belief in a distant (and uninterested) creator is an equally strong belief in the spirit world and spiritual beings who live alongside and work with or against mankind.[2]

Vodouisants honor Bondye, and other figures from Christianity, by attending Roman Catholic Masses. They sit quietly as the priest rails against "folly and superstition" and "devil worship," say a Rosary or two for the Virgin, then go back home. (Those who were raised Catholic will smile knowingly at this "cafeteria Catholicism" approach.) Certain saints are also called upon regularly. St. Michael the archangel is seen as a powerful protector and guardian against evil; St. Philomena is widely loved and St. John the Baptist is particularly popular with Haitian Freemasons. To people raised in cultures where particularly virtuous or powerful deceased ancestors look after their descendants, a belief that is widespread throughout Africa, the veneration of saints is logical.

Those who wish to draw clear lines between the saints and the lwa will soon be disappointed. Some saint images are used to represent the lwa: most Vodouisants who look at a picture of the denim-clad St. Isadore praying in his fields will identify it as Zaka, the hardworking peasant lwa of agriculture. Sometimes the saints are served in the same manner as the lwa: Philomena (Filomez), Clare (Klemezin), and St. John the Baptist (San Juan Baptiste) have all been known to possess people.

To make things even more confusing, John the Baptist can be honored as a saint and occasionally possesses people, but his image can also be used to represent Ti-Jan Danto, the son of Ezili Danto and a powerful lwa in his own right.

Whereas we are most familiar with the body and spirit dichotomy, Vodouisants draw a considerably more complex soul map. The *ko kadav* is the physical body; it is animated by the "little good angel" or *ti bon ange* (the ego and personality) and the "big good angel," or *gwo bon ange* (the soul), which acts in accordance with the *zetwal* (literally, "star": the closest approximation to the zetwal would probably be the Higher Self or "Holy Guardian Angel" of the Abramelin system). During possession the ti bon ange steps aside, allowing the lwa to take control of the ko kadav and use it as if it were their own. In addition, individuals have one or more lwa who "walk with" them, taking a direct and personal interest in their well-being.

Upon death, the conglomeration, which is the individual, dissolves and the soul goes "beneath the waters." (This most likely comes from the Kongo, where dead souls are said to reside at the bottom of the ocean.) If the individual was a member of a société, their *gwo bon ange* may be "drawn out of the water" after a year and a day and placed in a *govi* (terra-cotta container). From there they can look after and protect the société and their descendents. If the individual was particularly powerful and/or notorious, they may even return in possession as a lwa. Jean-Jacques Dessalines, the first ruler of Haiti, is honored in many peristyles as Ogou Dessalines. (As with saint and lwa, the lines between the two are not always clear.)

The slaves who were brought to Haiti in chains looked back with longing on Gineh (Guinea, or Africa). To their descendants, Gineh became a mythical holy land, the place where the spirits live, an Avalon or Land-Under-Wave. In keeping with African traditions, Gineh was placed beneath the ocean, yet alongside these African beliefs was the folk Catholic idea that heaven is above us. Vodouisants deal with this apparent contradiction by holding both beliefs simultaneously. Gineh, the home of the lwa and ancestors, is still seen as a place beneath the ocean—yet when the lwa come in a fet, it is believed that they come *down* the *poto-mitan,* the center pole that joins heaven and earth.

Technically speaking, Vodou (and most African-diaspora traditions) can be considered monotheistic, since they pay homage to one Creator God. In practice, they behave very much like explicitly polytheistic faiths. This gets us into thorny questions about what constitutes "worship." Vodouisants might say that they worship God by going to Mass; they honor the spirits by providing them with sacrifice and honoring them at fets and other events. Through Catholicism they fulfill their spiritual obligations, whereas their work with Vodou is focused on temporal needs like health, love, and prosperity. What these faiths most certainly are *not* is atheistic. There is no concept that the spirits are archetypes or symbols; the very idea would strike most Vodouisants as both silly and dangerous.

Other African-diaspora faiths have similar to nearly identical cosmologies. Santeria, like Vodou, has a distant and uncommunicative "Architect of the Universe" deity named Olodumare, to whom no shrines are erected nor much attention paid. It is Olodumare's children, the orishas, who command the attention of humanity. Unlike Vodou, in which a saint's name can be both an alias for a lwa and a deceased Catholic spirit (and either may ride a human being), in Santeria the saint and the orisha are considered to be the same spirit. The view is not so much that "the saint is a mask for the original African orisha" as that the saint and orisha are the same spirit with a different manifestation and name, a cosmological view that could be considered slightly more pantheistic, at least along certain lines.

There is also a greater emphasis on the orisha, or *santo,* having once been a human being who became a minor divinity because of (or in spite of) some personal qualities. While many of the original Yoruba deities do have myths that postulate them as ancient human kings or queens, the emphasis on this in Santeria is derived from Catholicism, thus strengthening their similarity to the Catholic saints. How is it that these spirits have two "human" histories—one in African legend and one in Catholic myth—yet are said to be the same spirit? Most *santeros* are comfortable with contradictions and just accept it as one of the mysteries of the Universe. The few who attempt to explain it will sometimes speak of those two historical humans both "merging" with the spirit that attracted each of them, and as they're entirely merged now, there's no point in worrying about what they once were.

In Brazil, Candomblé developed with the additional influences of Native American folk beliefs on top of the African cosmology and Catholic overlay. Working with plants is exceptionally important in Candomblé, to the point where some Candomblé groups have a tradition (borrowed from the locals) of using entheogenic plants in ritual, something that is not found in other branches of African-diaspora religion. The ritualized care and the usage of healing herbs are also a strong Native American influence, to the point where a local homily is "without leaves, there can be no Candomblé." Dealing with plant spirits takes on a more important level in Candomblé, as well as the local spirits of place, unusual in a diaspora faith and clearly the gift of native locals to the displaced polyglot religion. Similarly, while all the African-diaspora faiths have a certain amount of strong belief in the living energy and presence of all things—rocks, water, trees, and so forth—Candomblé is the most wholly animistic, in many ways just as animistic as Shinto.

> *If you all arrived at a Candomblé terreiro and talked about "cosmology" or "cosmovision," some people, especially the elders who have not had the formal study that we younger ones have had, would say to you, "Cosmology? What's that? No, I don't know about that." But their daily practice is completely permeated with a specific cosmology, a typical worldview . . . For us, what matters is that the rock is alive, the plants are alive, the earth is alive. Water is alive, animals. We ourselves are alive because of all this. There is an "energy" in the plant that nourishes us, that cures us. And this cure can be in the form of a tea, a syrup, something you drink,*

something you rub on your skin, something that you inhale. But also, you can take a leaf, for example, and you can say a few words and pass that leaf over someone's body, because we believe that the leaf is not just the leaf that we see—this form, this color, this texture—but an energy that exists in the leaf is capable of interacting with your body, with you, even with your mind. We are nature. Nature is the essence, the base of our belief and the base of our relation with the world that we see and the world that we don't see.[3]

—Valdina Pinto

Umbanda, sometimes modernly referred to as Quimbanda, is the most recently developed of the Afro-Caribbean faiths, conglomerated in the 1920s from African-diaspora deities, native Brazilian beliefs, folk Catholicism, and more strikingly the Spiritist movement (sometimes referred to as Kardecism, from Allan Kardec's writings on the subject). Like other folk-cultural religions, it varies from small group to small group in its hierarchy of spirits. However, each follows the same pattern of believing in one creator god who leaves humanity to its own devices, and then speaks of legion upon legion of spirit "nations," some under the purview of the orishas and some separate. Conceptions of the saints and orishas vary from group to group, but there seems to be more of a tendency to assume that the saints' names are simply masks for the orishas themselves, who take on more importance.

There is more actual musing on cosmology among Umbandistas, perhaps because it is so infused with the intellectual Spiritist movement. Umbanda has been accused of being a synthetic rather than a syncretic religion, self-consciously reinvented by the nineteenth-century Spiritists to look more "civilized" and "scientific" than Candomblé. It is no accident that among all the African-diaspora faiths, Umbanda is both the tradition with the highest levels of allowed Caucasian membership and the tradition with the most recognizable discussion of theology and cosmology. Some groups will accept the "polytheist" label; others will look over their shoulder at the watching Catholic Church and say that the orishas are only spirits, and subordinate to the Real God, which they then entirely ignore. A good deal of theory has been written about the nature of spirits and their ability to move in and out of human bodies, but most of it is in Portuguese and not available to English-speakers.

When Umbanda moved north with Brazilian emigrants in the last few decades, it took on a different character. North American Umbanda groups are more likely to utilize the sacrifices and props that Brazilian Umbanda has scorned as being "backward" and "barbaric" in competing Candomblé practices. Where some Brazilian Umbanda groups do not encourage possession by the orishas at all, considering it to be too dangerous for the horse, northern ones tend to have no problem with it, probably due to close interaction with and infection by the other African-derived religions in the smaller and less religiously segregated ethnic communities. In general, Brazilian Umbanda has striven for increasingly more "civilized" behavior; less possession, forbidding possession by spirits who are vulgar and use obscenities; and less traditional African atmosphere and paraphernalia, perhaps due to various tides of racism and classism in Brazil. Northern Umbanda, carried by lower-class emigrants, is often considered to have "backslid" somewhat. Northern Umbanda groups, especially those now run largely by non-Brazilian members, may allow random audience possession by the orishas, whereas southern groups reserve this for trained initiates.

There is also a lot more emphasis on being possessed by the souls of the Dead in Umbanda, which also harks back to its association with Spiritism. Like the related Spiritualists in North America, ghost-mediumship is a main form of divination in Umbanda, but unlike sedate northern mediums with their quiet circles in dark rooms, Umbanda ghost-possessions are likely to be as riotous as rides by the orishas. In fact, there is a line of thought in some Umbanda and Umbanda-derived Spiritist groups that giving one's body to a wandering, sundered ghost temporarily is a way to help teach it and aid it in moving on to a higher condition, and that doing so also gives good "credit" to one's own soul. An emphasis is placed on "helping the lower spirits," which is not necessarily present in other African-diaspora faiths. Umbanda practitioners acknowledge that this form of spiritual charity can be dangerous, but assert that it is reasonably safe when done in the controlled atmosphere of the rite, with skilled people looking on to intervene. Thus the orishas arrive to teach humanity, and humanity in turn aids sundered spirits, sometimes at the same bembe.

Another interesting point that is sometimes seen among Umbandistas is that they acknowledge different levels of trance-depth, and that the horse's mind and spirit may color the possession to one extent or another in a lighter trance. Unlike in the other traditions, the horse is not necessarily entirely unconscious during the possession trance, although they are not in control of their own bodies.

After reading these "explanations," you may very well be more confused than you were when you started. This is because you (like the authors) come from a culture that places a premium upon rationalism. One of the core beliefs drilled into us from an early age was "Everything has a logical explanation." When we use terms like "supernatural," we really mean "a natural phenomenon that hasn't been explained yet." Even those who accept the existence of a spirit world expect that it functions according to clearly delineated rules and regulations that can be understood, even if we don't have all the necessary data at hand just yet. Being comfortable with the kind of contradictions that seem normal to a traditional practitioner of aboriginal religion looks superstitious to us, as if people haven't bothered to think about what should be, in our eyes, the most interesting part of it.

Other cultures, by contrast, recognize the limitations of the rational. They don't expect the spirit world to make sense; they have no interest in a Grand Unified Field Theory Which Will Explain the Spiritual and Temporal Worlds. Instead, they focus on the practical applications of their work. While it goes against the scientifically minded brain to start with this way of thinking, it may be easier at first if you take this approach to the issues at hand: Accept that the spirits you are working with are real, then concentrate on the ways in which you can most effectively work with them. Much as you can turn on a light switch without a degree in electrical engineering, you can work with the spirit world without a complete understanding of its metaphysics. (Indeed, traditional followers of these religions would say that such an understanding would be impossible—they don't call them "mysteries" for nothing!)

If nothing else, starting with an open mind and a "black box" attitude about possession can prevent one's own unconscious (and often dismissive) assumptions from getting in the way and creating problems with other people's experiences. Most of us did not grow up in a culture where possession was accepted as possible, much less with an organized set of rules to handle it in community settings. It's a useful thing to suspend one's frantic quest for the metaphysical hows and whys until one has had time to objectively observe how things actually work. We suggest this as a useful beginning attitude not just for an individual, but also for communities as a whole that are new to the concept. Don't make policy based on "we believe this is why it happens"; make it based on "this is what is actually reported to happen on a regular basis," regardless of why that might be.

After all, think for a moment about the scope of the subject that we are talking about here, at bottom: the mechanism by which deities function and interact with our world. It's not as if humanity hasn't been trying to tackle that one for millennia, and it's hubris to think that we ought to be able to solve the mystery at dinner tonight over pizza, if we could just observe a couple of possessions, or perhaps nail down a god and interrogate him. (Not that there's much chance of that last one.) Let's have a little humility on the subject and keep an open mind, and we'll have a better chance of actually learning something.

4

Different Riders

Comparing and Contrasting

TO COMPARE AND CONTRAST the actual possession experience, from the inside and the outside, between the African-diaspora context and the modern Neo-Pagan context is something that can still be done only tentatively, with great caution. When scholars have written about the Afro-Caribbean possession phenomenon, they tend to be so caught up with the unusual (to them) behavior of the horses, or in searching for a mental health or social-delusion paradigm to fit around it, that they rarely give good, objective descriptions about such things as length of time and effect on the horse later. Modern Pagans watching Pagan possession have done little better, assuming that one can find any written accounts at all, which is rare. So for those interested in the possession phenomenon, there is a scarcity of material to begin with.

Also, possession experiences vary among African-diaspora faiths. At a Vodou fet, the lwa are called one by one, both verbally by the congregation and the houngan or mambo and rhythmically by the drummers who drum specific secret rhythms designed to call each lwa in particular. Sometimes the lwa will show up and ride someone, and sometimes they won't. Since these rites tend to be a fast "roll call" of lwa, the possessions tend to be very short—sometimes less than a minute, sometimes a few minutes, but it is unusual for them to go on for a particularly long time.

The orisha spirits, on the other hand, tend to like to stick around awhile. Individual groups may vary, but in most Santeria, Candomblé, and Umbanda groups, if an orisha shows up, they may stay for a minute or for an hour. There is usually more emphasis in traditional forms of these groups on having horses already on hand who are primed and ready to open to certain specific orishas, rather than letting possession happen randomly in the audience. (Some modern nontraditional groups, of course, don't mind having an audience free-for-all, but they are in the minority.) In Candomblé and Umbanda, possessions can go on for up to a couple of hours, usually one at a time. While there are bembes where several people are possessed at once, it is usually restricted to just a few, depending on who is especially wanted or whose feast day it is. Divinatory possessions—usually less public rites with only the horse, a small team of handlers and assistants, and a few querents—are especially likely to go on for quite a while.

Neo-Pagan planned possessions—in former days, generally "drawing down the Moon" sorts of things that just got deeper than expected—have tended to be more sedate. This seems to be partially about the sedateness of the ritual culture, which has tended to be crowded into a small living room rather than a big dance around the bonfire. However, it also seems to be about the nature and wishes of the European deities themselves, who have sometimes come through expecting a certain sort of ritual presentation. While this has often been difficult for the unprepared groups who inadvertently hosted them, it has also given us some useful information as to how it was done in ancient (and pre-literary) times, and how it should be done now. As things progress with this newly rediscovered religious activity, we hope to learn still more.

One thing that definitely creates commonality among possession experiences in all these varied communities is the self-related experience of the horses themselves. The words used to describe ritual trance-possession states are similar, regardless of the origin of the spirit involved. Sensory input seems to move farther away; there is a sense of "receding" from one's own body and senses; then a sense of the Spirit arriving in a rush of color, image, and pure feeling much larger than one's self. Afterward, there is usually a sense of exhaustion, emptiness, and sometimes confusion. There is also, permeating the entire experience from beginning to end, a palpable sense of awe.

> *It starts with me feeling the deity rising up behind me, and then I'm informed that they want to use my body. I relax my mental and emotional barriers, open myself specifically and only to that god or goddess. I usually feel Them moving into me from behind, sort of enveloping me and entering the sphere of my consciousness and the cloak of my flesh from the head/neck area. Then They flow into me, and I am pushed back to whatever degree the deity in question wants. I have certain warning signs that I am about to be taken. I will feel and hear buzzing about my head. My vision may start to gray, and I will feel myself become disconnected from the physical world. As the deities in question begin to seat themselves, I may become nonverbal or my speech may grow disjointed. Eventually I stop completely, and then They are in charge.*
>
> *Coming out of it can feel disorienting—my vision is usually odd, sometimes over-bright, sometimes fuzzy double vision. It depends on the deity and the length of possession. I will usually feel a cool lightness physically as though a heavy burden I have been carrying on my shoulders has been cast off. At the same time, sometimes there is a feeling of loss within, or conversely an extremely strong sense of enduring connection to the god or goddess in question. I may have trouble walking, as the disorientation often includes a lack of balance. Speech may be disjointed, just as prior to a possession, and I may be out of touch with my body. I may have something of an emotional high for some time*

after; disorientation, sensitivity to noise, fits of giggling, bursts of energy and vitality, all of which eventually plummets to exhaustion and a dire need to sleep.

—Galina Krasskova, Heathen spirit-worker

When I am waiting, I may feel twitchy and irritable. When the time comes, I start singing with the rest, and can in fact sing myself into trance. I may start to feel detached and woozy, sometimes my head jerks, then comes the rush, and sometimes a surge of energy that is released by stamping or laughter. At that point the deity comes in, body language changes, and s/he signals to others by putting on the regalia. I am in the back seat somewhere, and the deity has access to my knowledge as well as to his or her own. At the time I think I will remember everything, and that I could exercise control, except that the "me" thinking is not the usual one. At the debriefing afterward, I often find that there are major holes in my memories of the events.

—Odinsmeri, eclectic Norse/Umbanda spirit-medium

Assuming I have forewarning of more than a few seconds, I begin by disassociating with my body; I let my consciousness float and begin to disconnect. When the deity is ready, I can feel an enormous pressure behind me or all around me; their presence is always unmistakable. If I don't immediately relax and allow my "barrier" down, the pressure becomes very uncomfortable very quickly; the effect is rather like a sealed glass container that is dragged toward the bottom of the ocean—pretty soon the greater pressure shatters the container. I have never reached the shattering point; I just give in to the experience.

I know the deity is moving in because suddenly I feel like I'm eight feet tall! The shift in how the body feels is very marked; I feel physically different, maybe taller or with unfamiliar body parts. As I let them settle I may open my eyes, and I'm always surprised that I'm not staring down from a great height because my body is telling me that I am. I literally feel greater than life.

After the initial rush, the deity begins to settle and I let my awareness relax in the back seat. Sometimes the deity shoves me farther back if they don't think I'm removed enough; I'm not a particularly gifted horse, so sometimes this can result in a short struggle between us while it's discovered exactly how far away I am able to go. I am generally allowed some awareness, but I recall little or no conversation or action; I am aware of it on some level, though it's without any identification. I don't feel I take part in the events at all, I get no pleasure from the food or drink consumed, and my physical needs may or may not be taken into consideration. It isn't until after the deity leaves that I begin to order what I have witnessed, but the memories are very sketchy if I have any at all, and they feel completely irrelevant. They are the actions of a stranger, so my brain sees no reason to keep them on file.

—Silence Maestas, Pagan spirit-worker

I have done a good bit of guided trancework traveling down into my head, and that's where the images I use come from. The first thing that I do is to take a step back into myself. It's like stepping back from the controls of a big robot; I see my body as the robot, and I'm stepping back from the control panel. Next I step back and down even further, and open the door to let the god or spirit in, and while staying back I let them take control. At that point, they have the body and can choose to let me watch the interaction or not.

—Fireheart Tashlin, Pagan spirit-worker

Often the first thing I do is communicate with whoever is going to ride me: "I'm going to be coming in now." I close my eyes and try to will myself to let go of my body. It's like trying to force yourself to fall asleep. Often for me, there's the beginning of a falling sensation, or like submerging myself under water. Then I have the feeling of pressure, like something pressing on or through the back of my head, and that pressure forces me further away. If I'm going to be "behind the safety glass," the next thing I'm aware of is a jolt, and at that point I'm looking out through my eyes, but I'm not in willful control of my body. If I'm going to be in the trunk, there's a similar but more dramatic feeling of being turned upside down, and then nothing—no full awareness—until the deity has left or is leaving, although I sometimes have the feeling that I was aware of something, but I have no memory of what transpired. There's the feeling of a vacuum, or emptiness, or lessening of pressure, that I rush back in to fill, and I'm aware of another jolt as I take control of my body, although I may be dissociated for a couple of hours afterward, depending on how heavy a ride it was.

—Wintersong Tashlin, Pagan spirit-worker

When Yemoya comes in, I lose all sense of time. To me, that would be defined as full possession. There is an intensity when it begins that happens because I am initiated to her. I've been told my appearance changes when she enters. Since I normally walk with a cane, when Yemoya wants to dance, that can be lots of fun. Afterward I think that we might have danced for about fifteen minutes only to be told that much time has passed. With Lilith, I am aware of what I'm/we're doing as it is happening. I stand aside and she has control. Afterward, I do not remember much, but if someone talks about what happened, shows me notes, or plays a recording, the memories return. During a Misa, when a spirit enters, many times I stand straighter. I'm strong, and I can walk easily. To some degree, whenever one of them enters, there is a compulsion to act in certain ways. There are uncontrollable physical reactions. For example, my body may shake or I might laugh. My voice and personality change. The shaking has only happened within Santeria while the personality and voice changes occur across the board.

In spirit-possession, I feel the "knocking" of the spirit wanting entrance. I can refuse or I can let it in; my spirit guides can block the entrance. When spirit-possessed, I deliver messages or do the needed work, and then the spirit leaves because its job is done. During the possession, I walk differently; my inflection and phrasing changes. Although my appearance may shift, it is typically limited to stance, flexibility, and strength. However, that's not always the case. When a particular spirit enters, my body shakes all over. When a spirit leaves, my body can literally shake them off.

—Lilith ThreeFeathers, Olorisha

Deity-possession and spirit-possession look and feel very different to me. When Yemaya possesses me, I don't remember anything that happens during that time. I lose time, and that's a full possession. I feel like I am emptying and filling at the same time. That turned out to be accurate for seeing others get possessed by orisha; they seemed to light up from the outside and from the inside at the same time. When the lights "meet," the person is not in control any more—the orisha is. That's the only time that I have seen that phenomenon.

—Olorisha Omi Lasa Joy Wedmedyk

First, I get myself into a trance state, however that works at the time. I like to take some time about it, calming myself and feeling open and relaxed rather than closed and tense. I try to get my thoughts down to a flatline, a dull murmur. I mentally detach from my body, preparing for Someone else to take it. I like to paint my face during this time, as it has become a ritual activity, and it requires looking in a mirror. When the face paint is done, I stare into the mirror, and take a mental "snapshot" of that face which is now a vessel for a god or goddess. Then I slowly don the rest of my costume, or have someone else do it, and move into place. Then the god descends upon me—and that's actually what it feels like, a great form, like a bird, swooping down on me. Light, darkness, overwhelming sensation. They move into me through the back of my head and my spine, and I can just vaguely feel my hands and mouth moving without my volition, saying things that I can't hear. Then I'm gone, usually. Sometimes I'm still there a little, but it's as if I'm sitting absolutely still and daydreaming about something, my eyes fixed lazily on one point. Meanwhile the body is going about under the god's commands. Coming back is a reverse of this—I get control of the eyes first, as they recede, and I "lift my eyes" for the first time—occasionally just in time to see the floor rushing up, so it's good to have a handler about to catch me.

—Gudrun, seidhkona

During nearly all African-diaspora possessions, the horse loses consciousness entirely—in fact, it is something of a "litmus test" for possession by those spirits. The exception, as noted in the last section, is in Umbanda, where divination possessions are acknowledged to come through with varying levels of trance, and it is not unusual for the horse to remember some of the conversation later. In practice there are differing levels of possession; at a Vodou fet you will frequently see the lwa "pass through" people and leave them shaken but conscious, and it is not uncommon to see someone bellow as Ogou passes through them, or see someone drop to the ground as Damballah makes his way through the congregation. (For a more in-depth discussion of the controversy of full unconsciousness versus partial unconsciousness, see the section in chapter 13 called Mistaken Possessions.)

Among Neo-Pagans, because trances have tended to be spontaneous rather than trained, the results can vary wildly. Assuming for a trance deep enough to even be referred to as possession, the horse may be entirely unconscious, vaguely present in the background with only a fuzzy memory of the proceedings, distantly present but unable to hear anything, or able to see, hear, and remember everything clearly.

Anecdotal evidence from the horses in question seems to suggest that this is at least partly a matter of the wishes of the deity in question—some want their horse entirely out of the way, some could not care less, and some want them to watch for some educational purpose.

European deities also seem to be more controlled in their movement of the body. There is very little falling on the ground—we have generally found the transition to be smoother—and more of an immediate taking control of the physical motions, although the deities may move the body entirely differently from the horse. They dance less often, unless they are specifically associated with dancing, and tend to "sit in state" more often. Some prefer to interact with the crowd, some to let the crowd come to them, and some simply to look on and avoid the crowd. Both African and European deities like to eat and drink during possessions, and whether they "take it with them" depends more on the nature of the spirit than the pantheon.

They also tend to stay a lot longer; Western gods have remained at an event for some hours, although this is rather hard on the horse. Divine weddings are, as one might expect, a particularly long ride for them. Another huge discrepancy is that many European deities are willing to be sexual with worshippers (or perhaps even expect it in some cases where it was a major part of their ancient rites), where centuries of Catholicism has trained the lwa and orishas to a more chaste standard. (This tricky issue will also be dealt with in its entirety in a later chapter.)

What vague and fragmentary material we have on oracular and ceremonial ritual possession by European deities suggests that they tended to manifest with more decorum, generally "holding court" like nobility—which they do seem to have considered themselves—and true to form, they also seem to manifest that way today during modern possessions. Another sort of manifestation seems to have them specifically focused on one activity that was traditional for them—blessing the crops, giving advice, or, in the case of the Hunter, for example, leading a Wild Hunt. Generally, they will either show up and do that activity and then leave, or show up and be disappointed that this activity is not forthcoming (and sometimes render a tongue-lashing) and leave, or they may spontaneously trigger this activity into happening, which is another reason why communities need to get as much information from the gods as possible before asking them to show up for dinner.

Perhaps the biggest difference between the spiritual manifestation of the two cultures is that the African deities are accustomed to possessing more than one individual at a time. A Vodou fet may see three or four people possessed by Ghede at once; an Umbanda ritual may call on Oya to guard a boundary against evil spirits, and the request ends up with three women stalking the boundary, all chosen and possessed by her. There is a casual acknowledgment that the lwa or orisha are powerful enough (and big enough, cosmically) to be able to possess more than one body at a time without much trouble. European deities never seem to do this that we have personally witnessed. When asked about this (politely), their reaction has generally been something along the lines of "Yes, I could do that, but why bother?" They seem to like being the center of attention, and if there is more than one body manifesting them, the attention can be divided.

5

Gathering Culture

When Worlds Collide

AT THE BEGINNING OF THE 1990S, Neo-Pagan gatherings (and gatherings that weren't technically Neo-Pagan but catered heavily to that demographic) were bigger and more popular than they had ever been previously. There were national festivals that attracted hundreds of attendees, and thickly scattered smaller ones as well. If one wanted to, one could do a "festival circuit" that never ended, and indeed some vendors who specialized in selling to Pagan audiences did just that. The sorts of groups that attended, and the sorts of rituals that were run, also began to vary as a larger audience was drawn in. Before the 1990s, most festival Pagans practiced Wiccan or Wiccan-derived traditions, and their workshops and rites reflected that. Though the majority of people in the Pagan demographic still fall into those categories, the expanding diversity of these faiths has brought together practices and practitioners that might never have touched before. Traditional Wiccans are getting to see Norse and Hellenic reconstructionist rites, and Pagans used to "standard" circles are coming up against new and experimental ritual forms.

Somewhere in the early 1990s, Afro-Caribbean groups (Vodou, Santeria, Candomblé, Umbanda, and Palo Mayombe) began to take tentative steps toward allying with this demographic. After all, they shared a context with multiple divine spirits, bonfires, dancing, chanting, and a strong tradition of folk magic. More to the point, some people walked in both worlds, belonging to both kinds of groups. At first the Afro-Caribbean folk and the Neo-Pagan groups circled each other warily, each not sure what to make of the other. Neo-Pagans were uncomfortable with the custom of animal sacrifice, the vague background association with black magic, and the heavy Catholic overlay of some Afro-Caribbean sects. Used to a more sedate style of ritual, Wiccan groups of the time looked askance at all that wild dancing around.

On the other side, Afro-Caribbean groups were wary of potential racism from the predominantly white Neo-Pagans (and to be fair, most of the push to bring African-diaspora traditions into the festivals has come from white members), and some worried about attendees at rituals acting like tourists, or backlashing against practices that they did not understand. While things have generally gone smoothly and most of the potential trouble has not materialized, the Pagans who bumped up against African-diaspora beliefs and rites saw one thing that they hadn't seen before: serious deity-possession as an expected phenomenon.

Wiccans certainly had a tradition of "drawing down," or invoking the energy of a deity into the high priest or priestess to varying levels (which are discussed more fully in another chapter), but in general the experience was lighter—more about drawing the energy of that deity through them, or in some cases evoking an archetype from within themselves. The high priest or priestess rarely lost consciousness or control of their body, and the visitation always remained within decorous boundaries. Sometimes, like the botched Athena invocation whose warning tale begins this book, things would go further and the Presence involved would take over a body and act "outside the script." Almost always, however, these "anomalies" would be considered a "mistake," and quickly repressed. "We don't want that to happen again!" seemed to be the overriding opinion, whatever they thought that it was about. Yet the Afro-Caribbean lwa or orisha took their horses to the point of little or no control, and did things in those bodies that were not only outside of a script but also often completely socially unacceptable, if not out of character for those divine spirits. Their rites were designed with built-in allowances for spirits that might randomly decide that they wanted a certain food or drink, or that this person should be insulted or dragged off to dance, or that person should have booze spat in their face. They were very clear that no matter how bizarrely the bodies acted, it was not the humans who normally made them move and breathe who were in control.

Most Neo-Pagans reserved judgment on the matter. Afro-Caribbean traditions came under the "tribal religions" clause within the religious opinions of most educated Westerners. Under this mental clause, if (especially nonwhite) people are engaging in strange spiritual gyrations handed down from their ancestors, part of being "respectful of their native culture" is to pretend that you believe that what they're doing is valid, even when you think it's a load of bunk. "Acting as if" it's just another perfectly reasonable way to worship, and then sidestepping the issue into theories about the social uses of religious ritual when pressed, is considered to be the "polite" response. It's certainly more polite than saying, "Actually, if I have to think about it, I think you people are completely deluded." Instead, a vague "Well, they're doing their thing, and that's what they do" is much more acceptable. In some cases, the (mostly white) Neo-Pagans would accept the phenomenon of possession only when it was linked with Afro-Caribbean practitioners, ideally "authentic" ones, meaning nonwhite ones. This subtle racism—"our sort of people don't do that sort of weird and undignified thing"—is an attitude that uses a pretense of respect to cover up a bucketload of fear.

The problem came when ordinary Neo-Pagans would go to a bembe or a fet out of curiosity—after all, how often does one get that chance at a gathering—and get more than they bargained for. One Umbandista commented that when she brought her group to a Pagan gathering and held a bembe, there was a fair guarantee that one or two of the tourists were going to get snapped up and ridden by an orisha. She blamed this on the number of psychically gifted people attracted to the witchcraft-associated faiths, steeped in all the psychic exercises that some groups did to expand on their natural talents in that area, and yet with no training whatsoever in dealing with the phenomenon of possession. "Unclaimed open heads," was her comment.

> *Frankly, I am annoyed by the use of the term "horse" in Neo-Pagan traditions. Having worked both sides, so to speak, I know that there are differences and I don't think all of the people using the terms know those differences. Accuracy is necessary; borrowing terms can lead to confusion.*
>
> **—Olorisha Lilith ThreeFeathers**

At the same time that festival-going Pagans (who are still only a percentage of the entirety of the Pagan demographic) were occasionally running into Afro-Caribbean possession, small Pagan groups—and some solitary Pagans, the most common sort even today—were beginning to have their own troubles with gods and spirits demanding rides. Stories like the Athena debacle began to circulate, first as curiosities, then as warning tales. The phenomenon began to be debated and speculated upon. Workshops on the subject sprang up at the occasional festival, but generally gave only an anthropological view.

It has been speculated in some circles that the reason for this development is the increasing number of worshippers that these long-forgotten deities are gaining, thus strengthening their connection to this world. The way that the phenomenon has appeared and gained speed does have a "critical-mass" feel to it. Deity-possession, in particular, seems to have appeared in reconstructionist and reconstructionist-derived groups at a faster rate than it has grown in Wiccan-derived eclectic groups, although the majority of strict reconstructionist groups are still wary of the practice. This is significant, considering that "recon" groups, as they are known, are moderately recent as part of the Neo-Pagan demographic and still very much a minority. While there were a few scattered reconstructionist groups during the late 1970s and early 1980s, for the most part their groundswell has become noticeable as a force in the Pagan demographic only since the mid-1990s. The rise of their influence in modern Pagan thinking has coincided, eerily enough, with the growing numbers of reported deity-possession, even though most reconstructionists are not advocating the practice, and some are adamantly against it. There may be no direct correlation between these two phenomena, or if there is, it may not be based in actual practice so much as the "critical-mass" issue: the rise of reconstructionist groups may create a higher percentage of individuals who are actually bothering to learn the ways in which those deities were honored in the past, thus strengthening those deities' connection with this world through their worship.

In Wiccan and Wiccan-derived circles over the past two decades, especially those associated with radical politics, the main objections seem to be either complete disbelief or a fear that this practice could be misused. Some were also uncomfortable with the implied elitism of horsing (a point that will be discussed in later chapters). This put deity-possession in an objectionable light, to the point where a well-known Pagan writer faced down one of the authors of this book and accused the group's practice of ritual deity-possession as being "dangerous and self-indulgent." This attitude necessarily puts those horses who cannot refuse the call into an adversarial position with their communities, dealing with the (veiled or blatant) accusation that they ought to be able to tell the gods to boot off, and that their refusal to do so honors only their own ego.

On the other hand, most Wiccan and Wiccan-derived groups still have the tradition of "drawing down the Moon," which is a light form of trance possession, and some have begun to take that to further depths. A few such groups are now requiring their advanced initiates to show evidence of the ability to do some kind of trance possession, which has led to tales of some controversial tactics among minor groups with regard to "forcing" people to open to deity-possession, and some controversial discussion over whether or not this is wise, or effective, or actually even possible.

I have done the soul-condensing for people who are horses, to make it easier for them to be ridden. I have not done it to make people who are not horses able to do it, nor would I. I think that it is very dangerous, but there are ways it can be employed beneficially, and there needs to be significant discussion between the horse and the person doing the technique, and it should be avoided or used in extreme moderation whenever possible.

—Wintersong Tashlin, Pagan spirit-worker

I think that using these techniques in order to "turn someone into a horse" is dangerous, irresponsible and shows a level of hubris that is appalling. It's not just the idea that if you can't horse naturally, or by the intervention of a deity, that we will just squish you out of the way is one thing. That they have the balls to then pull through a god who may or may not want to do so—that's just playing with napalm.

—Fireheart Tashlin, Pagan spirit-worker

I think these techniques are very, very dangerous. I do not believe such training should be taught as a matter of course. I think that the ability to horse is either inborn or not. One either possesses the appropriate patterning or one does not. The gods themselves may choose to change that, but it's not something that we ourselves should muck about with. I think that possessory work should always begin with a god or goddess initiating it. Then, once the gods have made it clear a person is to be used as a horse, proper training can be given. That training really only consists of learning how to take care of oneself before and after the experience and to get out of the way during. I have heard of certain technologies, such as a group psychically condensing the soul and I think that not only are they ludicrous, they are very, very dangerous. Furthermore, even horsing just one deity can have irreparable changes in the horse in question . . . not bad, but irreparable. It can be emotionally and psychologically devastating if the person isn't ready for it.

—Galina Krasskova, Heathen spirit-worker

Look, we're talking about something that is basically divine intervention here. If a deity—a deity, remember!—does not have the power to come through Potential Horse X without help beyond a basic simple trance and relaxation, then maybe it shouldn't happen. Perhaps Horse X isn't suited, or deity Z doesn't want to come through them, and doesn't care about you and your assembled ritualers and your ego. Gods are not puppets to be summoned and yanked around. Frankly, anyone who claims to have forcibly brought a deity through a human being without that deity's active aid . . . well, I'd doubt whether it was a real deity they were dealing with. And if it is with that deity's active aid, then the deity probably did the trick themselves, regardless of your hand waving. They are more powerful than us, period. Keep that in mind.

—Ari, Pagan spirit-worker

The individual should be in control of when the possession happens. It should not be controlled externally by other mortal and fallible people. No person should make it happen for another person.

—Olorisha Lilith ThreeFeathers

In reconstructionist groups, the objections tended to revolve around whether or not there was enough written historical precedence to believe that those specific ancients practiced deity-possession or spirit-possession, and, if so, how it was "properly" done according to those ancient rules. This puts the horses that end up in those communities into a different kind of adversarial relationship: justifying what may be happening to them via personal experience in a forum that is extremely distrustful of such things. On the one hand, scholarship may actually aid in creating proper offerings and atmosphere for well-known spirits to visit; on the other hand, spirits with less documentation may be less welcome—and this is if the social norms find enough documentation to allow the practice of spirit-possession itself.

Many modern Neo-Pagan reconstructionist communities find themselves in a position that no other religion would tolerate—a venue where the most respected current writings on the subject of their faith are usually (if not always) written by academics who not only do not believe in that faith and those gods but also find the believers who hang on their every word ludicrous, bizarre, and deluded. In some cases, much of the original source material that these "experts" quote was written by long-dead individuals who felt these religions to be a source of evil. (One can imagine what the average Christian or Buddhist or Hindu theologian would say about centering all intrafaith religious debate on the words of scoffing nonbelievers, even if they were good historians.) The effect that this has had on reconstructionist theology has not yet been widely discussed, but its residue is evident. In this atmosphere, the unpredictable transpersonal experience that spirit-possession can become for both the horse and the community has little place and can become a source of conflict . . . yet as we've mentioned in the last chapter, anecdotal evidence seems to point to an odd link between reconstructionist practices and deities attempting to come through participants.

Despite the fact that possessory work is extremely controversial within Heathenry, I've never found it to be in conflict with my religious worldview. Perhaps this is because I'm a spirit-worker and god-slave, perhaps it is because I started functioning as a horse before I became Heathen and Odin was such a huge part of that—I'm not sure but for me, it's a uniquely cherished duty, the pinnacle of my service as priest and spirit-worker. It is as a horse that I know I am doing my duty to the gods, for the gods and for the benefit of the community in exactly the way that They intend . . . Within Asatru/Heathenry, there has been a great deal of ambivalent attention over the years given to groups such as Hrafnar and their rituals of god-possession. There are also Heathens like myself out there practicing possession in a more organic manner.

—Galina Krasskova, Heathen spirit-worker

I recently horsed Artemis for a Hellenic ritual—they didn't have anyone who could do it in their own group, so I volunteered. She was relatively easy to carry, but I was raised in the Greek pantheon so I was very familiar with her, and her personality meshes well with mine. Nonetheless, I spent months figuring out the best way to dress, and what to have at my disposal so that she would be more comfortable here, and also being celibate for several weeks beforehand and taking a purifying bath that morning. That was partially to make the ride easier, but also partially because the ritual that she was coming for was a reconstructionist-based ritual, so dress and "look" was more important than it might be in other contexts I've horsed in, such as one-on-one spiritual consultations.

—Fireheart Tashlin, Pagan spirit-worker

Possession in a reconstructionist context is a difficult thing, because reconstructionists are, in general, very conservative about what happens in their rituals, and when the gods come, your careful construct goes out the window. I started out doing possession rituals for a very small group who hadn't had contact with the larger community, and when our group got "absorbed" by a larger group, I knew that I had to make possession palatable for them in their own contexts, or it was likely that they would ban me. So I prayed to the gods and asked them for a favor. I would create a possession ritual that was as perfectly researched as possible, with all the correct offerings, and then I would run it past them. Please, I prayed, please, one of you who doesn't mind being temporarily confined within such a structure, please come and limit Yourself this one time to their expectations. I was lucky—Iduna spoke up and offered, with the divine equivalent of a sigh and an eye-roll, but she did it. I briefed everyone heavily beforehand, gave them all structured things to do, and it all went well. That was their first taste of possession—about as safe as it was possible to get. Then the folks in my smaller group could start talking about the less "safe" rituals we'd done, and I could start planning for bigger things. But it was important to walk them into the shallow end with baby steps.

—Gudrun, seidhkona

At present, Pagan groups vary wildly as to whether they practice possession, have seen it in other groups but do not practice it themselves, have only vaguely heard of it, or have no idea what it is. Individual Neo-Pagans vary wildly as to whether they believe in its existence as a reality, and to what extent. This issue may be hovering over the community like a tidal wave about to break through or it may creep up on it like the tide gently sucking at people's ankles, but there is no question that it will come. In a very real way, this is the biggest theological question that has ever landed on the doorstep of a religion that is currently very uncomfortable with serious theology, and it can only lead to what the Chinese curse refers to as extremely interesting times.

PART THREE

The Spirits

6
On the Nature of Spirits

ONCE WE ACCEPT THE EXISTENCE of spirits and a spirit world, we run headlong into a whole new set of questions: What is this spirit world like, and what sorts of beings inhabit it? There is no shortage of maps and guidebooks to the land beyond; most religious traditions have a multitude of stories describing their afterlife, Otherworlds, and the lands inhabited by their gods. But alas, there are frequently vast discrepancies in these descriptions. The heaven promised to devout Christians bears little resemblance to the Buddhist nirvana—and neither looks much like Asgard or Olympus. And, of course, there are several contenders for the position of One True God and quite a few Creators of the Universe.

It would be easy enough to say "My Revealed Truth is completely correct and everyone else is wrong." It would be even easier to say "Why bother with these questions, since we'll never come up with conclusive answers?" But if we are going to open ourselves up to possession, it behooves us to have some idea of what is taking control of our bodies. By examining the various descriptions of spirit and the spiritual realms, we may be able to come to a better understanding of the beings and forces that we are calling on and working with.

What follows combines research with informed speculation; it is not to be taken as gospel or revealed truth. We encourage readers to do their own research and exploration. Vast areas of the spirit worlds remain unmapped, and many of the spirits residing therein have not been described in detail (or, worse, have been maligned or misinterpreted). The divisions we've given here may be useful, but they're also somewhat arbitrary; one person's divinity may be another person's local spirit. What we have given here is not an authoritative guide, but rather a jumping-off point for your own work.

THE SPIRIT WORLD(S)

If the spirits are not just hallucinations, visions, or symbols, then nor are the worlds from whence they originate. Based on our experience and the experience of many other spirit-workers past and present, we believe that Asgard is as real as Albania and Tartarus as real as (if slightly more unpleasant than) Tulsa, Oklahoma. They are not just nebulous conglomerations of astral stuff that we can shape just by concentrating hard, nor are they "interior landscapes" or "reflections of our subconscious."

We don't know the exact boundaries of these Other Realms; we aren't even sure that one can map them with the sort of accuracy cartographers can achieve on this plane. Some aspects of Newtonian physics appear to be suspended or altered in these Realms, but some are not; other rules and systems may also apply and may cause a heedless astral wanderer a great deal of difficulty. Indeed, some of these Realms are unhealthy or even lethal to humans who venture therein, and many of the denizens of these Realms are indifferent or even actively hostile to human beings. Venturing about blindly in the Other Realms with no idea of where you are going can be as foolhardy as walking into the wilderness sans map, compass, or supplies. Injuries in the Other Realms can lead to difficulties, even death, in this world; if you don't believe us, check the available literature on any shamanic tradition you care to name.

While "faring forth," or spirit-journeying, is an invaluable shamanic tool, it is beyond the scope of this book. The important thing to remember is this: *These Realms, and the denizens residing therein, do not exist solely for our benefit.* As Raven put it in his book on Northern Tradition spirit-journeying, *The Pathwalker's Guide to the Nine Worlds,* the inhabitants:

> . . . are not there to teach you, mentor you, or even talk to you. Some of them might be friendly just because they're that sort; some will lie to you. Some will not want you there, and may try to throw you out, or prevent you from entering, or worse. Every animal you meet is not your potential totem or spirit animal. Some of them may consider you to be an intruder, or food. Every hall whose door you bang on is not going to let you in with no payment and no questions asked. Things aren't always aesthetically pretty, especially if you're among nonhumanoid types. People don't act the way you expect them to. In fact, they may be unable to—or refuse to—speak your tongue.

Those of us who want to world-walk for real need to get over the idea that Otherworlds exist for our own edification and amusement. They do not, any more than the denizens of foreign cities exist to help you find your way around, teach you the native arts, let you invade their homes to gawk, and politely ignore your rude and crass ignorance of their manners and customs. We also need to get over the idea that we have an automatic right to be there, which we don't. We are there by the sufferance of the gods and spirits who order those realms, and those worlds are their territory, not ours. We need to stop acting like superior tourists; it is not in our best interest to play the archetypal Ugly American all over the multiverse.

This is equally true of those spirits and deities who have come down to our world. They may have other plans in mind when they arrive in possession, and those plans may or may not work out to your ultimate personal benefit.

GODS VERSUS SPIRITS

In Neo-Paganism, most of our important spirits are what we refer to as a god. To us, that generally means an entity who is bigger, older, and wiser than we are (and perhaps more than we'll ever be). It is an entity who sees further down the threads of Causality and Possibility and may guide or protect or teach us, or in some cases owns us. Whatever their nature, they partake of a nebulous energy that we refer to as "divine," and we can't seem to define that at all, but we know when we've touched it by the way that it affects us. Divinity seems to be more a matter of consensus emotion about the spiritual effect of a particular entity, rather than something based on a concrete knowledge of what they're really about—which is to be expected, considering that the gods generally refuse to show up to be stuck under a microscope.

Different gods have different levels of what one might refer to as "differentiation." If one assumes for an extremely transpersonal and undifferentiated "divine energy" at the very top of the hierarchy something so far from human that we can recognize no petty human traits in it (and a concept that nearly every religious context carries, although some ignore it more than others), then the gods or goddesses can be conceived of as the "differentiated Divine," as opposed to the "undifferentiated Divine," which doesn't have personal interactions with humans the way that the gods do. Of course, some gods are more differentiated than others—Demeter, for example, is a more differentiated deity than Gaia, who may blend into the even less differentiated culturally nonspecific Earth Mother. Ullr and Herne are more differentiated than the Hunter, as another example. Differentiated gods are more personal, more human, with histories and motivations that we can more clearly understand. The more undifferentiated a divine force is, the more "archetypal" it is—although that does not mean that it is merely an archetype. It's also harder for a human body to contain very much of an entity that's higher up that ladder—archetypal gods tend to have only a small amount of themselves in someone during a possession, and sometimes calling on one of them will get you a more differentiated personal deity instead. It seems to be entirely impossible for a human to be possessed by the undifferentiated All That Is/Architect Of The Universe, for theological reasons that are outside the scope of this book, and which we would not be able to do justice to here.

Another possible axis in attempting to define deities (always a dangerous act, but something that it seems we humans are driven to do) is *transcendent* versus *immanent*. This is a division between deities who are more concerned with actively bringing humans to a connection with the All That Is through them and those who are more concerned with the sacredness of this world's activities. Examples of the former are the modern version of the Judeo-Christian YHVH (the ancient Hebrew totemic god was much more personal and immanent, but he seems to have evolved toward being entirely transcendent today) or Allah (who may or may not be YHVH), and Hindu deities like Shiva, Vishnu, and Brahma. Examples of the latter are the various earth-based gods and goddesses. Although they are capable of possessing human bodies—thus the Christian sects whose members are filled with the Holy Spirit and speak in tongues, or Shivaite priests who dance the Tandava and are filled with Shiva's essence—they seem less comfortable with bodily incarnation in general, by nature of, well, their nature. On the other hand, immanent deities seem to honestly enjoy getting down and dirty in a flesh form.

So here's the first big question: What's the difference between a god or goddess and a mere spirit? Frankly, that's not something that we can answer clearly here. First, it's not as if there's a nice simple line that can be drawn; it's more like a huge gray area that's very open to interpretation. It is, after all, a concept that we humans are attempting to use to box up entities who are not we, and don't use or care about our petty boxes. It's also true that our boxes are based on personal preferences and a wish to picture the Universe in a particular way that works with our varied theologies. A Neo-Pagan would call Yemaya a goddess; a Santeria practitioner might say that She is "only" a spirit, and that the only entity worthy of the word "God" is the impersonal one at the top. Trying to define levels of "big" gods, "demi-" gods, and so on, into a coherent hierarchy rarely works well, especially across pantheons and cosmologies. It may be best just to treat everything with respect and leave it at that.

In addition, these definitions are often drawn across who the individual in question happens to be worshipping, or not; all too often "Gods" are who I worship, while "not-Gods" are those gods I don't. In the Norse pantheon, there are many giants, and some are Giant-gods and some aren't. Which are which becomes a matter of great debate, depending largely on whether the arguers are followers of the hereditary enemies of those spirits. Trying to definitively draw that line will get you in trouble more often than not, especially when you fail to show respect to the very real entity on the other end of the interaction. A friend once said, "If it's bigger, older, and wiser than I'll ever be in this lifetime, then I treat it as a God." This may be easier for polytheists, as we do not expect our gods to be either omnipotent or omniscient.

Another difficult issue is figuring out which god it is that you've got trying to come through. Putting aside the issue of whether this spirit is what it claims to be (which we will discuss in chapter 12), what about the issue of syncretism? With the names of all the world's pantheons at our fingertips, how can we tell which god blends into another? Is it all right to use an epithet of Diana for addressing Artemis? What about all those academic works saying that these goddesses are really the same figure?

Pre-Christian worshippers typically paid homage to the deity of their village, city, or clan. There were significant differences between the Diana worshipped at Ephesus and the Diana worshipped at Corinth; among one Germanic tribe, Tyr might be seen as King of the Gods while another gave that title to Odin. Conquerors often inherited the gods of the vanquished, or renamed them to better fit them within their own familiar pantheons. (The Romans were particularly fond of this approach: when they weren't venerating the Egyptian Isis or the

Persian Mithras, they were claiming that Gaelic and Germanic tribes really worshipped Mercury and Mars.)

This makes for some confusion when dealing with many of the differentiated gods. Are we dealing with separate entities that have a common name? Is the Apollo of Delphi the same as the Delian Apollo, and how does either relate to Helios? Is Ogou Ferraile the same as Ogou St. Jacques or Ogou Osanj? If we are assuming that "all gods are aspects of the One God/dess" or "all gods are mental constructs," this poses few problems. If, on the other hand, we attribute actual independent existence to our gods, it becomes an issue that must be addressed before going any further.

In some cases, what we consider the "name" of a god might more properly be considered a surname. This is particularly true of the spirits who are served in Haitian Vodou and other African-diaspora traditions. The Ghede, for example, are related in that they are all spirits connected with death, sex, and raucous good humor, but there are as many different Ghede as there are different dead people. Most will be fond of *piman* (raw rum in which twenty-one Scotch bonnet peppers have been steeped), but some will prefer red wine, some will prefer soda, and some will prefer another drink altogether. Most will tell dirty jokes, but some will be dead (pardon the pun) serious and somber. Most will dance the *banda* (a hip-grinding, pelvis-thrusting dance) but some will sit quietly and at least one, Ghede Zaringuey, will crawl about on the floor like a spider. Most are known as La Kwa, or "of the cross"—but I know a Jewish Ghede who will object loudly and profanely if anyone associates him with Christian imagery.

One theory is that the Apollos, Zeuses, and so ons of various temples might be seen as brothers or cousins. They are not the same person, any more than you are your sister or your maiden aunt, but they share a certain "family resemblance." If we accept this, that means that calling on a deity without specifying a particular name, offering the sacrifice given at a particular temple, for example, means you will have no idea which specific deity is going to show up. You may even get one of the family who has never been served up to this point—which is how all those various temples got set up in the first place! Yet another theory holds that various names are "aspects" that represent the deities at different stages of their career. Odin Way-Tamer (the traveling Odin) is going to appear quite differently from Odin All-Father or Odin Bolverk (Evil-Worker). Because time in the Other Realms is nonlinear when compared to our own world, it is possible for spirit-workers to encounter different "aspects" of the deity; one may encounter a god in his youth and later as an elderly man, for example.

Others have compared these different aspects to differing channels on a radio; Ares and Mars are in the same band but are broadcast on different frequencies. Still others have spoken of different "badges" or "hats." You fulfill different roles during any particular day—father, husband, lover, employee, boss, subordinate, customer. The way you act in any one of these roles may be radically different from the way you act in another. (You probably don't coo and make funny faces at your coworkers, for example.) In a similar vein, calling on a god in his role as "avenger of wrongs" will get a very different response from calling on him as "lord of poetry" or "bringer of fire." If one were to use this as another theory, one could say that the different titles of deity X are ways to get hold of deity X's different job specialties without confusion. It does seem to be a Law of the Universe that deities themselves cannot disobey—when you call on a deity by a specific title, that's the one you get, every time. If you call Aphrodite Porne, you don't get Aphrodite Urania. It seems to be one of the few ways in which we can affect the way that the gods manifest to us, using universal laws that are bigger than everyone, human and deity alike.

But back to what's not so certain. It could be that all these models are correct, depending on which deity one is talking about; perhaps none of them is right. What does seem correct is that deities can appear very differently to different people, or in different times and places. We should also note that there are forgotten deities, deities who have never been worshipped, and deities who have little or nothing to do with humankind. Hence, you shouldn't be surprised if the deity who arrives doesn't act exactly like the one you've studied. And whatever model is true, our experience suggests that you are wisest to treat each possessing deity as an individual and honor them on their own terms.

NON-DIVINE SPIRITS

While there are many deities in the Other Realms, there are many more beings that are not and which do not claim to be divinities. Among the most famous examples of these are the Faeries of European legend and the Djinni (genies) of Islamic lore. The animal totems encountered in vision quests could be seen as non-divine spirits, as could the spirit guides of Spiritualism; the angels and demons of Judeo-Christian tradition; the dryads, naiads, and satyrs of Greek mythology; and the Alfar, Duergar, and Jotnar of the Northern Tradition.

These spirits may not be divinities, but they can be extremely powerful nonetheless. It's another example of why it's difficult to tell where the line between "deity" and "non-divine being" should be drawn, and why in practice the best approach may be to treat any spirit with caution and respect. A smiting from an offended dryad or angry djinn can be every bit as painful as chastisement from a deity. That doesn't mean you should kneel down before any spirit that demands your worship; indeed, you should think long and hard before you promise eternal fealty to *any* spirit, divine or not. You should also keep in mind that in most situations, treating any spirit with the respect and dignity you would use when dealing with a Very Important Person will be sufficient. (In fact, quite a few deities and non-divine spirits will be offended by groveling in their presence, if it's not what they had in mind.)

Of course, with non-divine spirits it's even harder to figure out what you've got. One of the big disadvantages of dealing with non-divine spirits as opposed to known deities is that it can be very difficult to check your experience against the available primary sources. If "Thor" comes down and demands champagne and a pink frilly tutu, you can be reasonably sure you're not dealing with Thor. But what do you do if there is no known primary source on the spirit? These cases demand a bit of extra caution and a firm hand. If your new spirit companion is a lying spirit, a parasite, or something innately harmful to humans, you will need to be able to eject them at the first sign of trouble. (We'll discuss this in a later chapter.)

Non-divine spirits can and frequently do possess people. One of the most common forms of small spirit-possession in ancient (and modern) tribal societies with a shamanic culture is the shaman's use of spirit-possession with entities that we would not generally consider gods (although god-possession happens in some shamanic traditions as well). One example of this is the shamanic use of spirits to pass through their bodies and hands and heal or otherwise fix their clients. Some shamanic traditions also send smaller spirits temporarily into the body of the client in order to do the job. Shamans have also traditionally used a technique that some modern shamanic practitioners have referred to as "reverse-possession," which allows the shaman to utilize the spirit's qualities for his own purposes while being completely in control of the situation. It's not so much that a shaman possesses the spirit-worker as the spirit-worker possesses him. It's been referred to as "wearing them like a hat," as opposed to deity-possession, which would be like trying to wear a refrigerator like a hat. This can be used to augment one's shape-shifting abilities, or temporarily lend some important quality necessary for an act of magic. In order to pull this off, you have to have the consent of the spirit in question, even if it is technically smaller and weaker than you.

Smaller non-divine spirits are all different, but the experience of the ride is often similar. With some of them, ones whose personality are more like mine, I have to be careful not to let too much of myself spill onto them while they are here and pollute the message they are trying to convey. That's tricky, because it means consciously giving up more control in some ways than with a god. I have to be more passive with them, where a god will just squish me into a little ball and move me out of the way.

—Fireheart Tashlin, Pagan spirit-worker

Animal spirits are probably the most commonly used for this purpose. A shaman or shamanic practitioner (or whatever the name for spirit-worker is in the given culture) might make an alliance with the Grandparent Spirit of the Wolf, who will come through their body and reach into a sick client and "take out" something that the spirit-worker can't reach—for example, the life force of inhabiting "evil" bacteria or viruses, the actual "evil spirits" that attempt all too often to mess with us. The spirit-worker might also make an alliance with the spirit of an actual dead animal, rather than the overarching Grandparent Spirit; Greywolf, a Celtic shaman, writes of his experience with doing this. At a yard sale he found a rug made of the skins of young wolves, and he wore it as a cloak; the first time that he wore it to a feast where venison was served, the wolf-souls who were still attached to the rug "woke up" and demanded to be fed through the medium of his body, even though he was a vegetarian. "As I ate the first mouthful I felt the hides on my back begin to ripple with life and heat that radiated through my body. After forty years in a bag in an attic, my wolves were eating again. . . . After the wolf-skin cloak came to me I found that I had a pack of six young wolves that I could call on for assistance. I became their alpha male, the pack leader."[1]

Although lycanthropy is a complex phenomenon that is beyond the scope of this book, one rather rare form of "shamanic" lycanthropy might also be considered a form of spirit-possession. In this practice, rather than actively shaping the astral body into animal form, the spirit-worker "trades souls" with an animal spirit, allowing them to use the human flesh for a time while they travel in the animal spirit's shape in the Otherworlds. While all such accounts seem to come from the point of view of the spirit-worker doing their journeys, and there is very little written about what the animal spirit does with the human body while it has it, such a situation is a form of possession—perhaps even "double" possession. One correspondent describes her experiences with modern possessory lycanthropy:

> *I am a therianthrope, someone who identifies nonphysically as an animal, specifically a wolf. I first became aware of being a wolf when I was about two years old, and it's something that's always stuck with me . . . I've never determined the source of this; I'm more concerned with the functionality of it and what I can do with it. While I don't believe it is entirely totemic in nature, nor is it wholly psychological—but both play a strong role in it, particularly as it relates to my spirituality and magical practice. If you wanted to talk in terms of personality aspecting, you could say that Wolf-the-totem corresponds internally to my ego, which is also lupine-identified. However, that which is wolf in me is not limited to my ego and the human consciousness; as with most therianthropes, I go through shapeshifts at various times in response to a variety of stimuli. In these cases, my consciousness and perception ceases to be that of a human, and becomes primarily that of a wolf, though there is enough of the human mind-set to keep me from doing something entirely stupid, such as bite someone or run naked down the street.*
>
> *While this wolf-nature is something that is wholly a part of me and always has been, rather than being due to an external entity possessing me, the extremely strong bond with Wolf makes invoking them very easy. Generally if I try out a new form of animal magic, I'll ask for help from Wolf or a wolf spirit, simply because that is what's most familiar. For example, for about 5 years now I've been dancing in a wolfskin at drum circles at various Pagan festivals. What I have found is that when an animal dies, the soul leaves the body, but there remains a spiritual residue of sorts strong enough to have a personality of its own. I am able to work with this spirit when I work with animal parts artistically and*

magically, and when I dance with the wolfskin (or any other skin) I invoke that spirit and allow it to use my body, while getting a chance to find out what it's like to live in their head and feel what it's like to be them. I figure that's about the closest I'll ever get to an actual physical shift.

We have a small ritual we go through every time we dance together. First I slip my arms through the holes where the front legs once were—my arms fit perfectly. That establishes a bond between us. Then I fasten the skin at my ankles, then my arms and hands, and as I do so I can feel myself spiritually/energetically/astrally shifting to wolf, feeling the spirit of the skin entering into my body at each point of contact. Finally, I pull the head over mine like a hood and tie it, and at that point the spirit fills my body entirely and we share flesh and fur. Once we get started dancing, the barriers between our respective consciousnesses dissolve and we meld in mind as well as in spirit. The outer wolfskin spirit never entirely overwhelms me; he may call up and meld with the internal wolf, but I am not taken over to the point that I forget myself.

—Lupa, animistic Pagan magician

Plant spirits, too, have been used shamanically in this way. A spirit-worker who has an alliance with the Grandparent Spirit of a particular plant may take the spirit of that plant into them, or put it into the client, in order to do healing. This is particularly effective in that one can actually ingest some of the body of the plant, and thus take it quite literally into the body. If there is an alliance with the spirit, it will travel along and "aim" the action of the plant's alkaloids where they will do the most good, creating an extra "kick" for healing. This is a mild form of possession, the oldest and most common method of fighting against the "evil spirits" of disease that also inhabit, both physically and astrally, a human body.

Entheogenic plant spirits have also been propitiated historically in order to achieve altered states, generally with those powerful plant spirits as guides through the Otherworlds in order to do spirit-work. Again, the fact that they can be taken physically into the body as well as astrally can create a highly effective kind of possessory altered state. Plant-spirit possessions don't look like the possessions of most other spirits—plants are sessile, and plant-spirits have little interest in running around in the body, so the interaction is usually entirely internal, between the plant-spirit and the spirit-worker—but their presence can be palpably felt working through the hands and body of the practitioner in question.

Plant and animal spirits are good examples of egalitarian allies, in that you can't force them to do what you want, but nor are they generally strong enough to force you to do anything, unless you have made deals with them that allow them that liberty. They are also likely, when it comes to alliances, to require you to take on certain taboos as payment for their aid. These might be rules around what you can and cannot do with their meat or skins, or how you treat, eat, or recreate with animal or plant substances in general. If you agree to these taboos and then break them, they have the lawful right to mess with you, so be careful what covenants you make.

> *Aside from deities, I have done possessory work with a number of plant spirits. Skullcap moved inside me to teach me some of the things I needed to know about her powers; she was quite solidly in me and my awareness was kept in line in order to learn from her. The fly agaric spirit, Father Redcap, hasn't slipped completely inside, though he has overshadowed me on a few occasions. In a sort of reverse possession, I have been taken into the ruling Wormwood spirit and was held inside him for a time. My awareness has been allowed inside redwood trees to sit next to their slow steady spirits and to see the world through their ancient perspective. Being inside Wormwood was very healing and comforting; being inside the redwood trees was simply one of the most moving experiences of my life.*
>
> **—Silence Maestas, Pagan spirit-worker**

Local elemental spirits are another sort of entity that occasionally (but rarely) possesses people. The largest spirits on this scale are the land-spirits, the guardians of specific areas of the Earth. They vary in size from the one that might guard your back field to the one in charge of an entire mountain range. As a rule, the bigger they are, the less likely they are to pay attention to you. Even local land-spirits will generally ignore human beings unless they are A) doing harmful large-scale things to the land, such as clear-cutting and strip-mining, B) making overtures to the land-spirit for some reason, or C) doing magic or ritual on the land, which attracts their attention. This is why it's good policy to check with the land-spirits before doing something power-raising on unfamiliar land. Generally the land-wights will possess someone only in an emergency, if they feel that their land is being seriously threatened and they find an unguarded "open head."

Some smaller elemental spirits are the various air, fire, water, and earth elementals. These are a similar class of being to land-wights, although somewhat smaller and bound up in the expression of one sort of natural essence. They are not the same as creatures such as giants and elves and other sorts of elementally affinitive being, although the latter categories can "backslide" into being little more than an elemental spirit if they burrow too far into their elemental nature and lose the depth of their soul. Elementals have a short attention span and are further removed from humanity than the giants and Faeries; their natures are simpler, although they are not stupid. Local sprites are one form of elemental, although they may not be lined up with any of the "classic" four elements. Others can be dryads (tree elementals), naiads (river and lake elementals), nereids (ocean elementals), and other various entities described in myths and folktales. As with land-wights, possession by such creatures is possible, but rare and unlikely, and will usually be as brief as their attention span and only happen to the unshielded open horse with no other protections.

On the other hand, there are powerful and intelligent "nations" of spirits such as the various forms of elves—the Sidhe, the Alfar, the Tuatha De Danaan. There are the Giants, some of whom—as with the

Norse *etin/jotun* and the Greek Titans—scale up to godhood. There are the dwarves, and the satyrs, and many other forms of creatures with their own Otherworlds, cultures, and power. Again, usually they'll leave you alone unless you're courting them, or they've taken a special interest in you for some reason, but they have been known to possess people, consensually and otherwise. Sometimes this is for a teaching alliance, sometimes because they want to experience this world in a "heavy" body. Like the gods, they may sometimes take psychically gifted humans as lovers, and although those connections are usually made on an astral level, they have been known to "borrow" human bodies for ways to make that connection physical if only for an hour.

According to some legends, they may also utilize possession as a way to fix the personal and psychic qualities of their species into a human bloodline, through possession during the physical mating and embryo-conception of two human beings who may be simultaneously hosting one or more nonhumans. According to the theory, if these entities are astrally present in the bodies at the time of the conception of a new human, they are able to slightly alter the child's genes so as to make it more like the inhabiting Faery/Giant/what-have-you, and this is how nonhuman "blood"—and nonhuman gifts and flaws—get into human genetics. Legends and folktales abound with stories of mortals bearing children to immortal lovers, and the gods get into those stories as well; certainly Zeus spread his "seed" far and wide among mortals, including Alexander the Great, whose mother, Olympias, claimed that her child was the son of both her husband, Philip of Macedon, and Zeus himself. (Frankly, it seems not at all unlikely that Zeus would choose the great warrior King Philip for a vessel.) The dynasty of Yngling rulers, who gave their name to England, claimed to be descended from the god Ing/Frey. Are Marsson, one of the great seafarers of Icelandic legend, was said to be fathered by an elf on his mother, Katla (described in the sixteenth-century Icelandic poem "Koetlu Draumar").

It has also been noted that when a member of one of these nonhuman species approaches a human being out of nowhere, the reason most often given is that this individual has some small amount of their genetic ancestry, and this makes them "interesting" to the nonhuman involved. However, even humans with these bloodlines should be careful of such alliances; while they can be highly rewarding, it is important to remember that they are Not Human, and their values, worldviews, and cognitive differences must be taken into account when dealing with them. Some nonhuman species can be quite easy to offend, if you make human assumptions about their motives and reactions. If you are approached by one—and especially if there is impending negotiation about being ridden by them—try to find a spirit-worker who works specifically with that race and ask them for advice and possible mediation, before you misstep.

Another subcategory of not-quite-gods, if we can even make that hubris-filled statement, is that of divine servants. This encompasses such entities as angels, Valkyries, Odin's ravens, and formerly mortal messengers who work for a particular deity. Often, when they come, they explain that they are here to speak and listen for their divine masters, who do not choose to come directly for whatever reason. Treat them with the respect that you would treat their masters, as you can be sure that everything you say, do, and possibly even think will be reported. However, it is generally considered fair to do a quick divination to make sure that this messenger is really reporting to god X, before you open negotiations.

THE DEAD

The idea that deceased people can sometimes return to this plane is as close to a Universal Myth as we are likely to find. Ancestor worship is the oldest form of religion, and funeral rites may have started not as a way of assuaging the grief of survivors but as a means of ensuring that neglected dead spirits would not wreak havoc on those who did not provide them their due respect. Even today, possession by the dead is commonplace in many cultures. Francis X. Hezel S. J., a Jesuit scholar living and working in Micronesia (a collection of islands and atolls located between Melanesia and Polynesia in the Pacific Ocean), gives us a contemporary account of dead relatives returning to intervene in the affairs of the living:

> Just as the family members crossed themselves to begin eating, M. shouted, fell back off her seat and lost consciousness. She awoke and started to scream. An uncle who was knowledgeable in Chuuk medicine was called. When M. saw his arrival, she struggled to escape. She was so strong that her older brothers could barely keep her down. The uncle saw the spirits of the mother and the aunt "on her" and explained that they were angry and wanted to take M. away. He knew why the spirits came: there were bad feelings between the oldest sister and a brother. For his medicine, the uncle chewed certain leaves, perfumed them and washed M's body with them. While he was bringing out the medicine, the spirits left and M. calmed down. Since the uncle had already brought the brother with him, he and the oldest sister were reconciled. The bad feelings were caused by a land dispute. M. had another three incidents after this, all within a month. Each time M. would cry and take on the expressions of the dead mother, both in voice and in facial expressions. M. said in her mother's voice, "I want to take her [M.] away because you don't love her."[2]

Other Micronesian shamans work with dead spirits: on the island of Puluwat, a boy who was said to be possessed frequently by a spirit of the dead "prophesied" the arrival of a South Seas Expedition steamer, while on the island of Ulithi a baby who died soon after birth in 1839 returned to work as a powerful prophet and healer for his father, who would call him down by drinking coconut oil and chewing mint leaves. When possessed by the baby's spirit, the father would speak in a high falsetto voice and would diagnose disease and warn of oncoming typhoons.[3]

The dead can sometimes return to take care of matters left unfinished when they departed. The second half of Dion Fortune's *Moon Magic* was completed by a trance medium who channeled Fortune after her death.[4] The "restless dead" can also attempt to possess the living so that they can continue to enjoy the benefits of life on our plane. Many practitioners of African-diaspora religions have encountered these possessions/infestations by "haints," *spiritos intranquilos* or *morts;* they can be among the most difficult and dangerous possessions to break, and are a major reason why sensitives must take proper precautions when visiting graveyards, "haunted areas," or locations where paranormal or poltergeist activity has been detected—or avoid these places altogether.

And when the dead don't come of their own accord, those they left behind frequently call on them. The Spiritualist movement is a well-known example of this, but it's far from the only one. Despite official proscriptions against "superstition," Vietnamese "soul callers" do a brisk business channeling the spirits of departed loved ones,[5] while the Bible records King Saul's visit to the Witch of Endor when he wished to gain counsel from the deceased prophet Samuel. (As frequently happens during possessions, Saul didn't get the reassurance he was hoping for: rather, Samuel predicted his downfall and defeat.[6])

> *The difference between horsing dead human souls and gods? Dead people are much smaller. Most of my horsing dead people were for teaching purposes—either me being taught from behind the safety glass, or that spirit teaching someone else, with or without me watching. I found that horsing a spirit doesn't take nearly as much out of me as horsing a god, but it can be harder to maintain the horsing—finding myself coming back to my body before they were ready to leave. There isn't that divine power holding the door open. It takes more of my conscious effort to open for a dead human spirit, whereas a god can just shove me out of the way and take over.*
>
> **—Wintersong Tashlin, Pagan spirit-worker**

When a spirit or Egun comes in, I feel a pressure on me, or an entwining feeling within my body. An old medium once described it as feeling like being a mailbox, and the spirit comes in like they are a letter entering the slot of the mailbox. I experience this on the back of my neck and down my spine. Sometimes the coming possession of a spirit feels like the body of a spirit walking into my upper torso, or my whole body. I don't experience the feeling of "light" that I do with a deity-possession.

Most possessions that I have witnessed are the spirit-possessions that I have described. I have also seen elevated beings come in who are not orisha and are not the dead; maybe they are some form of deity. It does not look like what I described when I see orisha possession, so I consider them spirits. I am being very cautious about this. In my tradition, they say that an orisha will sometimes send a spirit on their behalf to manifest an aspect of themselves. Perhaps it is the same with Western deities, or perhaps there are elevated levels of deity that we as a community are experiencing. I am still learning and watching and finding language for all of this.

—Olorisha Omi Lasa Joy Wedmedyk

Like many of the other distinctions drawn here for convenience, the line between revered ancestors and divine spirits can be a blurry one. The people of Bǎo'ān (a village in southwestern Taiwan) believe that after death, people who were especially virtuous and important become gods, and that most of the gods they speak with through trance mediums were once living people like themselves.[7] In Vietnam, Ly Phuc Man, a historical personage from the sixth century, is worshipped in many villages; so too is a more recently deceased ancestor, Ho Chi Minh.[8] Many practitioners of Ifa and Lukumi identify Chango as a mighty chieftain and warrior who was promoted to orisha status upon his death, while Ogou Desallines, the spirit of Jean-Jacques Desallines, Haiti's first ruler, often appears at fets. Mongolians revere Genghis Khan as something between a dead ancestor and a demigod, and call on him often for protection. Similarly, Korean mudang shamans revere and call upon (and are often possessed by) ancestral shamans and ancient rulers who have now become godlike and impart their wisdom. During a mudang initiation, the mudang will be dressed in a wide variety of costumes dedicated not only to gods but also to ancestral spirits, and she will be possessed by several of them, as their way of claiming alliance with her.

What Westernized people need to keep in mind while reading this all-too-brief chapter is that there are many, many more sorts of spirits than the few that we list here. Every ancient and aboriginal culture had—and has—its pantheon of spirits, and some of them could name literally hundreds, often by name. As people raised in a monotheistic culture, we may have absorbed some of the Western assumption that having one god is more "advanced" than having multiple gods, and some of this assumption seems to have continued even in less monotheistic communities with unspoken ideas that having fewer gods and spirits in one's world was more "rational," less superstitious, less like those primitive people, than having multitudes of them. If one couldn't be a monotheist, then by God one should at least have a "decent" number of gods, which translated to "as few as possible." This seems to be at least part of the motivation of many scholars to conflate and merge deities into piles of vaguely similar entities and decide that they are all one rather than many.

There's no easy answer when it comes to figuring out what sort of spirit you've got, and how to best behave toward it, although in this book we will give you what wisdom we've gleaned on the subject. Some spirits blur the boundaries of the above categories—how many of us are only one thing?—and some may be in other categories we didn't even get to. Still, the basic rules apply: courtesy, thoughtfulness, and keeping your wits about you. We aren't expected to have plumbed all the mysteries of the spirit worlds, and they know that. We are expected only to do our best, and to keep a mind open to wonder.

7
Spirit and Flesh
How Possession Works

It is one of the best ways to experience divinity. It shoves your face in the fact that there is something bigger than you, right in front of you, every day. It is a far wilder and more personal experience of divinity than other methods I have experienced.

—Summerwind Tashlin, Pagan spirit-worker

SO HOW DOES A SPIRIT get into a human body? First, it's important to remember that unless the body is dead, there is already a spirit dwelling in it. The soul, with all its various parts and accessories (descriptions of which vary depending on cultural context), usually resides in the area inside the flesh envelope, taking up the space we refer to as the astral body. The aura is to the astral body as an atmosphere is to a living planet, and extends beyond it. This means that there is already a "space" carved out, so to speak, to seat a spirit in. Possession is the (ideally) willing action of moving over and letting another spirit share that space. It may be much larger than you, and thus only a small part of it will fit in, leaving the rest to swirl about the body or (more likely) not enter into the space at all. (Gods can do that.) It may be much smaller than you, and need coaxing to do what needs to be done. It may be unfamiliar with a body—or, at least, your body—although some are a quicker study in that area than others.

What you have to remember with deity-possession in particular is that the gods are much, much bigger than we are. Only a small part of their being actually lodges itself into our limited physical bodies. The entirety of a god or goddess simply wouldn't fit in our tiny space, no matter how much we were squashed. Of course, some gods are bigger than others. The more "personal" and "humanlike" deities are not as huge in comparison to us as the older and less "human" gods. One individual who had been an aide for several public ritual horsings wrote to us:

> *I can see auras; I've always been able to. The aura of a god is much bigger than that of a human being. If a human is about two or three feet across—coffin-size, as one friend put it—the aura of most gods is more like ten feet across, and it has a brightness that's the visual equivalent of standing near an electric fence. You have to keep averting your eyes. Of course, the first time that I was at a horsing of the ancient Hunter, his aura was so big that it encompassed the entire field. That meant that his horse looked, at first glance, like it had no aura at all, just a moving dark figure in furs and antlers. Then I realized that the horse's body was the central anchor point for this utter hugeness, and I was totally awed.*

It seems that people who are natural horses—those whom the gods and spirits choose outright, often without warning or consent—are "wired" psychically (and possibly neurologically) to be that way. We have noticed a higher occurrence of certain neurological disorders among natural horses (meaning those who are plagued by god-possession without ever striving for it), including Tourette's syndrome and some seizure disorders. Many of the conditions that are currently classified as schizophrenia also appear to be concomitant with the ability to horse naturally. However, some natural horses have no such indicators, and many people who suffer from one or more of these conditions have no natural ability to horse.

In many religious traditions, only skilled and trained professionals practice possession; in others, it is more egalitarian. It is not uncommon for bystanders at a Vodou fet or an Espiritismo *misa* to become possessed, for example. We suspect that many of these cultural and religious taboos originated with the gods themselves, as they were only willing to use a body that fit their rigorous specifications. We would also note that not everyone in these cultures can experience possession either. Even in Haiti there are a significant number of houngans and mambos who *travay klere* or "work clear"; they serve the lwa but are never possessed by them. Of those people who can become possessed at a fet, most will experience them as comparatively light and brief. (Those whose possessions are more intense, frequent, and long lasting will generally be encouraged to *kanzo* and become full-fledged priests of the religion.) The ability to completely "let go and let the gods" is not something that you can learn from a book, or even from a teacher.

This doesn't mean that those who are not natural horses can never experience possession, although it does mean that it will be unlikely. People whose genetic dice gave them tin ears and a poor vocal range are less likely to be professional singers, although a few will get lucky anyway. However, this is still one of the rarest of the psychic gifts, because it isn't one that you can just set out to master via willpower. It is entirely dependent on the gods and spirits, and if they don't want you to use this path, then it simply won't happen. That's another reason for the greater community to dislike it; it is (like becoming a classic shaman) rather an elitist situation. The gods and spirits decide who gets to do it, and we have no say over that. We can't even really understand their choices and reasoning; being nabbed as a horse doesn't seem to be contingent on any standard of intelligence, sanity, morals, or even devoutness. In the egalitarian views of the modern alternative spirituality movement(s), any spiritual experience ought to be available to anyone who works hard enough at it, and the unfairness of being chosen (or not) as the gods' own limo driver can rankle terribly.

In ancient times, this was less of a problem because people didn't expect spiritual things to be egalitarian. They also didn't expect spirits to be kind, or loving, or in the immediate best interests of the humans whom they might grab. In fact, the average person in a traditional tribal society today will generally avoid "spirit-ridden" sacred places as taboo; they don't want to be noticed by the spirits. They know what happens to the people who get noticed, and they would prefer to keep living a life with a full set of choices. This contrasts wildly with modern people who desperately want to "bring more magic into their lives," without knowing what that meant to our ancestors. The gods, however, still work along the paths noted by those ancestors. They are untouched by, and immune to, our exhortations that spiritual attention be distributed fairly, by our own standards, and they will continue to work in ways that bewilder and confuse us, and are mysterious to our limited understanding.

> *It's not a problem that most people can't be horses. It's an asset. What would happen if everyone at a ritual was a horse and there was no one who could make sure that it stayed safe for them and anyone who happened along at the wrong time? Also, not everyone can handle being in the presence of the gods, and that's OK. The idea that everyone can do everything is dangerous and ineffective and is just going to piss off the gods, and hurt the poor people that are forcing the issue when they shouldn't be. On the other hand, if the person has already been grabbed by gods or spirits, then it is our obligation to teach them to do it safely.*
>
> **—Fireheart Tashlin, Pagan spirit-worker**

> *Possession is a skill that must be developed by the person who is born with that kind of energetic pattern, developing a relationship with all of Creation. It should not be taught to anyone who*

wants to learn. I have seen extreme damage to a person's energetic field when they have forced a possession or had one forced upon them. It is a true gift that takes the right person, the right god, and the right set of sacred circumstances. It also takes a lot of training, knowledge about the nature of possession, and personal spiritual commitment. I believe that what I do works because I have established relationships with the seen and unseen worlds in a consistent spiritually based way. I could not do all the work that I do without the continued support of all Creation.

—Olorisha Omi Lasa Joy Wedmedyk

That said, one person who is grabbed as a horse may be offered a different deal from someone else. Some spirit-workers are required to horse when the gods tell them, and their only bargaining points may be time and place. Others have greater leeway and can refuse, although if they refuse too often, the gift may be withdrawn entirely. Some offer and are accepted; some offer and are refused; some refuse and are taken anyway. Some may horse only their patron deity; others might be "lent out" by their patron to horse other gods (we call this being a rent-a-horse), and yet others may have no patron and no restrictions except for which gods are willing to show up and use them. (This situation will be discussed more thoroughly in the Horse section; see page 168.)

I think that anyone can learn to channel, or to let something ride along with them to shadow, but not everyone can horse. Some people just can't let go of control, some people just aren't wired for it, and some spirits just won't horse a particular person. They're picky; they like a particular body type or brain type or personality. There's no judgment there; it's just not a fit with them. I think that anyone can be taught to be an energy channel, but we would never accept anyone as a divine energy channel who hasn't had some kind of experience with being touched by deity. And just being a divine energy channel is the lowest, simplest level of horsing. I think there are cultural factors as well, so I'm undecided on the issue. I don't think everybody can naturally do it. In fact, I think some people are forbidden and precluded from doing it by their patrons. I think that you can teach people to have the channel open, but you can't force the deity through. You can teach them relaxation, mental preparation, awe, and such, and you can practice that, but that's not the same as deity coming through.

—Lydia Helasdottir, Pagan spirit-worker

People who horse regularly generally say that they definitely have a sense of a "hole" or "door" in their astral body, where the spirits can enter. The most common sites for these holes seem to be either the crown chakra at the top of the head or the base of the skull (what some Afro-Caribbean faiths refer to as the *aché* point). A small minority reports the gods coming through the middle of their back, at about heart chakra level. Some are not able to pinpoint any particular "entry point," but just report that the spirit slides into them, and they slowly lose consciousness to one extent or another.

I consider myself extremely fortunate in how I first came to learn about and experience divine possession. My first experience with a god choosing to temporarily inhabit my skin occurred in the early 1990s, when I was still working with Fellowship of Isis. At the time, I was serving as psychopomp for someone's initiation ritual. The woman in question was dedicating to the Kemetic goddess Neith, and as I was guiding her through the various challenges and keeping her as grounded as possible considering the circumstances, I felt a quiet, reserved presence touching my consciousness. I had honored Anubis many times before, and I recognized the feel of that presence, so I didn't panic. He slid gently into my consciousness, and I allowed Him to take over my mental and physical reins. The possession wasn't very deep—a light shadowing, really—but it started me down the road of a horse, one whose primary spiritual "job" is allowing the gods to speak and act directly through the medium of one's human flesh.

While possessory work is neither common nor encouraged in Fellowship of Isis, my priestess had some experience with the Afro-Caribbean religious traditions, enough to understand what was going on. She neither encouraged nor discouraged the practice. If it occurred, that was good and if it did not, that was good too. Thanks to her practicality in the matter, I was able to view possessory work as simply one more manifestation of my spiritual evolution. It had no particular weight attached for good or for ill. This has served me extremely well over the years. It allowed me to approach it as an act of service from the very beginning without becoming attached to either the practice or the outcome. I never sought out possession, but when it occurred, I was able to step back and allow the god or goddess in question to come in without too much difficulty. Some people experience possession as violating in the extreme, but I was fortunate that for myself, this was never the case.

—Galina Krasskova, Heathen spirit-worker

There are generally five main reasons why someone would horse a spirit of whatever size and intensity. There might also be a couple of smaller reasons, but these are the main ones:

1. **Training purposes**. Sometimes there are skills that can't be taught to you through words but instead require a wight to enter your body at least partially and "motor you through" the skill. (For example, Loki taught Raven pathwalking in this way.) This also includes being horsed in order to train someone else, when the wight in question needs a willing body to be his sparring partner, or to show the person how a type of energy is moved, or a type of magic done.

Once I was taken in hand by Loki and Odin, possessory work became one of the training methods that They commonly used with me. In teaching me journey work, or certain aspects of magic, galdr, *and* seidhr, *Loki would often ride me lightly, enough to overlay his consciousness with mine and to guide my hands in the techniques he was attempting to teach me. Eventually, Odin gave me a spirit song and over time used this to pattern my head and mind to Him specifically. I didn't realize precisely what He was doing at the time though, not until much later. Using the receptive state the song put me in, He would modify me slowly over a period of about a year until He could slip into me deeply and without difficulty. For that year of training, Odin became the only deity other than Loki that I was allowed to be ridden by, but eventually He permitted me to do so for other gods and goddesses.*

—Galina Krasskova, Heathen spirit-worker

I have experienced both god-possession and spirit-possession; most of the time when I am being possessed by a spirit it is for the purpose of training. Sometimes the spirit-teacher will come forward and go through a lesson with someone else and I will be allowed to follow along, thus learning the lesson as well. When they are teaching through me, it is like watching someone else do something with your hands. It makes sense at the time, and sometimes I can do it when they leave. Often I have to do the thing that they have taught several times in a row or I will lose it. Gods are somewhat different when they come to teach—the lesson seems to come through much more clearly. If they were written down, it would be like all of the letters were outlined in light, glimmery and more clear.

—Fireheart Tashlin, Pagan spirit-worker

Freya has come into me and walked me through various techniques. This is sometimes a partial possession—she gently glides in, does something with my body and my hands, and then glides out and says, "Do that." I try to copy it, although sometimes she has to repeat it a few times before I get it right. Luckily she is patient with me.

—Gudrun, seidhkona

2. **Information purposes.** If a client comes to a spirit-worker with a question and one of the gods wants to answer that question themselves, you could just take verbal dictation and relate the words, but it's useful for the spirit-worker to be able to temporarily horse the client if need be. That way they can speak to the client face-to-face, as it were, and you're less likely to muck things up with an unclear signal.

Being possessed by my Orisha is a joy and an honor. Being possessed by Yemaya and the spirits is part of my work for many reasons. They wish to work through me in that way to help others in their lives. Sometimes it helps with clarity of message. Sometimes it helps other people know that the truth has been given to them, because they recognize and trust the spirit that is speaking.

—Olorisha Omi Lasa Joy Wedmedyk

Usually I can talk to a deity myself—I've got a good phone line, as it were. But sometimes the signal is unclear, because I'm sick, or tired, or in a bad place, or—to my shame—ignoring the answer because I hope that it's something else. If praying before an altar isn't getting me anything clear, I may look for someone who is a horse and can carry that deity in order to talk with me one-on-one. Sometimes I can't find anyone who can carry that god or goddess, and that's just life. Sometimes I can—and it's amazing to have that god look you in the eye and tell you what you need to hear. All the internal arguing just melts away. It's a great gift. While I can't carry gods myself, I am grateful that there are those who can. Once one of the gods deigned to do a ritual for me, in the body of a friend, and that was a great honor.

—Ari, Pagan spirit-worker

3. **Public devotional purposes.** For some people, a spirit-worker horsing a deity at a public ceremony is the only chance that they'll have to see and speak with a divine force. This is very important, both to the gods and to the worshippers. This was driven home to me after a Lammas gathering when Raven horsed Frey and another spirit-worker horsed his wife, Gerda. Both of us remembered little about what happened during the horsing, but afterward people were coming up to us and thanking us for allowing them to speak to the gods directly for the first time. The number of people who were genuinely moved made it clear to both of us that this was not just done because our gods had demanded it of us. It was a real public service, and a valuable one.
4. **Errands for the deity.** Sometimes a god or wight will want to do something in our world that requires a cooperative human body. Most often it seems to be a one-on-one meeting with one of his dedicants. This could be just an important conversation or something as formal and intense as a marriage to a mortal god-spouse. Occasionally it will involve an interaction with another deity that needs to happen in mortal form for some reason (usually unknown to us, as we don't necessarily get the whole story), or even no one else at all (such as the time that a wight wanted to use me to taste meat, or gather seawater).

This kind of body-sharing is somewhat rarer, and can be very dangerous. In these cases, the spirit rides a body to experience the human condition for some purpose or another. In my experience, there have been several spirits who ride bodies to understand what cars and the Internet are like. On the other hand, a spirit might ride someone to accomplish a purpose entirely of his own (siring children, for example).

—Summerwind Tashlin, Pagan spirit-worker

5. **Channeling spirit-energy.** This is doing work on someone who

requires you as a channel, as we've described in the last chapter, about animal and plant spirits. Channeling spirit-energy is rather more of the "classic" shamanic work, where the shaman asks his spirit-helpers to come through him and aid an individual who needs help. Most often this is simply the energy of the spirit in question coming through, which is beginning to be commonly referred to as "aspecting" (see below), but on occasion it requires full-on spirit-possession.

LEVELS OF DEITY ASSUMPTION

Some time ago, a list started circulating around the Neo-Pagan community, attributed to Willow Polson, with regard to levels of deity presence. While we found it to be useful, we also expanded it a bit to include levels between levels that only people who've had a lot of experience horsing deities could know. Therefore, we present the expanded list, with apologies to Ms. Polson.

1. **Enhancement.** This is speaking about a deity: for example, giving an invocation in the third person or telling a story. Doing this enhances people's understanding of that deity, their immediate connection with them, and the feeling of their presence at the event. Enhancement requires only knowing about the deity, rather than having any sort of connection with them. Example: A priestess tells the story about the birth of Aphrodite, as part of a rite, in such a way that people will always remember the image of Aphrodite stepping off the shell onto the shore, and what that really meant.
2. **Inspiration.** This is similar to enhancement, in the sense that you are giving an invocation or telling a story, but the difference is that with inspiration you speak from the perceived viewpoint of the deity. In this case, you speak for rather than speak about them. Instead of "Aphrodite did this," it's "Aphrodite wants

this." Inspiration is both a matter of knowledge about the deity and imagination about what they might want.

3. **Integration.** Integration goes one step further; here you speak as the deity in the first person. This is generally done only as the highlight of a ritual. One example of this is the classic Wiccan "drawing down the Moon," in which the high priestess steps forth and speaks as if she were the goddess herself. "I am the beauty of the green earth and the white moon among the stars and the mystery of the waters . . ." In a way, this is like making of oneself a votive figure to represent the deity.
4. **Aspecting.** Up until this point on the list, the human being involved has been in full control of the situation, and the presence of the deity as an entity may not even be involved at all. One can do enhancement, inspiration, and integration without actually having an astral connection to the god or goddess one is honoring, but the jump to aspecting brings one to a level where the deity is involved. From this point on, the choices and control of the human being diminish and the choices and control of the deity become more important. It is difficult to impossible to go further without the active cooperation of the entity in question. Of course, there is also the point that at any of the three stages already discussed, the deity can step in and establish a link; two-way communication can happen spontaneously. Inspiration can suddenly become channeling and integration can become aspecting or even full possession.

   In aspecting, one is a full channel for the energy of the deity, and often their words, but the deity has not fully taken over the flesh body in order to walk around in it and treat it as their own. The individual is being a vector for their energy, but not their actual presence. Some refer to this as "co-consciousness," meaning that the deity's mind and energy and their own are equally present and share command of what will be said. Aspecting is often mistaken for fully being ridden by people who have never dealt with full-on possession. Many people can aspect a deity that they cannot necessarily fully horse, and aspecting is less exhausting and much easier on the body and the soul.

Often at this stage, I find that I am sometimes able to (or allowed to) explain sensations, thoughts, or emotions that I pick up from the deity to whomever the deity is speaking to for greater clarification. There are those possessions where I am sure it's co-consciousness and later find out that while I may have thought so, large portions of time are simply blanked from my mind, so that what I think is a full memory of the experience is in reality piecemeal.

—Galina Krasskova, Heathen spirit-worker

When I first read about the practice in Ceremonial Magic *of "assuming the god-form" of a deity, I felt certain this was something I had experienced. I have never been possessed, but I have connected very solidly with the archetype of a deity while in ritual space. I didn't connect with the deity as an individual entity, but I did connect to the role of that deity and I had some small level of access to the deity's wisdom and a deeper understanding of its mysteries. I was fully conscious, but my judgment and preferences were strongly skewed to match the deity's. It was like seeing the world through the deity's eyes, rather than the deity seeing the world through my eyes. I would call this aspecting a deity's archetype, but I've also heard it described as wearing the deity's "hat" or "mask." It is very different from the sort of connection one would make doing oracular work or channeling, because the deity isn't directly communicating with you. It is much more abstract and archetype-based.*

—Joshua Tenpenny, Pagan spirit-worker's assistant

5. **Shadowing.** This is when the deity "rides along in your head," as many folks have put it. There's a feeling of them being just

behind your shoulder, and able to speak clearly to you (and some may keep up a running commentary during a shadowing experience), but they are not using your body, and you are in full control of your reactions. You may "take dictation" and relay their words, or rephrase them, or keep silent as the situation requires. Shadowing can happen as an individual experience (e.g., you're walking through the mall and your patron deity comments on which trinket they'd like you to buy for them), or as part of a ritual or spiritual consultation; in the latter case, it can shade into channeling.

6. **Channeling.** Made famous by the New Age folks, channeling is a form of partial possession in which the entity is allowed to make use of a human being's voice or hands but does not actively take over the whole body. This tends to be more common with "lesser," non-divine spirits, as it is more of a partnership between the channel and the "guest." Deities are more likely to want to take over the whole body, although this is not a hard-and-fast rule. Some may settle for channeling if there is not enough connection, or letting go on the part of the horse, to manage full possession.
7. **Possession.** In this situation, the strongest connection of all, the deity comes into the person's body, displacing their own personality/soul for a time, and speaks directly to the audience or client. Depending on the god and the situation, the deity may commandeer the body for other things as well. Generally the horse's consciousness at this point is either extremely distanced (horses have reported seeing and hearing things as if underwater or from a long way away, in a very dissociative manner, or the sound might be turned off entirely) or they are completely unconscious and have no memory of the experience. Raven's Pagan group Asphodel, with its wry sense of humor, often refers to the former as being "in the backseat behind the safety glass" (while the deity is "driving") and the latter as "locked in the

> trunk." (For a more in-depth discussion of the controversy of full unconsciousness versus partial consciousness, see chapter 13, which discusses mistaken possessions.)

This is what we know, so far, about how spirit-possession works mechanically. Of course, when one is describing something that ties together the physical, the esoteric, the cosmic, and the theological, you're going to be able to be only vague at best. There is no clear-cut boundary demarcating where Inspiration becomes Shadowing becomes Aspecting—and if you ask ten practitioners, you may well get fifteen different answers, with several of them being presented as definitive! It may be that someday we will know more about this, but the above is our information gleaned from years of observation and experience. It is, of course, full of gray areas. Nailing down the gods is like trying to squeeze water, or sunlight, or shadow: one may fool oneself into believing one has done it, but one's hands still remain empty.

8

Hearing Gods

A Guide for the Head Blind

YOU'VE WORKED HARD ON DEVELOPING a close personal relationship with your gods. You have a solid, committed group that meets regularly to worship Them. Now you'd like to invite one of your tutelary deities down in a possession ritual, and you've come to this book hoping we can show you how to do it.

However, we did not write this book as a How To Become A Horse In Ten Easy Lessons. We wrote it more for those who are already dealing with the phenomenon, close up or from a distance, and want to know what to do about it. We can offer you some pointers based on our experience; we can give you some safety tips and some things that will increase your chances of success. But ultimately the possession experience is a personal one. Each horse is different, and so is each spirit. Only your gods can tell you exactly what they want when (or if) they come. Indeed, the best way to "get" a horse for your group is to ask your gods to send one over . . . if this is actually what they want for your group. So how do you find out what your gods want?

You ask them.

Of course, this is easier said than done. Gods are notorious for being an uncommunicative lot. What's worse, many of them enjoy riddles, paradoxes, and irony—and more than a few will lie to you if it suits their purposes. If you don't yet have someone horsing your deity regularly, it's hard to know what she or he wants. And even if you do, the obvious question arises: How do you know that your horse isn't feeding you a line of horse puckey?

There are a rare few people who can chat with spirits as freely as they can speak with corporeal people. Some are born with this talent and some acquire it later in life as a gift or a curse. With training and practice, most can develop their intuitive and spiritual facilities to a greater or lesser degree, but by and large our interactions with the Divine are through a glass darkly. Indeed, various world myths suggest this is a defining part of the human condition. Some connect this with a "Fall from Grace," while others recognize that prolonged face-to-face contact with deity is hazardous to their physical and mental health. Remember that story about Zeus and his mortal lover Semele? He offered her any gift, and she asked to see him as he really was. And then, when after some arguing she held to her case, he appeared to her in the full extent of his divine glory and she was burnt to a crisp. Well, that myth isn't all hyperbole. Too much direct exposure to the gods in all their energetic intensity (as opposed to being buffered by a human body, or your mental constructs, or their willingness to extend only a finger to you) will fry your astral circuits just as crispy as Semele.

To counter what spirit-workers have come to call our "head-blindness," humankind has developed numerous work-arounds. These have become an integral and important part of most possession cultures. Mastering them before going forward will help ensure that your possession ritual is a beneficial experience for you and for your gods.

DREAMS

We spend approximately 30 percent of our lives sleeping—and all the caffeine in the world won't change that fact. Sleep is an insistent drive; whereas people can deprive themselves of food and water until they die, people cannot voluntarily sleep-deprive themselves to death. Indeed, they will drift into sleep even if they are in a situation that demands wakefulness, such as driving a car.[1] During sleep our breathing becomes more shallow; our muscles relax and our heart rate slows; our pituitary gland releases hormones that aid in growth and healing. We also experience rapid-eye movements and increased activity in various portions of our brain; these manifest as vivid multisensory experiences, or dreams.

Much of humankind's oldest surviving literature deals with dreams and their import. Enslaved in Egypt, the Hebrew patriarch Joseph rose to prominence thanks to his skill at dream interpretation. In the *Iliad* and the *Odyssey,* Homer used dreams to further the plot and provide succor to his mortal characters. Socrates was drawn to a life of philosophy by a recurring dream, and the Pythagoreans and Orphics taught that during sleep the soul left the body, took trips, visited gods, and communed with other spirits.[2] The author of the *Aitareya Upanishad,* one of Hinduism's oldest and holiest texts, said, "The Self being unknown, all three states of the soul are but dreaming—waking, dreaming, and dreamless sleep. In each of these dwells the Self: the eye is his dwelling place while we wake, the mind is his dwelling place while we dream, the lotus of the heart is his dwelling place while we sleep the dreamless sleep."[3]

But skeptics have long questioned these night visions. Aristotle scoffed at the idea that dreams have a supernatural origin; according to him, "the faculty by which, in waking hours, we are subject to illusion when affected by disease, is identical with that which produces illusory effects in sleep."[4] Following in his footsteps and in those of Sigmund Freud (who saw dreams as a release valve for the subconscious), most scholars today believe that dreams are a purely biological phenomenon with little or no spiritual importance. Those who work with the gods on a regular basis will beg to differ. Aspiring spirit-workers are well advised to take their dream life seriously: as Edgar Cayce, the famous "sleeping prophet" put it, "Dreams, visions, impressions, to the entity in the normal sleeping state are the presentations of the experiences necessary for the development, if the entity would apply them in the physical life. These may be taken as warnings, as advice, as conditions to be met, conditions to be viewed in a way and manner as lessons, as truths, as they are presented in the various ways and manners."[5]

When we enter a sleep state, our brain is no longer quite so bombarded with outside stimuli. Our consciousness is thus free to concentrate on things that had been drowned out amid the noise, light, and general chaos of the material plane. This allows us to interact with beings whose presence might otherwise have gone undetected, and allows them to get their point across to us in a face-to-face manner. With every sleep cycle, you enter a state that allows for direct communication with the gods—and all that it demands, ultimately, is that you lie down, close your eyes, and relax.

"But I never remember my dreams!" you may protest. This is a common complaint. Freudian psychologists suggest that this is due to repression; we forget our dreams because they deal with material that our conscious mind does not wish to address or acknowledge. (By this token, we "remember" our dreams once we are able to deal with those hidden issues.) Others blame interference from waking sensory input—the beautiful gossamer creations of our mind are too delicate to survive the concerns of the mundane world. Still others blame as yet undetermined neurological quirks that keep us from storing dream-information in our memory circuits. But perhaps the most important reason for forgetting dreams is that we attach little or no importance to them. As Freud himself pointed out, "Anyone who for some time applies himself to the investigation of dreams, and takes a special interest in them, usually dreams more during that period than at any other; he remembers his dreams more easily and more frequently."[6]

One of the first things you can do to ensure an active dream life is to get enough sleep. Dream deprivation follows close on the heels of sleep deprivation . . . and your dream periods get longer as you sleep. While your first dream of the night may last no more than ten minutes, after eight hours of sleep the typical dream period increases to forty-five to sixty minutes.[7] You may improve your dream recall dramatically merely by going to bed an hour earlier. If that's not possible, you may want to devote some time to quiet meditation or relaxing before going to sleep; you should also avoid alcohol, caffeine, and heavy or spicy foods at least six hours before bedtime, since all these can interfere with your dream life.

In China, Buddhists seeking enlightenment through dreams would spend the night in the Jiuxian (Nine Immortals) Tower of the Shizhusi (Stone Bamboo Temple) in Fuqing, Fujian Province.[8] In Greece, invalids came to an Asklepieion (temple dedicated to Asklepieios, Greek god of healing) to seek dream advice. After purifications and fasting, the patient would be placed on a pallet in a darkened room. During sleep, the god would come and offer advice and healing. Grateful patients who recovered thanks to this treatment would frequently leave models of the healed limbs and organs. Archaeologists excavating the site of the Asklepieion at Epidauros discovered some ten cubic meters of terracotta offerings, including legs, feet, arms, hands, ears and eyes, torsos, heads, female breasts and reproductive organs, and male genitalia.[9]

You may also want to prepare a special dream chamber of your own. If you can set aside a sleeping place to be used solely for dream work, do so. Lacking available space, you can dedicate bedding (sheets, pillows, and so on) to dream journeys. When you clean your room and make your bed using these special sheets, you will put yourself in a frame of mind conducive to vivid and memorable dreams. If you want to commune with your patron deity or deities in a dream, you can sleep in front of their altars or shrines; alternately, you can place their statues or images near your bed that night and return them to their usual place in the morning.

Recording your dreams immediately upon awakening will help immensely in achieving dream recall. Many dreamworkers keep a notebook by their bedside, and make a point of jotting down everything they can recall about the previous night's dream activity, no matter how fragmentary or nonsensical it may seem. Others use a tape recorder or a sketchbook, while still others recount their dreams in detail to their partner.[10] What is important is that you bring your dream experiences into your conscious mind immediately, rather than allowing them to dissipate as you awaken.

Keep these records handy, and resist the urge to throw them out. Aleksa, a Maryland spirit-worker who works with the Lakota deity Grandmother Spider and does extensive dreamworking, says, "I've had Medicine dreams that weren't confirmed for years after the fact so I can never forget or ignore them." You may discover that your dream excursions are affecting your mundane skills. Wintersong Tashlin, another spirit-worker, learned to drive a stick shift in his dreams. "He had recurring dreams about practicing shifting just before we got a manual car, and by the time that we had the car he was fairly familiar with the basic ideas and motions, enough so that it took him only a matter of days to become proficient," explains his partner, Fireheart Tashlin. "Similarly, I had a very vivid dream about knitting one time, and when I woke up I not only knew how to knit, I desperately wanted to do so."

Dreaming, like everything else, improves with practice. When you treat your dreams like trivial nonsense, you're likely to have trivial and nonsensical dreams. If, on the other hand, you treat your dreamtime as an important part of your spiritual and mundane life, you'll soon find your dreams growing increasingly complex and memorable while your communication with the Divine grows apace. For more thorough information on using dreaming as a psychic tool, Raven recommends the book *Psychic Dreamwalking: Explorations at the Edge of Self,* by Michelle Belanger.*

Exercise: Iluminasyon

In Haiti, Vodouisants seeking dream guidance from their spirits will frequently perform an *iluminasyon,* or illumination. This ceremony is

*San Francisco: Weiser Books, 2006.

adapted from Kenaz's *Haitian Vodou Handbook** and can be adapted to any tradition.

Begin by cleaning your sleeping area thoroughly and putting clean sheets on your bed. In Vodou white sheets are used almost exclusively; if your patron deity is associated with other colors, you may use those as an alternative. Create sacred space by your preferred method (see chapter 9, Sacred Spaces: Permanent and Ephemeral, for suggestions). Fill a basin with clean, pure water. Haitians typically use white enamelware, for this, but if you cannot find enamelware a ceramic bowl or other fireproof container will do. Place a seven-day candle in the basin, in a color appropriate to the spirit with whom you wish to commune. If you are just seeking general guidance, use a white candle; since white incorporates all colors, it can be used as an all-purpose candle. Feel free to add other things to the water if the spirit moves you—a dash of perfume for Aphrodite, some oak leaves for the Green Man, and so forth.

Wrap your head in a white cloth or head scarf. This shields you against negative influences while allowing positive energy to pass through. Say a few prayers of your choice, light your candle, and get into bed. You may focus on the flickering candlelight and allow it to lull you to sleep; you may also meditate about the spirits you wish to contact as you drift off. When you awaken, be sure to write down any dreams or waking visions you have had.

OMENS

In preindustrial societies, people lived by natural cycles. Their diet was tied to the trade winds that carried the ships to the fishing banks and the spring rains that ensured that crops would thrive until first frost and harvest. An interruption in these rhythms could mean famine and death for the entire community, hence any aberration from the usual order of things was seen as an event of major importance, a message to

*Rochester, Vt.: Destiny Books, 2006.

be deciphered by those wise enough or inspired enough to see deities at work and one to be ignored at great peril.

Outbreaks of plague, invasions, and bad weather were signs that someone had done something to piss off the Powers That Be; particularly good fortune and bountiful harvests were evidence that the gods were (at least for the moment) pleased with Their followers. A deformed colt could mean the overthrow of a kingdom; a white buffalo calf might herald a new era of peace and prosperity. Simply put, almost *anything* unusual could be taken as an omen—and it was generally best to spot and deal with the small anomalies rather than clean up after the larger and more spectacular ones.

Today most of us follow in the footsteps of the Enlightenment-era Deists. We may imagine the world was created by someone—but we assume that after putting things in order, she or he stepped aside and let the machinery run itself. We seek "rational solutions" (meaning explanations that are wholly grounded in the physical world and in known scientific laws and axioms and which do not rely on spiritual intervention) to the anomalous or unusual. We explain disease in terms of viruses and bacteria, and eclipses in terms of orbits and planet placement; why do we need recourse to some Divine Puppeteer yanking the strings?

This is not entirely a bad thing. Blaming an epidemic on tainted food is probably more productive than accusing unpopular neighbors of devil worship or blasphemy. Setting up a satellite watch to detect incoming hurricanes will save more lives than human sacrifices to the storm spirits. The scientific method of inquiry has allowed us a greater understanding of many things that once were considered "Sacred Mysteries" eternally beyond the ken of mere mortals. But all those gains have come at some cost. To our ancestors Divinity was ever-present; to many of us she or he is little more than an abstraction, an amorphous generalization that has little relevance to our daily lives. By learning to recognize and respond to omens, we can recapture our ancestors' connections to the Divine.

To start looking for omens, the first step is to ask for them.

Formally request of your gods or goddesses (or perhaps one specific one whom you are currently working with) to send you clear and unassailable omens. Second, do your homework on your patron deity or deities. What are some of the colors, animals, objects, and expressions that are commonly associated with your patron? Once you know these, you can look for unusual situations involving these symbols. If someone who honored the Morrigan awoke to find a murder of crows* resting comfortably outside his window, he might take it as a sign that he had attracted Her attention. If you ask one day "Should I honor Artemis?" and then find a stray hunting arrow on the sidewalk, you can take that as an affirmative.

Omens may also be situation-specific. The first time that Raven utilized the practice of asking for an omen, he asked his patron deity for an answer as to how long his then living situation (which was very stifling) should go on, and whether the change he was sniffing in the wind was real or imagined. An hour or so after asking, some family members coaxed him to come with them to the mall. He hated malls, but the request was odd enough that he accepted, figuring that a mall was a busy enough place to provide plenty of omen-opportunity for Divine meddling. When they walked in, a coin-and-stamp fair was in full swing. The first table that he passed held a grab-bag box of historic coins—pay your dollar, pull a little plastic bag at random, and take what you get. Sensing a divinatory setup, he immediately fished out a buck and gave it a shot. The coin that he pulled was light and thin, and bore a double-headed ax and crossed sheaves of wheat, a very Pagan motif.

The coin dealer told him that this was minted in France during the German occupation of World War II; it was the last minting a few scant months before the Germans were expelled and France set free, and its light weight was due to the lack of coin metal available. The omen was, as requested, clear and obvious: this situation had worn thin, and he would be set free in a matter of months. By the end of the sea-

*Traditional term for a gathering of corvids.

son, another living situation suddenly presented itself, comfirming the omen.

Once you have the divine request for omens sent off, you can also look for other anomalous events that may not be connected to your patron but which are difficult to ignore. Keeping a diary can help with this. As you examine what appear at first to be the trivial minutiae of your daily life, you may detect certain recurring patterns or themes. You may note, for example, that you have regularly had good (or bad) luck on or around a certain time of year; you may find that you keep running into similar situations repeatedly when you are in a particular place or taking a particular action. Recognizing these themes can help you to determine what spiritual forces are at play in your life, and allow you to work with them rather than stumble into them.

While one must be open to finding omens, a bit of healthy skepticism will also be required. If you see soldiers in the street, it may be a sign that you have attracted the attention of Ogou, Ares, or some other war god . . . but it may also be a sign that you've stumbled into the annual Memorial Day parade. That lightning bolt may be a message from Zeus, or a sign of an incoming thunderstorm. To discover divine messages amid daily life, one must first be sure to filter out the background noise.

To further complicate matters, omens are rarely clear-cut. Did Artemis lay that arrow in your path as an invitation—or as a warning to stay away from her? Did the Morrigan's crows come as a sign of her favor, or because the birds were waiting to feast on your corpse should you offend her again? Seeing an omen may prove that a deity is speaking; understanding the context in which this omen arises will help you to understand what she is saying. The better you understand your deity or deities, the more likely you will be to catch their omens and read them correctly, but ultimately interpretation is an art as much as a science. It requires both a keen eye for data and data irregularities and the ability to put aside your own preconceptions and let the events speak to you as they will.

One thing that will help you to establish whether or not you are dealing with an omen: Does it make the hair on the back of your neck stand up? Does it move you to the core of your being? You'll know an omen in your belly and in your bones, even if you don't like the message it delivers. The gods cannot help but make their presence known . . . and once you've experienced them sending you a few messages, you're not likely to mistake them for coincidence or wishful thinking. As Dagion, a priest of Hela, says, "Omens stick in one's mind very pointedly, at least in my experience; they seem oppressively important. It won't leave me alone until it is fully assimilated."

Elizabeth Vongvisith, a spirit-worker and Lokiswife, describes some of the ways she incorporates omens into her practice:

I have a kind of totemic relationship, for lack of a better description, with three or four animals and so when I see them in my immediate environment, I pay attention since much of the time it's an omen of things to come (i.e., spiders turning up in my bed, moths hanging out on the car window when I walk up to unlock the door, crows flying up everywhere I look). I often get really weird and stupid omens that have no meaning to anybody but me, and thus aren't always readily interpretable, but they tend to be SO weird that they could only be a sign of things to come, if that makes any sense. True omens tend to be statistically very unlikely and may often reflect something so weirdly personal and applicable to one's life at that particular moment that there's really no other way to take an event but as an omen.

A priestess of Artemis, Thista, got a reassuring message from the animal kingdom:

Once I did a festival for Artemis that had a pretty small turnout, and I was disappointed. As I was packing up the supplies after the ritual, I wondered if Artemis was pleased or not, and then a doe and her fawn walked out of the woods. I was able to get pretty close to them and just watch. The location was in the woods, so it's not all that unusual to see deer, but the fact that it happened right then, and that it was a doe and her fawn (which was particularly relevant to the ritual I had just held), clued me in that the sighting was a sign of her approval.

With practice and study, you will learn to sort out omens and recognize the Divine Nudge before the Cosmic Bitchslap becomes necessary. But before doing that you need to recognize that your gods and spirits are not confined to some inaccessible celestial kingdom—they are with you right here and right now. As you learn to spot the signs of their presence, you will begin to understand their power and their direct and personal concern for you. This moment of enlightenment may leave you reassured, terrified, or some combination thereof; you can rest assured that it will not leave you unchanged.

Exercise: A Period of Omens

Victorian mage, philosopher, and *enfant terrible* Aleister Crowley gave us the Oath of the Abyss: "I swear to interpret every phenomenon as a particular dealing of God with my soul.'"[11] Taking this oath is no small affair; according to Crowley's dire warnings, "Should one rashly dare the passage, and take the irrevocable Oath of the Abyss, he might be lost therein through Aeons of incalculable agony; he might even be thrown back upon Chesed, with the terrible Karma of failure added to his original imperfection."[12]

Purple prose aside, there is very real danger in this oath. One of the primary symptoms of schizophrenia is "delusions of reference," defined by the *DSM-IV* as "when things in the environment seem to be directly related to you even though they are not. For example it may seem as if people are talking about you or special personal messages are being communicated to you through the TV, radio, or other media."[13] The mage-in-training may see the Divine in seemingly random events—or she or he may fall into madness like David "Son of Sam" Berkowitz, who interpreted the barking of his neighbor's dogs as a command to go on a killing spree.

Perhaps the safest course is to experiment with declaring a defined period of looking for omens, which can range from anywhere from "for the next hour" to "for the next week." Declare this to the gods, and ask them to send whatever they think you need to know during this time, and you'll do your best to interpret it. For the duration of this period, imagine that this world and everything in it is a personal message to you from the Divine. What is the Divine saying to you? Have you been listening to these messages, or have you been ignoring them or making excuses for your inaction? Do you have a friendly, distant, hostile, or strained relationship with the Divine . . . and what can you do to improve that relationship? Look for the answers around you, again assuming that *everything* around you is a direct message of some sort.

Look for the answers, and write down those answers, but don't act upon them just yet. Wait until the term of your oath has expired. Then give it a rest period of several days, and go back through your notes. Determine what you learned from this exercise, then act upon it accordingly.

DIVINATION

Ultimately, dreams and omens are based upon anomalies, upon things that differ from the norm. Divination works from a different place. The diviner seeks recurring patterns, and sees them as a reflection of events in the spiritual and mundane world. The Ifa of West Africa discovered that by studying the way that coconut shells or cowries fell, they could learn about the forces acting upon their current situation and plan accordingly. In China the ritual of casting yarrow stalks to determine the future was codified in the I Ching; Roman augurers sought answers in the flight of birds and the entrails of sacrificial animals.

Teaching an appropriate form of divination is beyond the scope of this work, as writers have produced volumes on tarot, I Ching, runes, pendulums, and various other divinatory methods. A quick trip to your local (or online) bookstore will provide a wealth of opportunities for learning just about any system you can imagine. Instead of reinventing the wheel, we'd rather entrust your divinatory education to more-skilled folks. But since you are here, we might be able to offer you a few pointers on things you can do and mistakes you should avoid.

Our first bit of advice would be, "Find a system that works for you and stick to it." If you are drawn to the tarot, use the tarot; if geomancy tickles your fancy, learn geomancy. While you may want to experiment with various methods of divination to find the one that fits, ultimately you will probably do best by focusing on a particular system and mastering it. If you already have a patron deity, you should ask for her input on this; you may also do some research to ascertain what divination methods, if any, were historically used by her followers. A priest of Odin should probably learn to cast runes, for example, whereas someone initiated in an Afro-Cuban tradition will use cowrie shells for the same purpose.

Of course, many professional diviners do utilize several different divinatory methods, especially if they deal with clients from many different spiritual walks of life. As a shaman and professional diviner, Raven does this; the spirits of his tradition required him to learn twenty-seven different forms, and he has been known to do divination before seeing clients to determine which form of divination would be most appropriate for that person's oncoming problems. He has also found that in stubborn situations, switching to another form of divination can give a clearer take on the matter. However, this seems to work only if it is another form that you are also very proficient with.

Most nonprofessional folks who want only the occasional reading to find out what's going on with them are not going to be in the same position as the professional (paid or unpaid), who will be faced with a variety of different situations to read on, possibly not at the most opportune moment, or with the most time to make sure that one is rested or is in a good space. For the beginner, we suggest getting competent with one form before taking on a second one.

Our second bit of advice would be "to take your divination *seriously.*" If you're going to perform a divinatory ritual, you should listen to the results and put them into practice—even if they aren't the answers you expected or were hoping for! The idea is to discover what the future holds, not to repeat the procedure until you get a favorable reading. If you get an unfavorable reading, you can do another reading for clarification, but that does not invalidate the first one. (In other words: the second reading may show you what to do to avoid the troubles foretold in Reading #1, but it will not say "ignore the first reading, you gloomy Gus; here are all the good things that are going to happen if you follow your original course!")

A good way to ensure that you take your readings seriously is to do them in the context of a ritual. Casting sacred space (see chapter 9, Sacred Spaces: Permanent and Ephemeral) is one good way of doing this; not only will it put you in a properly reverent frame of mind but it will also help to drive away malicious spirits and tricksters. Keeping your divinatory tools on your altar in a closed container will also help. With practice, the simple act of removing them from their place will help to trigger the divinatory mind-set. If there are already traditions connected with your method, don't jettison them without careful thought—casting the yarrow sticks according to Chinese custom is more involved and time-intensive than simply throwing coins or dice, yet many diviners find their work with the I Ching becomes far more effective after they begin working within the traditional manner.

For the purposes of spiritual work, you may want to avoid divination by *scrying,* which means "crystal-gazing, mirror-viewing," and the like. These techniques are very powerful and, if used properly, extremely effective. However, the images produced are subject to contamination by the scryer's subconscious mind and desires. The line between crystal visions and wish fulfillment can be very unclear, particularly for beginners. (Scrying is also very knack-based; people tend to be innately good at it or not, and a lack of talent in this area can be improved only so far. This is in contrast to "sortilege" methods like tarot or runes, which require only random selection from a group of different objects and then interpreting the results, which works for almost anyone.) What we want is a source that is not subject to the diviner's mental state. Dreams and astral images are intangible, while visions are easily manipulated or misunderstood. Yarrow stalks, rune staves, coins, and the like are physical, material objects: the diviner's ability to control them is far more limited.

That being said, you cannot have divination without interpretation—and the interpreter's prejudices will certainly come into play during that process. As any good postmodernist will tell you, there's no such thing as "neutrality." Many of the best diviners I know cannot read for themselves; they simply cannot achieve the proper emotional distance. When you're dealing with events that carry a powerful emotional payload—and any omen or god-dream worthy of the name carries a hefty charge—it's hard to keep yourself from shaping the reading to suit your desires and preconceptions.

If you have a friend who is also a competent diviner, you will probably be better off getting her to do a reading on your behalf. Otherwise you should hire the services of a skilled professional. (A caveat: Divination from an incompetent or an unethical reader is worse than no divination at all.) You may want to appoint the best reader in your group as "Official Diviner," responsible for casting lots and interpreting the results. This is an office with a long and honored history; however, it is also a position of considerable responsibility, and should be held only by a trustworthy person.

Exercise: A Month of Divination

For the next thirty days, start every day with a reading using the divination method of your choice. Write down the results and your interpretation of the results. At the end of the day, look back on your predictions. Which ones came true? Which ones were not quite right but suggestive?

Which ones were way off the mark? Which came true, but perhaps only because your morning divination affected how you did things? Which failed to come true because you were warned in time and did something about it? Try to figure out what you got right and where you erred. This will allow you to put your divination into practice, and will make these symbols come alive for you. Instead of studying what others have to say about Thurisaz, the Six of Cups, or Hexagram 27, you will experience them in your life. At the end of those thirty days, examine your progress. See where you have improved and where you still have opportunities for growth.

When faced with really huge questions, such as "Should I leave my marriage and family and move to Faraway Place X to study Strange Art Y for much of the near future? Is this meant to be my path?" we suggest a "Four-Fold Signal Clarity" divination method, which is used by many professional spirit-workers, whose responsibilities are such that they cannot afford to be wrong too often in their divinations. This method utilizes both omens and traditional divination methods, and it goes like this:

First, do a divination yourself.

Second, have a friend who knows you and the situation do a divination.

Then have yet a divination done by an outsider who does not know you, your situation, or anyone else involved.

Finally, directly after the third divination, tell the gods that you are going outside into a busy and populated area, and that you want a clear and obvious omen *immediately,* within the next hour. Go out and look for one.

If all four steps give you basically the same message, then you've got something worth moving to Kamchatka over. However, if you start getting widely disparate messages, stop right there. Don't go to the next step or repeat things. It may mean that the future is heavily conflicted and things could go many ways. It could also mean that the Powers That Be want you to figure it out for yourself, or that now is not the right time. Give it a period of days or weeks and then start over from the beginning. And remember also that sometimes signal clarity just doesn't come, because we are complicated beings with complex and ever-changing lives, and that's just the way of it.

9
Sacred Spaces
Permanent and Ephemeral

IN VODOU MOST FETS TAKE PLACE in and around the peristyle, a temple that has been specially consecrated to the lwa and which has been used for years in their service. In Greece the Delphic Oracle declaimed from a spot that had long been held sacred to Apollo and which was the site of regular ceremonies. Possession cultures generally set aside a space in which possessions took place. If possible, you will do well to emulate their example.

Sometimes the gods or spirits will pick out a sacred space for you. They may inform you that a spring or stand of trees near your house is one of their favorite spots, and tell you to bring your offerings and petitions there. Death gods may choose an old graveyard, while warrior spirits may favor a monument to a heroic soldier, and deities of healing may choose an abandoned hospital or a field that served as a medical facility during some local tragedy. A study of both primary sources and people's personal gnosis suggests that this is how temples and sacred groves were originally founded—by the gods making their wishes known by various means.

You may live near a "power site"—Mount Shasta, Sedona, and Glastonbury Tor come to mind immediately—but there are many other powerful spots that are not so well known. If you can hold your rituals at or near these locations (if your deities are amenable to this), you will be able to tap in to this land energy and use it to make your rituals, including your possession rituals, more powerful and effective. Although of late a good bit of silliness has attached itself to the idea of "cosmic vortexes," the concept is sound. Those who are sensitive or who have done energy work will quickly notice the difference between a dead area and one that contains an abundance of chi, prana, orgone, or whatever you want to call it.

(Note that this does *not* mean that you should try holding your rituals in areas that are reputedly "haunted" or which are known for their negative or harmful energy. Unless your deities specifically ask you to use such a spot—and unless you have confirmed their wishes via divination and other means—you should avoid these places, not seek them out. As discussed earlier, negative entities can follow you home from an infested area and wreak all sorts of havoc in your life and in the lives of those around you.)

Just because you don't know of any power places in your area doesn't mean they aren't there: it just means that you will have to locate them yourself. The usual methods of divination (as described in chapter 8, Hearing Gods) can be consulted. If you are good at communing with nature spirits, a spot-on method is to meditate and ask the local land-spirit for their advice on the best place for this sort of thing. One warning, though—in some more-urban areas, the land-spirit has been killed off by, morphed into, or been replaced by the city-spirit, and you will have to talk to them. Start by making an offering to them, perhaps of food and drink put into the ground. Once you have your land-spirit-approved site, remember to make offerings to them before and after rituals. Those who are in line to open themselves to possession there should also begin with an offering. Land-spirits can be quite useful in grounding a horse after a ride.

When you have found your sacred area, do *not* end your rituals with banishing. Instead, invite your deities and spirits to stay there and be welcome. As you continue working within the space, the energy will grow and your rituals (possession and otherwise) will grow increasingly powerful and effective.

DOWSING

One other technique that can work well for determining whether or not a spot is your deity's chosen space is dowsing, an earth-focused method of mapping the energy of a region and locating areas of particular power. Traditionally, dowsing was used to find underground water for a well. An Ozark water witch explained the process to Fred Roe:

> *First, you have to wait until spring when the sap is risin'. Then you get yourself either a peach or cherry tree and select a fork in the branches about the width of a pencil. Break or cut the limb about 20 inches (or half a meter) in length below the fork and strip off any leaves or extra branches, as you only want just the forked section. Then, holding the 'y' of the branch splayed in your upright palms, the stick pointin' forward, you walk very slowly until you find water.*[1]

Mr. Roe was skeptical, until he experimented with dowsing himself:

> *Wild cherry grows in these woodlands, and I hunted down a small tree growing near the road and selected a branch, just as he told me, and held it in my upright palms and clamped down hard with my fingers. I walked around my home, I walked around in the pasture to the curiosity of the cows, I walked along the road to the bewilderment of my neighbors until I was some distance away when suddenly, something began to happen. I renewed my grip upon the twig as the tip began to angle downward!*
>
> *I stepped back, half believing what I just experienced. I*

wondered if this was a truly weird experience, or if it was like the Ouija board. I returned to the point when I first began noticing the movement in the stick and repeated the process, stepping slowly. Again, the stick began to point downward. Amazed, I ran back to the house and found two pairs of metal pliers used for gripping and returned. Grasping the forked branch in the two pliers, I repeated the process. The force was so powerful it literally stripped the bark off the wood as it twisted downward until the point of the stick was pointing straight down toward the ground, a full 90 degrees from the starting position.[2]

You may use this technique to discover where your gods want to be worshipped. If you have a location where you regularly pay homage to your deities, consider dowsing and see where you get a strong reaction. If you don't have a stick handy, you can also use two L-shaped lengths of heavy copper, wire, or bend a copper hanger into a Y-shape. (If you use copper you will probably want to insulate the handles with cardboard, duct tape, or something else that will keep the energy from flowing into your hands and overwhelming you.) State your intent to locate sources of positive energy, then walk about the area slowly, paying close attention to the dowsing rod. If it dips notably in or around a particular area, you may want to set up your rituals with that energy point as the center.

As an alternative, you can also try a pendulum. Like a dowsing rod, a pendulum can be used to map the energy of an area. To do this, walk slowly with the pendulum hanging free. If it begins moving unusually, you can assume that you are on or near a power spot. By continuing to walk about, you can determine the approximate size and shape of that area. You can use that spot as a central point for your rituals—or place your prospective horse there. This will encourage possession and help your group to experience the land's sacred energy rather than merely paying it lip service. Some dowsers favor pendulums while some prefer dowsing rods. Either will work if used properly. In practice, pendulums tend to be most effective indoors where there is no wind to disturb their movements; dowsing rods offer a response that is more difficult to miss and may be better for outdoor work.

Exercise: Dowsing 101

At first scientists theorized that water witches were actually sensing electromagnetic currents caused by water running underground. Then they discovered that some dowsers were able to locate metal deposits by holding a pendulum over a map—and because they could not explain this, they immediately wrote the whole thing off as fraud. But whatever the mechanism, it is clear that the technique of dowsing can achieve real results in the hands of a skilled practitioner.

If you want to train in dowsing, have somebody hide an object. Start small—a single room or a small clearing, for example. With the dowsing tool of your choice, walk about the area and see when you get a response. If you have success here, try again in a bigger area. If you have a knack for dowsing, before long you'll have no problem marking the ebb and flow of the land's power. In any event, you'll almost certainly gain a heightened sensitivity to and knowledge of energy that will serve you well in your spiritual work. Once you learn how to feel the difference between a holy place and a plain old mundane room, you'll find it easy to recognize when the gods are coming and when They are staying away.

TEMPORARY SACRED SPACE

Not everybody has a spare bedroom that they can dedicate to their gods, or an area that they can regularly use for their rituals. Those who live in urban areas may not have enough space for themselves, never mind putting aside a room or even a closet for their divinities! If you are long on devotion but short on space, you need not fret: there are a number of work-arounds that will allow you to create sacred space on the fly.

In New York a good-sized *sevis lwa* (Service for the Spirits) can attract upward of three hundred people, far more than can fit in even a large house. Kenaz has attended fets in restaurants and banquet halls that were rented for the occasion. The lwa came down and appeared quite satisfied with the proceedings, even though they were not being held in a peristyle. While some might protest, we favor the approach generally taken by Vodouisants: If the spirits are pleased, your service was "correct."

Although these services were held in rented space, the altars were set up using statues and implements that had long been dedicated to the spirits. Perhaps the spirits were able to use these tools like a beacon, making it easier for them to locate a place and come in: perhaps they traveled with their tools. Whatever the case, there is ample evidence that things which have been repeatedly used in spiritual ceremonies gain a "charge" that can be felt by psychometrists and energy workers.

If you regularly do ritual, you should already have some tools that you normally use for that purpose and only for that purpose. If you don't, consecrate the appropriate implements to your tasks and set them aside when they aren't being used. They needn't be incredibly costly: in fact, if you have the skill to make your own tools, you will generally find that they are more effective than the most expensive store-bought items. But it is important that you dedicate them *solely* to ritual and service to your deities.

For purposes of possession, it is particularly important that we have items that are dedicated to the deities and are only used by Them when they come. Even if you cannot have a permanent dedicated space for your deities, you can have permanent and dedicated tools. Consider the care taken by Tibetan Buddhists when they call on Dorje Drakden, an ancient oracle whose *kuten* (medium) serves as a deputy minister in the Tibetan government cabinet-in-exile. Although the monasteries where Dorje Drakden was originally served are now inaccessible, they are still able to call on him thanks to specially prepared items that help to call him down.

On formal occasions, the kuten is dressed in an elaborate costume consisting of several layers of clothing topped by a highly ornate robe of golden silk brocade, which is covered with ancient designs in red and blue and green and yellow. On his chest he wears a circular mirror that is surrounded by clusters of turquoise and amethyst, its polished steel flashing with the Sanskrit mantra corresponding to Dorje Drakden. Before the proceedings begin, he also puts on a sort of harness, which supports four flags and three victory banners. Altogether, this outfit weighs more than seventy pounds and the medium, when not in trance, can hardly walk in it. As the first prayer cycle concludes and the second begins, his trance begins to deepen. At this point, a huge helmet is placed on his head. This item weighs approximately thirty pounds, though in former times it weighed more than eighty.

Now the face of the kuten transforms, becoming rather wild before puffing up to give him an altogether strange appearance, with bulging eyes and swollen cheeks. His breathing begins to shorten and he starts to hiss violently. Then, momentarily, his respiration stops. At this point the helmet is tied in place with a knot so tight that it would undoubtedly strangle the kuten if something very real was not happening.[3]

DEFENSE OF YOUR AREA

If you are going to be opening yourself up to possession, you will have to ascertain that your space is free of spirits other than the ones you want to call up. You may be able to start out most ceremonies with a desultory "calling on the light," casting of quarters, or what have you: for a possession ritual, you will need something stronger.

Vodou fets start with the *priye gineh,* a long invocation that begins by saluting God, Jesus, the Virgin Mary, and various saints, then pays homage to the various lwa and spirits and asks them to watch over and protect the ceremony. It can take as long as several hours to complete the priye. The lwa provide further protection; with the likes of Ogou and Ezili Danto watching the door, very few uninvited guests will try to sneak in. The people attending these ceremonies have a long-term, frequently multigenerational relationship with the spirits they serve; they can rely on them for protection and defense.

For working with possession, you will need a similar level of protection and defense. If you have a solid, serious, and verified relationship with your patron deity or deities, you should be safe from most spiritual nasties when you are working with them. Keep in mind that "solid, serious, and verified" is something quite different from "I feel strongly that I am connected to X and so I am sure they will protect me against anything negative." By this we mean that you have been chosen by your deity, that you have been working with them for some time, and that you have verified this connection through solid evidence like multiple divinations, repeated omens, and so on. You may think Loki is cool and Kwan Yin is very nice—but that in and of itself is no guarantee that they hold you in particularly high regard or that they will protect you. (And even if they do like you, don't expect the gods to step in and save you from your own carelessness and stupidity.)

There are numerous ways to ward, cleanse, and protect a space. Draja Mickaharic's *Spiritual Cleansing: Handbook of Psychic Protection,* Ivo Dominguez Jr.'s *Castings: The Creation of Sacred Space,* and Jason Miller's *Protection & Reversal Magick: A Witch's Defense Manual** are all highly recommended for further research. What is important is that you protect yourself and your congregation from negativity. Good intentions will not protect you if you run a red light or grab a live wire; things are no different when dealing with spiritual matters. All the sincerity in the world will not take the place of a well-defined set of boundaries.

To prepare your space for a possession ritual, cleanse the area physically and spiritually. The act of removing debris and rubbish, plucking weeds, dusting, polishing items, and such does more than just make the place look nice; it helps get rid of unwanted energy and discourages stray spirits from sticking around. Once you've cleaned the area, fumigate it

*Weiser Books, 2003; SapFire Productions, 1996; and New Page Books, 2006; respectively.

with incense and perfume appropriate to the deity being honored, decorate it with the appropriate colors and images, and otherwise prepare it for the party. Ideally this cleaning and preparation is a ritual in itself. If you have problems getting into that mind-set—and it can be hard to feel worshipful when you're scrubbing a floor—a soundtrack of tunes appropriate to your deity can do wonders toward making a chore an act of worship.

While you are in sacred space, be it permanent or temporary, treat it like sacred space. That doesn't necessarily mean you have to be solemn as an undertaker (although some gods will indeed expect that), but it means that you should recognize that while you are there, you are in the presence of the Divine. It doesn't matter whether it is a temple, a sacred grove, or a temporary altar erected in your dorm room. It is a holy place, and anything you do therein is (or should be) a holy activity.

As a final entreaty: If you are doing ritual in space that is not to be permanently dedicated to ritual space and nothing else (as most Pagan rituals will probably end up), please do the next person a favor and thoroughly psychically clean the space afterward. Leave nothing of your energy, your gods, and your disturbance of the ether. It should feel clean and sterile, and no one should be able to tell what has happened there. Why? Because the energy of that ritual might conflict with something that happens later in that space. If the folks who did ritual at the gathering mentioned in chapter 12, where we chronicle a possession gone wrong, had thoroughly cleaned up everything and banished any stray spirits who were hanging about, having been attracted by the energies raised, the accidental possession might not have happened. Similarly, if you are doing a possession rite in a temporary space, do not assume that no one else has ever done anything ritualized in that quaint and pretty natural spot, and don't assume that they had the courtesy to clean it up afterward. Most modern Pagans are taught that it is acceptable, and even desirable, to raise all sorts of magical energy and leave it randomly floating about. Don't assume that people know what you know. Be careful, and be safe.

PART FOUR

Possession

Kenaz's Story

August 1999

Geometric figures dance on my eyelids. This isn't dehydration. I had that on my second day here; since then I've made sure my urine is clean, clear, and copious. There's no nausea, no dizziness, just an electric anxiety and a feeling like I'm falling upward, like something is trying to pull me up and out of my body. Given that I'm presently on a cot near a *peristyle* (Vodou temple) outside of Jacmel, Haiti, this could be only one thing . . .

"You're getting the lwa," says Vivian, one of my fellow travelers.

Lightning bolts and unfamiliar *vévés** dance up and down my spine. I tried to get out to the crossroads before. I thought maybe Legba could take it away, but two of the men who live on the peristyle saw me wandering in the darkness and brought me back here. I close my eyes and try to stop the electric anxiety from turning into screaming terror.

"That ain't no lwa," Houngan Aboudja, another guest, says in his Gulf Coast drawl. "It's that *mort* I saw around him before. It knows it's getting sent away soon and it don't wanna go."

I look up, like I might be able to catch my soul before it falls into the screaming bright vévés. Dunni's coming in now from the guest room next door, wearing a nightgown that exposes her not-inconsiderable assets to best advantage. I try to ride a wave of lust back into my body but the vévés are too strong, I'm still falling away.

"I don't care what it is," Dunni says. "It doesn't need to be here now."

She mutters something in Yoruba. In addition to studying Vodou, Dunni is an Iyalocha in Lukumi, a child of Oshun who was initiated in Cuba. As she blows in my ears the terror fades to anxiety. "You go to sleep now, baby. I'll see you at breakfast in the morning."

I fall back on my cot. The anxiety turns to bone-weariness: I'm

*A vévé is a ceremonial drawing used to symbolize and call upon a lwa.

already falling asleep even before Dunni closes the door. The vévés flicker before my face like embers, then shimmer to nothing in the Jacmel night.

Raven's Tale

1996–2006

My body has danced with Oya moving it, as she whirled in ways that I certainly never could . . . out on a rooftop, which horrified me when I found out about it later. "She went right out the window and danced on the roof!" the onlookers told me in hushed voices. Lilith has danced in my body, too, swinging her curved sword in a dervish spin, brashly asking hard questions of the onlookers. Ariadne, wreathed in serpents, walked with my feet in my battered sandals through woods and fields to a sacred rite, bare-breasted, her skirt with its rows of ruffles swaying around me. I relaxed into her, smelling pungent incense even though the air was clean and clear.

But that was before. Before I had my breasts removed, before the beard grew completely in, before the injections of testosterone poured hair all over me like a pelt, before the fat and muscle arranged itself into a shape that says Man. Now none of them will enter me. There are no hard feelings from them; they know the deal, but they require a horse who is physically female enough for them. "Enough" is a subjective quality that only they can say, because I have always been an intersex being, but once I was "female of center," and now I'm the opposite.

Hela, who owns me, will still take this body when she chooses, in order to do something for someone who needs her hand upon them. If it is to be a particularly deep ride, she has me shapeshift my astral form to female first, sometimes weeks in advance, as if to prepare the inside of this vessel for me. That's hard for me, but she tells me: *Just get your issues out of the way and do it. I know you can do it, you're made for this. You're both.* And I can, even if it feels strange and dissonant with this now mostly male body.

10

The Horse

Safety, Sanity, and Consent

THE HORSE'S SAFETY

When it comes to the phenomenon of possession, we have to honestly say that talking about "safe" possession is like talking about "safe" sex. There's really no such thing as absolute safety in either of them. Both are amazing and intense experiences that can cause all kinds of trouble if and when you get involved with them. It's no accident that experts are now pushing the use of the term "safer sex." Not only is there no such thing as a foolproof birth-control or disease-prevention method, there are also the emotional repercussions of having sex, and of not having it. Sex can open up your body and heart in ways you didn't expect, and leave you vulnerable to psychological damage, just as it can equally possibly heal you of such damage. Some people can thrive on celibacy and abstinence; for others, that causes more emotional problems than having sex. The gift of the Love Goddesses is sacred, and anything that is that sacred is also powerful and beautiful and terrible and awe-inspiring . . . and never, ever completely safe.

Possession is like that as well. Opening one's flesh to be a container for something of the realm of spirit is indescribably amazing, as is being the close outsider who is able to see those things of the spirit in fleshly eyes for once. It is also impossible to make completely safe, because the gods and spirits are never safe. However, like sex, one can at least take some basic precautions to eliminate most of the dangers, and accept the other risks as a possibility.

Being a "human suit" for something that is not human is a physically and psychically stressful activity. Even calling smaller spirits down through yourself can be wearing on your soul-stuff, and when the astral body is stressed, that reverberates into the physical body, in as much as the two are tied together until we leave the second one behind entirely at our final death. When it's something even bigger than you are, it can leave you weak or tattered or hollowed out, at least temporarily. A horse whose physical and psychic safety needs are well taken care of is a horse who won't get burned out nearly as quickly.

To this end, the horse needs to start with taking care of his- or herself. First, they should take stock of their condition. Are they physically capable of the demands? If they are just getting over the flu, or had a terrible argument with their partner, or got no sleep the night before, it might be wise to see if it can be put off. Do they have a heart condition, a seizure disorder, or any other physical condition that might be exacerbated by possession? That doesn't mean that possession can't happen, but they will need to pray and speak first to whoever wants the ride so as to be careful of the physical issues. Some spirits—especially gods—can do things with a body that one wouldn't think that body could be capable of. Then when they leave, some leave it in good condition with no sign of what was done with it (and perhaps even better than they found it, as deities can give healing energy if they're that sort), and some leave it trashed and dragging around. If there are potential problems, a good staff can sometimes alleviate the worst of them, but the horse needs to be honest and immune to pride. If they aren't in a place where they can safely act as a horse, and they have the choice not to do so, then they shouldn't.

Remember that the gods may define "as safe as possible" quite differently from how we do. They may put us into situations that threaten life and limb—and when they do, there is no guarantee that they will save us should we get into trouble. There are many stories of good spirit-workers who came to a bad end not because they disobeyed the spirits, but because they followed their instructions. You may see martyrdom as something to be avoided; they have no such qualms. On a less spectacular level, they may rearrange your life in very uncomfortable ways. Understand that by being a horse, you are putting yourself into a very intimate, and sometimes very frightening, relationship with Divinity. Approach this relationship with caution and reverence and you will be safer than if you approach it carelessly or negligently.

The ideal situation is for the horse to have a prep and aftercare team. Usually (at least during our rituals), these are the same people, chosen by the horse, who trusts them and feels comfortable with them and knows that they are competent at the job. For the full job description of the job of Prep Team and Aftercare Team, see the appendix, Asphodel's Ritual Structure for Public God Possession. Here, we will just say that a well-trained and dedicated team (which can be only one person for small rites where the ride is a familiar one) makes a huge difference in the physical and emotional preparedness of the horse.

> *Having a crew of people to help is vital, if nothing else because then the god has attendants, and people who know what is going on and can explain it to others. Also, having ground crew can be essential when the gods start shedding garments and leaving them about! They seem especially fond of getting rid of glasses that the horse finds vital but the god, in the same body, doesn't need. The ground crew can pick up your shoes and glasses and put them in a safe place so that when you come back, they aren't off in the woods somewhere and lost for ever and ever.*
>
> **—Fireheart Tashlin, Pagan spirit-worker**

It is always good to look out for the person who is possessed. There is always a community present for Orisha possession. During the Spirit's Mass, I work with other skilled mediums, and we look out for the people in the service, and for each other. There is always a danger during possession that something may go wrong, such as a spirit refusing to leave, or a lower spirit causing harm to someone. You need to have people present who know how to deal with these issues. During my private consultations I do not have a crew, but the possessions are not as total at that time, and I request that the spirits let me come in and out to make sure that all are safe. Myself, the client, and the spirits all need to be safe and protected.

—Olorisha Omi Lasa Joy Wedmedyk

Working with experienced people who can provide assistance and backup is definitely the way to go. I've done it both ways. Having even one experienced person who knows what to do makes all the difference. Once in the past, Lilith got very annoyed with the person working as assistant. Because he had no experience of what to do, when she entered, he was flustered and forgot what was supposed to happen. After a long period of silence, she finally turned to him and brusquely suggested that he ask something rather than waste time.

—Olorisha Lilith ThreeFeathers

I did it alone, for a long time, because there was no one around to help me. I was carrying the gods for a small group of people, none of whom had any experience with possession. I was also young, foolish, and inexperienced myself. I had prideful feelings around the whole event which got in the way—I didn't want to be seen as weak or needing help. Sometimes, though, it would leave me physically and psychically devastated for days afterward. I was egotistic enough that when Freya told me flatly that I needed to train people to help me, to be my ground crew and aides, I brushed off the suggestion. So Freya took matters into her own hands and completely side-stepped my prevarications. The next time that she rode me, which was a ritual a few days after she spoke to me, she simply picked out the people that she thought would be the best choices, and informed them of what they were to do in the future when I was possessed. When I came back, how could I deny Freya's public demand, eh?

The funny thing was that she knew exactly who would be good at what. The people that she picked were not the ones that I would have picked, and I was apprehensive, but they turned out to be really good at those jobs. The woman that Freya instructed to "watch closely" during my pre-possession ritual eventually turned out to be able to be ridden herself, once she had gotten over some emotional issues. Lesson for me: The gods want their horses to be safe, and They know better than we do.

—Gudrun, seidhkona

Good attendants make the process before, during, and after go far more smoothly than it otherwise might and can contribute greatly toward the comfort and well-being of the horse, especially in the exhausting aftermath. For many of us, coming to possessory work in traditions that lack a cohesive framework for such things, having a skilled team of handlers is a luxury. I've only had the advantage of working with an experienced team once in all the years I've been doing this work, but that experience both before and after the possession itself was markedly easier than any other. I recovered faster and had fewer aftereffects. Furthermore, good handlers are calm during the onset of the possession and know what to do to help coax and entice the deity in, which makes the whole process far more comfortable. Having knowledgeable people in attendance helps the horse relax, which goes a long way to quickly facilitating the entire process.

—Galina Krasskova, Heathen spirit-worker

Sometimes, of course, the god or goddess who takes the ride is just going to be somewhat rough with the horse's body, either because that's the way they are, or in some cases because they have a specific lesson for the horse. This is one of those situations where it's really good to have a patron deity who owns your ass and can set firm limits with other deities and spirits, preventing them from going too far. If a particular spirit is known to be a "rough rider" and the chosen horse is not up for the task, see if it can be rescheduled for later or for another horse. Of course, if the horse is a god-slave (a situation discussed in this chapter under The Horse's Consent) and a visiting deity trashes them, it's because their patron allowed it to happen for some reason that is between the horse and the patron, and the community would be wise to stay out of that argument. In a similar vein, a horse who is a god-slave may be required by their patron to offer themselves even when not in the best of shape, and this too is not something the community can change, although it may do what it can to aid the horse's physical comfort.

If you are the horse and you have been informed that a possession will be happening (see the Community section for advice on negotiating possessions ahead of time), and you feel that you can't get out of it, it is your responsibility to do what you can to prepare your body for this honor. It will be housing a denizen of the Otherworlds, and you should take the time to get it in as good a shape as possible. Besides the usual taking care of your flesh temple in whatever way works best for it, a horse can and should ask a deity that they are soon to horse (assuming that there is decent lead time) what they think ought to be done in order to prepare the body for them. Some gods ask for a specific diet for a few days prior to the event, or fasting, or particular sorts of cleansing and detoxing.

Someone who horses regularly—and by this we mean anything like three or four times a year—needs to do regular psychic cleansing exercises on their astral body. Possessions are rough on the entire psychic system, so learning to do magical cleansings—with sound, with water, with heat, with whatever works for you—is important. Some spirit-workers recommend exercises such as t'ai ch'i in order to keep the energy system resilient. Developing a daily practice of grounding and centering is useful as well; if the horse can learn to do it quickly and reflexively even in times of crisis, it will aid them in grounding themselves after being ridden.

As to the dangers of horsing . . . well, I don't think that people should do it at all, not unless they're forced to. In Western magical tradition the concept of "assuming a god-form" is a mild type of horsing in which you identify with a god-form, invoke that particular kind of energy into yourself, and embody that energy. It's not the same as horsing, but the danger even from doing it is that the god-energy leaves, but the person forgets to divest themselves of the god-form, and they get stuck in that space "being" that entity—first of all, to the exclusion of all else, and usually to the great annoyance of the people around them who are tired of them "being" Ra all day long. It's just not good.

Other obvious dangers are that they'll do something with your body that damages someone or is illegal. "Oh, cool, it's a car? Is this like chariots used to be? Yes?" and they smack you into a tree, or run a red light, or have unsafe sex, or make you ingest things you're allergic to and don't take them with them, or beat someone into a bloody hospital-ready pulp. I think there's also a psychological danger from sharing mind-space with a deity. They're so huge and you're so small. If they come forcefully, and you're not ready for them, you can tear. It can rip your soul.

—Lydia Helasdottir, Pagan spirit-worker

Some Neo-Pagan groups are starting to work with various levels of spirit-possession, but there is a disturbing trend of the occasional training group insisting that anyone can horse regardless of innate wiring (and in some cases, that anyone can horse any deity with no ill effects). In order to make this happen, some are utilizing the process of the group psychically "condensing" the individual's soul and stuffing it into a corner of their being, and then reaching through them and pulling the deity through into their body. We find this trick to be rather concerning for a variety of reasons, assuming that it even works for full possession and not merely aspecting. First, it is our experience that horsing can be a psychically strenuous activity. The individual's psychic "sphincter," for lack of a better word, is stretched wide open. Just as with physical sphincters, the best way to receive something large is to be in a state of relaxed, accepting openness. Someone else forcing the issue may or may not get the horse open enough, but even if it works, it may cause lasting damage, which can manifest as mental illness. We would rather go with the idea that if the horse can't seem to open up enough, they either don't have enough of the inborn psychic wiring for it (which is no one's fault) or they aren't ready for some internal reason of their own, which must be dealt with in its own time and way. Horsing is shock enough to the soul; having a bunch of people shoving it around is more trauma to the soul complex than is good for anyone.

We have also found that not everyone can be ridden by just any spirit. There has to be an element of "like calls to like," or at least some sort of compatibility. Sometimes that compatibility is subtle and not something that the horse can know until they try and succeed or fail. As the Northern Tradition equivalent of a "black shaman" (that's in the Siberian sense, not the Western black = evil nonsense), who is owned by Lady Death, Raven never thought that he would be able to horse Frey, the Golden One of the Vanir . . . but Frey has a standing date to take him around Lammas, and it works well . . . even leaving a residue of light and health in his dark insides. On the other hand, Baphomet fits well as a ride for Raven, as he is also third-gendered and is associated with the rotting-down part of the cycle, as is his Lady Hela. The old primal Hunter also rides Raven on a yearly basis, and his predator nature works well as a fit. But when a bride of Anubis asked for someone to horse her husband for a ceremony, Raven asked to see if he would be an acceptable fit and the cosmic answer came back no, even though he is associated with Death.

There are certain deities that are incompatible with me (I have been told flat out that certain Loa and Orisha will never be able to ride me, for instance) for reasons of my own emotional patterning and utter lack of compatibility, or because to horse certain deities would inadvertently destroy too much of the patterning Odin put in place. Over the years it seems that more and more I horse primarily, if not only, the Northern pantheon. I am also not permitted to horse lesser spirits, but only certain deities on what I like to call Odin's "approved list."

—Galina Krasskova, Heathen spirit-worker

Being ridden by male deities is not something that I do well, at least not the ones that are very sexually male, like Thor and Frey. I have a special relationship with Mimir—I may be the only human person around that he actually likes—but he's got no body, so gender isn't an issue for him riding me. Odin is really good at shifting his "shape," I suppose you might say, in order to fit into someone; I don't know how he manages it, but he doesn't seem to trigger the gender barrier for me the way that other gods do. Well, actually, I have an idea how he manages it, being as a female friend of mine who has carried Loki (a poor fit for me) noted the same thing about him. But we won't talk about that here! Anyway, I tend to only be "afflicted" with goddesses—Frigga, Freya, Iduna, Nerthus, the Handmaidens. Once all three Norns rode me at once, or perhaps it was one at a time switching off very fast, but that was grueling.

—Gudrun, seidhkona

Sometimes the problem isn't mental fit but rather physical. Before Raven transitioned to a more male physiology, he had horsed Lilith. She is a fairly masculine and hairy goddess, but she is still female of center, and when Raven crossed the middle line she would no longer use his body. Some deities will horse bodies of a different gender, or very different physique or state of (dis)ability, from their own with no problem. Others are extremely picky—all the Love Goddesses, for instance, and many of the more "macho" and physically oriented war gods. No horses should take it personally if they aren't a good fit for a particular god or wight. (For that matter, since most people aren't wired to horse at all, they shouldn't take that personally either. I'll never be a pro basketball player or a genius mathematician. So what?) The gods have their own preferences, and we just have to go with them. Some modern Pagans do hold that any trained horse ought to be able to carry any deity, but we haven't found that to be true. And, frankly, if you are horsing any deity with no ill effects—or little in the way of serious aftereffects at all—we seriously doubt that you are doing full possession. It's not something that is ever done easily or lightly. On the other hand, even if it's only Aspecting, that's a good thing in and of itself and much easier on one's astral body.

Another reason that someone might not be able to horse a certain deity, or a type or pantheon of deities, is because their energy clashes with that of the spirit-worker's patron deity. This could be an issue of two deities who are enemies, or who just don't get along. A Lokisman likely wouldn't be able to horse Heimdall, for instance, nor would a horse dedicated to Pan be attractive to Hestia. In general, if one has a patron deity to watch one's back (which we recommend), that deity will have a list of who can and cannot use you drawn up for their own reasons, and you will be expected to go along with it. That's a matter of courtesy and respect.

Afterward, I'd often feel run over; my back would be sore. At first I'd think that it was just from sitting in that position for a long time, and then I'd try to just do that, and it doesn't hurt a bit. It's like a massive vibration has gone through you and rattled you at a cellular level . . . or like someone has ripped your spine out and put it back in again with two channels instead of one, and then afterward they yanked the second channel out and loosely stitched it back together. It's sore. But that's also a "throughput" issue, because if you're only used to 110 volts running through your spine, and now you've got deity energy running through you—ten thousand volts and several more million amperes than you're used to—it can fry your circuits. Doing it a lot, you grow fatter wires, fatter pipes, until you can manage the deity energy easier. But then it starts to seep into everyday life; you can be in a constant state of being shadowed, a walking pair of eyes for your deity to ride along with.

—Lydia Helasdottir, Pagan spirit-worker

THE HORSE'S SANITY

Sane can be a loaded word. Often it means "able to function in polite society without making too many waves" or "able to behave in an appropriate manner." Those who do not measure up to this standard—the "insane"—fill a role once played in medieval times by the leper. The insane are outcasts, figures of simultaneous pity and mockery. Like lepers, they are diseased and potentially dangerous. To protect themselves and their community, right-thinking citizens may call upon whatever judicial or extrajudicial measures they deem necessary. "Sane" people may mock these poor souls, or they may pray for them and offer them help, but they certainly aren't expected to treat them as equals or take them seriously.

The gods, on the other hand, may define *sane* quite differently from how we do. When they appear in a human body, their logic may appear skewed and their behavior bizarre. They may not act in the ways that you expect, and they may well act in ways that make you uncomfortable. They may appear unreasonable or be downright unlikable. They may even act silly and treat your whole ritual like a big joke. (Trickster spirits are notorious for this, and more often than not there is valuable information hidden amid their antics.)

Be very careful about dismissing a possession because you didn't like what the spirit had to say or how they said it. Be especially careful about dismissing spiritual advice or orders just because they conflict with your preconceptions. You may think that staying in your comfortable but boring job is perfectly rational, but the gods may decide that you're putting your soul and spiritual health at risk, and take care of the problem by terminating your employment. While this may sound sensible on paper, those who are living through it may have difficulty finding the rationale.

To much of the "real world," horses and spirit-workers are all crazy anyway, and not in a good way. What's more, many of the residents in said real world aren't shy about telling us exactly how they feel about us and our "delusions," "imaginary friends," and "attention-seeking behaviors." When dealing with strangers and casual acquaintances, you probably don't want to be seen as insane. At best it's going to make things very uncomfortable for all concerned; at worst it may get you beaten, institutionalized, or killed. (If you are part of the percentage of the population who actually suffer from a brain-chemical mental illness, you already know this all too well.) So discretion about your path and your practices may be in order. This may smack of "going back into the broom closet," or treating your religion as something shameful, but try instead to think of it as reserving your sacred things for people who can show due respect. There's also that if this is a sacred act—and it is—there's no need to go around bragging about it. When a horse is chosen by the spirits, that doesn't mean that they are necessarily better as a person than anyone else, and using it as part of your "coolness résumé" demeans it and insults the spirits who have put their trust in you. If necessary, ask yourself, "How would the gods want me to act?" and if there is still confusion, ask them directly.

While encountering the assumption that they are mad can be discomfiting for a horse, actually accepting it can be far more dangerous.

It may be tempting to decide that "this is all an elaborate delusion," but soon thereafter you may find yourself asking, "Why are these delusions continuing and making my life miserable?" Editing your own experiences to conform to someone else's version of reality is a fast way to making yourself actually crazy. Besides, if you've been tapped as a "natural" horse—meaning that you are experiencing spirit-possession on a regular basis, perhaps whether or not you want it—deciding that it is not real will not stop it, nor will you be able to negotiate properly, protect yourself, or prepare your body while in a state of denial. You certainly won't be able to give the spirits the ride that they deserve, and you can go only so long doing the denial trip in the face of actual rides before you either have to accept it or spiral down into a pit of madness.

There's also the fact that the aftermath of a possession can leave a horse with a "residue" of the spirit that spent time inside them. They may find themselves liking or disliking things that are uncharacteristic of them but quite characteristic of that spirit. Although the effect generally fades over a few days or weeks, it can be crazy-making for the horse who is not open and flexible and doing this out of love for the gods and the community, or who is unsure where their own edges begin and end.

I think the main thing is not to panic. Yes, you will think you are going crazy at first, you will think that something is wrong with you, you'll feel sick, you'll feel out of touch, but if it's a god who has chosen to use you as a vessel, you should feel honored. At the same time, though, don't get too full of yourself; you are not the only tool the gods choose to use in this fashion, and you are expendable and can be replaced. It will take some adjustment, but the best thing to do is to find a qualified teacher. If none is available to you, as was the case with me, then it will be more difficult, but either way the key is communication, communication, communication. Talk to the spirits/wights/gods/angels/etc., and listen. If you keep the lines of communication open, you might find that you'll learn a lot, and that the spirit may be willing to compromise as far as when, where, and how often they take over. But whatever you do, check your ego at the door. Nothing turns a deity off more than hubris.

—Abriel, Pagan spirit-worker

It's important that your possession work be done from a place of reverence, openness, groundedness, stability, and mental equilibrium. Possession is high-energy, high-intensity work that can exacerbate mental conditions and underlying psychological weaknesses. You don't need to be a pillar of mental health (Kenaz comments, "Gods know *I'm* not!"), but you should be aware of and working on your issues. (That said, sometimes when a deity temporarily shares your head, they may also see your mess and decide to move the furniture around a bit in order to help you with it. This can bring up all sorts of things as soon as the ride is over, things that Ought To Be Dealt With Now, at least in the opinion of the Power that passed through you.) More to the point, you ought to be able to stash your emotional baggage until the ritual is over.

If you have an innate hunger for attention, you will have to get over it. When the spirits come, it's all about them, not you. Trying to turn yourself into the star of a possession ritual can have real and painful consequences, such as the rider becoming offended by your attitude and leveling a punishment. The easiest punishment, of course, is to simply refuse at the last minute to show up, and to leave you high and dry after you've made all that fuss and everyone's waiting. Possession by the gods, especially, is a very submissive experience. They have ways of bringing down the proud and chastising the arrogant, most of which are quite unpleasant.

We're not saying this just because of leftover internalized Judeo-Christian ideas on humility and groveling before God, either. If you bother to do research in ancient religions, or existing tribal ones, you will soon find plenty of anecdotes showing just how kindly gods of any pantheon deal with the problem of hubris in their servants. And yes, if you are a horse of gods, you are first and foremost a servant. Work on having a good servile attitude. People who are desperate for importance in their spiritual community and think that this is a way to achieve attention and prestige are really not good for this job. It's more like being the divine limo driver, actually. It's grunt work, and if you go into it with ego issues, the gods who use you may find ways to slap you down . . . perhaps leaving you to clean up their Divine messes. If you can't be humble about it, don't do it . . . and don't let your community give you lots of special head-pats for being the suit that the god wears, either. It encourages the wrong mind-set.

> *In retrospect, the manner in which Odin trained me as a horse leads me to conceive of the whole process as one of learning to welcome a deeply internalized crisis. Essentially, possession is a crisis situation. One's entire ego is put aside or pushed aside so Someone/Something else can enter and take control. That is a difficult thing for many people to deal with, and the reason that some horses find the whole process very violating. I do not find it so, but I suspect my erotic/romantic attachment to Odin as well as the very organic way in which I was first introduced to the whole thing has helped me immensely there. This is also the reason why I believe a certain degree of self-knowledge and psychological stability should be a prerequisite for a horse. Of course, sometimes the gods just don't give a damn and will utilize a person anyway, but in the ideal situation, a firm, solid sense of self is foundational toward ensuring the continued psychological health of the horse. Personally, I would not train someone as a horse unless it was patently clear from the get-go that the gods were hell-bent on using them in that capacity.*
>
> *This is the reason that not only cannot everyone do possessory work, but not every one should. It's not just a matter of having the right brain chemistry/psychic patterning for it, though that*

is the most important thing, but the secondary crux of the issue is the ability to get beyond that initial trauma of having one's consciousness moved aside. It's apparent from all outward appearances of the horse that the beginning manifestations of possession reveal themselves to be a crisis situation, and this is perhaps the primary reason that horses need skilled, experienced, and knowledgeable attendants to minimize difficulties. Possessory work can be grueling, not just mentally, emotionally, and psychologically but physically as well.

—Galina Krasskova, Heathen spirit-worker

If you are going to shunt aside your ego and allow Someone Else to take control of your body, you are also going to need to know where your Self begins and ends. Highly sensitive individuals with poor boundaries can get badly hurt by possession experiences, and it is contraindicated for anyone without good boundaries and a strong sense of self. If you suffer from schizophrenia, dissociative identity disorder, or other ego-dystonic psychological conditions, you should approach possession with extreme caution, and probably should avoid it entirely. These preexisting disorders will not necessarily disqualify you entirely from being a horse; some spirit-workers do have continuing struggles with mental illness. (Kenaz counts hirself* among that number.) However, they must be addressed and, where necessary, accommodations must be made.

At the very least, the horse with a history of mental illness should be highly functional and very experienced in figuring out which voices are the voices of the illness and which are not. In general, someone with mental illness should not seek out the role of horse, and it is especially contraindicated for people whose grip on reality is tenuous and easily thrown off. For those with dissociative identity disorder—also known as multiple personality disorder—there may also be a consent issue if some of the personalities consented to the ride and others didn't. If the

*"Hirself" is a gender-neutral pronoun.

gods repeatedly choose them anyway, then the gods think that they are sane enough, and that is going to have to be enough for anyone who believes in Them, assuming that experienced people have agreed that it really is a proper possession. Horses with mental illness should also try harder to find other spirit-workers who can see the psychic results of an actual possession, and can step in should the bad brain soup get the better of them, and make them believe that a psychotic episode is a possession. If the horse knows that they have a history of impaired judgment due to neurochemical conditions, they should be humble about having experienced people to second-guess them.

In general, people with trust issues are contraindicated for this path. If you find it difficult to trust even people who love you and are reliable, you will not have the ability to hold yourself open for the god to enter. You may react instinctively, slamming the door shut instead of being responsive. Work on your trust issues, including any anger you may have toward the Powers That Be. If you are blaming the Divine Will for your problems, you won't be comfortable with letting any aspect of it run your body even more closely.

You can work on trust issues with the aid of other human beings. Ask the people whom you trust the most to blindfold you and take you somewhere unknown, perhaps to do something that you have never done and have no knowledge of. If the idea makes you recoil, you're not ready to work with possession.

So far we've discussed how the horse's sanity can be threatened merely by the intense experience of the gods, but we have not yet touched on the very real dangers to one's sanity of possession by destructive or amoral random spirits, which is another matter entirely. This will be discussed further in chapter 11 under Harmful Possessions, but suffice it to say here that anyone who is haunted by such an unpleasant entity is in real danger of insanity, more even than bodily harm. The entity who is feeding on them probably doesn't want them dead, but they are easier to control while insane, and so they may be pushed in that direction. Being possessed by reasonably benevolent deities is one thing;

being possessed by something that has no vested interest in your health is another thing entirely.

THE HORSE'S CONSENT

Our Western culture places a high value on freedom and free will. We like to think that we are masters of our fate and captains of our soul. We try to "give each other space" and (at least pretend to) bend over backward to avoid "compelling the will of another." But all this emphasis on autonomy is of comparatively recent vintage, certainly no later than the Enlightenment era. To our ancestors, the idea of untrammeled freedom would have seemed ludicrous. Accidents of birth decided their social status and profession; matchmakers determined their life partners; kings and lords shaped the society in which they lived. Above all else, Nature laid down a harsh and unbending law about what they would be doing at any given time of year, a law that had to be obeyed if they wished to survive. Understanding this is vital to understanding how the gods view the question of "consent."

But the gods and spirits are also aware that things aren't what they used to be, or at least some of them are. They know that their temples have crumbled and their armies of worshippers have been reduced to a mere handful. Hence, they are often willing to bargain with the followers who remain. This is not to say that they are desperate—they have survived very well without us for a millennium, thank you—or that they should be treated with contempt, as they can easily choose to ignore us if they think us unworthy of attention. But it does give you a bit more flexibility when dealing with them. You have every right to say, "No, we are not going to offer you a human sacrifice," or to set other boundaries when asked for something that is unacceptable under present-day legal and social climes. Nor is it unthinkable for most people to bargain with the gods. You do not have to take everything that every spirit says as gospel, and follow it without question. Most people have the right to bargain and negotiate with spirits, and the right (and responsibility) to say, "I'm sorry, I can't do that at this time." Like any sane relationship, the interactions between you and the gods should have appropriate boundaries. If the gods are not indulgent parents who exist to fill our every whim, nor are they mad tyrants.

Modern-day worshippers frequently fall into one of two camps. Either they think the gods exist solely for their benefit and will happily do their bidding upon call (or at least act benevolently toward them) . . . or they believe that the gods are all-knowing and all-powerful and we should be blindly obedient before them. The truth, as is often the case, lies somewhere in the middle. While the gods are certainly more powerful and more far-seeing than we are, they are neither omnipotent nor omniscient. When presented with a divine demand that will be the opposite of beneficial for the community, you may well be able to make alternative arrangements.

> *I do generally have a good bit of warning—they don't usually just pounce on me, although that has occasionally happened. Where and when depends on the spirit and the purpose of the ride. If they need to get a message across to that person right over there right now, then no, there's not much choice in the setting. However, to be fair, I would say that the times that I have felt that I had little to no warning were the times that I wasn't really listening.*
>
> **—Fireheart Tashlin, Pagan spirit-worker**

In most possessory traditions, a great deal of framework and structure is used to make possessions less random and nonconsensual, or at least nonconsensual-appearing. In some branches of Santeria, for example, nonconsensual possession is much less acceptable than in other sects. Possession, in those groups, is to be done only by initiates, and only under specific ritual circumstances. Some even split terms, using *possession* for an orisha entering an initiate in the accepted place and manner and *horse* for the (unacceptable) inadvertent or misplaced possession. Olorisha Lilith ThreeFeathers relates that her *Ile* (House) does not use the term *horse* or *ridden* to describe the Santeros who carry the Orisha: "Personally, I don't use the term 'horse' either; however, that may be because I associate it with Voudoun. To me, 'horse' implies an unavoidable happening—that is, the Loa decides to come in and it doesn't matter if the person is initiated or prepared for the possession. In my branch of Santeria, possession is not done that way. Initiation is required before possession by Orisha, and others can stop the possession."

While some spirits—and especially the gods—are capable of taking and riding an unwilling horse, it appears to require far more effort on their part than coming down on someone who is open and willing. It is in their best interests to establish a cooperative and mutually beneficial arrangement with the horse and the congregation. They don't want to drag you along kicking and screaming, any more than you enjoy dealing with a stubborn and ill-behaved toddler. Of course, while they may not like taking nonconsensual control of a situation, that doesn't mean they aren't capable of doing so if their hand is forced, only that it is a last resort on their part. Academics have written numerous books attempting to learn the sociological and psychological rationale behind our religious instinct and the ways in which it influences our behavior. Perhaps their questions should be answered thusly: *Religious ritual is an ongoing contractual arrangement between humans and the Divine Powers by which we interact with each other to maximum mutual benefit.*

However, it would be simplistic of us to say that the issue of consent when dealing with possession is easy and clear-cut. Some would-be horses are unable to achieve possession, and some "natural" horses are unable to avoid it. For them, consensual possessions would be an enormous step in the right direction. The gods don't always ask our permission before calling us into service. (Some say that we agreed to the task in some forgotten past life, but that's cold comfort when you are suffering in this one, and well-nigh impossible to prove anyway.) This may not jibe with our modern views on "free will" and "free agency," but it's quite in keeping with history. Our ancestors would have laughed heartily at the idea that the gods need to ask our permission before intervening in our lives.

While natural horses may not be able to stop possessions, they may gain some control over when and where those possessions take place. In fact, it is vital that they do so as soon as possible. Thankfully, the spirits are generally amenable to setting up mutually agreeable rules and regulations for that, as long as they get what they want. If you're suffering from nonconsensual possessions, you need to get in touch with a qualified spirit-worker who has experience with possession, and ascertain what actions you must take in order to get things under some semblance of control. Keep in mind, though, that we've never seen "control" for someone in this position to mean "making the gods who are bothering you go away and leave you alone until you decide that you want to deal with them." If you are a natural horse and you've already been chosen and are being actively used, that isn't going to stop until the spirits say that it will. You can't walk away from that job. You can, however, set up terms that make doing that job easier and more comfortable for you.

> *Possessory trance should only be done in a disciplined way, but it's no use trying to suppress it. If a deity is determined to come through, you have to arrange appropriate situations, and train yourself to allow to trance only in response to cues. Doing automatic writing can relieve some of the tension . . . I am trained to go into trance when cued by specific songs or regalia, and not to go in unless I have those cues.*
>
> **—Odinsmeri, eclectic Norse/Umbanda spirit-medium**

> *I feel them coming in, and I do have time to give consent. Sometimes when I don't want to give consent, the being becomes insistent, and it becomes extremely difficult to resist. In those cases, I've learned that there is a valid reason for the entry. In other words, I need to do specific work and the merger will assist that work. Other times when I don't give consent, they leave gracefully.*

With Lilith, I go through a formal procedure before she enters. With Yemoya and the Misa spirits, I know where and when the possibility exists that one would come through. In other words, I know that certain situations will likely bring one through. If I'm around the drums, or working in a Misa circle, I know something is likely to happen. They don't come through unless I am doing work within the religion, or have set up ritual space for them to do so. In a Misa, other spirits may ask entrance, or may insist on it. When that happens, I am still protected by my known spirit-guides and Egun. They often permit this other spirit to enter, but there have been times when my known spirit guides have stepped in and prevented it.

—Olorisha Lilith ThreeFeathers

I cannot control a full Yemaya possession. I depend on my religious community for that. My work with other spirits happens in a ritual context. In the case of the dead or Egun, I can usually stop if I need to, but not always. Usually that happens when they feel that there is more for them to say, and want to finish something already started. The Orisha have their own way of controlling the event, but it is always in the context of a certain time and place for them that is appropriate to their energy and safety.

—Olorisha Omi Lasa Joy Wedmedyk

Lacking a strong ability to set boundaries makes you a poor candidate for a horse. You need to be able to set boundaries, or you'll just become a powerless vessel, living your life around the visitations of your patron deity. It's hard to do things like hold down a job or have relationships or care for children when you're constantly being used in this way. If you want to take this path, you will need to work on the firm mental negative. It's difficult, because it can be an amazing feeling to share your vessel with a Power, and it's hard to turn down, but if it's getting in the way of your daily activities, it can damage your life and health and make you a less worthy vessel. This is in addition to the fact that a deity can better be served and honored if the right situation is prepared for it in advance—which is something that most gods can understand when you use it as a reason—"If you wait until next week, I will have a ritual set up, with your favorite foods and people to interact with! Please allow me to honor you properly!" The idea is not to let it take over your life, because it can burn you out psychically if you do too much of it. If you're the ultrasensitive type who is easily swayed by the strong emotions of others, do work on keeping your boundaries clear before opening yourself to an even stronger and more intense experience.

People with small children, or other full-time responsibilities that cannot be shirked, may also have difficulty with this path. Being a horse can take up a sizable chunk of your life. If you are needed on a moment's notice by dependents whose care hangs on you and you aren't home in your own body, it can cause problems. You might want to wait until some future date when you are no longer responsible for them and your time is your own. If the gods are not going to let you off, you can pray to the Mother—that's the Big Mother whom all mother goddesses draw their sacredness from—and ask her to intervene and give you space in which to raise your child. Raven did that, and it worked, although he paid for it later when his daughter was grown.

However, to more fully address the aforementioned fact that "consent," when dealing with the gods and spirits, is an ambiguous thing, we should briefly deal with the concept of the god-slave. This is yet another concept that the greater Neo-Pagan demographic is generally horrified when faced with, yet it is flourishing quietly in small corners among people who don't speak much on the subject. The god-slave (Galina Krasskova uses the term *godatheow,* Venecia Rauls uses the ancient Cretan term *doera,* and some prefer the Greek term *hierodule*) phenomenon is much more thorough than the usual idea of a "patron deity" who watches over you from afar, is kindly and benevolent and helpful, and may point out your path while not forcing you to tread it. The god-slave, in comparison, is very much the total servant of his god(s), who may turn his life upside down, strip away anything that does not serve the spirit-worker purpose, and usher him by force onto a specific path, not shrinking at punishments up to and including death if he rebels.

While Western sensibilities may bridle at that idea, it's not at all unfamiliar to tribal spirit-workers around the world. Many tribal shamans will say bluntly that their spirits will make them ill or even kill them if they quit or dishonor their job, or offend the spirits in some way. Some god-slaves volunteer for the duty out of love and reverence for their patron deity; others are grabbed up without their consent, much like the classic tribal shamans who are driven ill by their spirits until they accept the call, and must continue to do the work indefinitely or the illness will recur. While not all (or even most) god-slaves are natural horses, we have noticed a higher percentage of natural horses among their (admittedly tiny) numbers. This isn't too surprising, considering that being able to physically carry a deity would be an advantage in a bound servant.

Like many relationship arrangements, there are advantages and drawbacks to being a god-slave. One possible drawback is, obviously, about consent and how choices are taken away from you; They run your life, down to the details. This may include food, sex, clothing, human relationships, career, living location and standard, and anything else. The effect of this on a modern Western individual, used to independence, can well be imagined. The advantage may be that there is a certain amount of comfort in knowing you are being pushed to be the best that you can be, whether you like it or not; that you are a part of something larger; and that you are burning off karmic debts at a much faster rate than that of most people! (Indeed, a "bankruptcy-level" amount of karmic debt seems to be the most common reason why some people are taken as slaves by gods without their consent.) You also get a higher "security clearance" when it comes to getting pieces of cosmic information, because your bosses know that They can gag you at any time.

In terms of negotiating, Hela does whatever she wants with my body. Other deities, if they want to speak through me, have to clear it through her, and they can never go as far into possession as she does. The negotiations with me are usually about not doing anything that could send me to prison, or that would damage me. Sometimes astral spirits, lineage spirits for example, tag along to go for a ride. I don't consider that to be full-on possession; they'll just come along and sit in the body and experience what it's like to be incarnate. We'll go to the movies together, or drive a car. They'll get the sensation of being in the body, but they're not in control.

—Lydia Helasdottir, Pagan spirit-worker

I do this because it's part of my job. How much say I have over where and when varies from deity to deity and circumstance to circumstance. My Lady extends me some decision-making power, but that's clearly just a courtesy—she could take me any time she wants, but she lets me have some say when it's not inconvenient to her. It varies with other deities that I've horsed, but it's always been clear to me that she always has a say in it. The few times that I've been ridden without any say-so or consent, I can clearly remember a touch of her power in there someplace. I don't think that being a horse makes someone more of a spirit-worker, or a spiritual person, and I don't think that being a horse is something to be envied or aspired to, nor is it necessarily a sign of mental weakness or spiritual submissiveness.

—Wintersong Tashlin, Pagan spirit-worker

My advice to someone who is becoming uncontrollably possessed by various spirits? Develop a strong relationship with a god or goddess, and preferably be taken up by a patron goddess or god. This provides a great deal of protection to the horse; otherwise, there is no divine "owner" to make sure that spirits and gods do not harass and over-use the horse. And if you happen to already have a patron, maintain your devotional practices. This is important.

> *That relationship has to be strong, nourished, nourishing, and reciprocal. It will sustain you.*
>
> **—Galina Krasskova, Heathen spirit-worker**

If you are a natural horse and you are suffering from uncontrollable possessions, and you absolutely cannot get control of the situation any other way, this is very much worth the price as a last resort, because you as a mere mortal cannot guarantee to protect yourself against random spirits who might want to come in, nor can you guarantee to be able to control their actions once they get inside you. With a patron deity at your back setting rules of use and screening out the unsuitable, you can guarantee that you will not end up in prison, the mental bin, or dead from random spirit use of your flesh. Of course, this can be fairly said to be trading one uncontrollable situation for another (more benevolent) one, and should be called upon only if there is no other option. It definitely does decrease the amount of limits that you can place on rides by your owner-deity and their friends, but it means that you won't have to set the limits, nor enforce them. Even god-slaves can generally get leeway by asking for those things that make the visiting deity's experience better—plenty of warning and a safe context, for example.

The concept of the god-slave is discussed in more depth in the final section of Raven Kaldera's book *Dark Moon Rising* (Asphodel Press), but here we excerpt one section of the relevant essay on the subject from that book:

> When I fish for the big cosmic reasons—why me, why not someone else?—what come to me vaguely, over and over, are the twin concepts of Dire Necessity and Lawful Prey. I know that those labels are confusing, but they are the best that I can do to explain such fuzzy concepts, ideas that seem too big to be contained in my head. I suppose I should first start out by saying that the gods are not above the laws of the Universe; they are bound by rules just as we are. Consequence happens to them, too. Therefore, the taking of god-slaves cannot be

done frivolously or to no purpose. The first principle—that of Dire Necessity—seems to indicate that it can be done only when there is some hole to be filled, some job to be done, that would benefit the greater good in a manner so as to outweigh (at least in a larger cosmic sense) the needs of the individual.

The second concept is even more difficult to explain in words. It just seems that some people are the "Lawful Prey of the Gods" for some reason, and others are not. Freely offering your oath to a deity, having the deity accept, having them offer at least once to free you, and your subsequent refusal, makes you Lawful Prey and they are allowed to take away your rights and choices. Also, some of us seem to be Lawful Prey without our consent, perhaps due to karmic debts or other reasons, about which I'm not certain. However it goes, I was Hela's Lawful Prey from the moment of my birth, while my sister, for example, was not.

SAFETY FOR THE SPIRITS AS WELL

Worrying about the health, safety, and general well-being of the arriving spirit may seem strange—after all, most gods are quite capable of taking care of themselves. However, we need to remember that even the gods are neither invulnerable nor all-powerful. Many of them have weaknesses or taboos, and others have complicated or hostile relationships with other members of their pantheon. If you trip these triggers, the results may be spectacular and unpleasant for all concerned. Inviting Loki and Heimdall, Oya and Yemanja, or Hera and any of Zeus's concubines to the same party is a Bad Idea. Providing alcohol for Obatala, meat for Vishnu, or iron implements for the Sidhe will get your event off to a bad start and an even worse finish.

Not every spirit who arrives at a possession ritual is divine; Spiritualism, for example, concentrates largely on communication with deceased human beings (also popular in Umbanda, which was strongly infected by Spiritualism), and possessions by land or nature spirits are also not unknown. These spirits may be just as prone to injury and error as you and I; just like us, they may stubbornly refuse to recognize their limitations and weaknesses. They may act in a way that is harmful for them and for those around them, or they may become confused or disoriented and then react with terror or anger.

Be prepared for the possibility of a rough spirit-descent. Have some of that spirit's favorite items on hand and be ready to offer them. Vodouisants know that a good cigar and a swig of rum will calm an angry Ogou, and some nice perfume will soothe a weeping Freda. Often giving a spirit some of their favorite food and/or drink seems to help "seat" them and anchor the possession, taking "their" substance into the body along with their energy. (Again, be aware of all appropriate taboos and ritual requirements for preparation and serving.) If all else fails, treat the spirit as you would treat a friend who was panicking: talk them down and make them as comfortable as you can. If that fails, end the possession. Allowing it to continue will be hazardous to all involved. (See page 206, Aborting a Possession, for some pointers.)

If you were raised in an Abrahamic faith, you may recoil at the idea that spirits might actually need our help, or that we might be able to do them harm. It seems blasphemous; we are far more used to seeing the spirit world as an all-powerful cornucopia from whence all things flow, but in many spirit-working traditions, gods and man work together. Orion Foxwood, a Faery-tradition seer, has referred to our relationship with the spirit world as one of "co-creators" (*The Faery Teachings,* R. J. Stewart Books, 2007), whereas Brazilian Spiritists believe that our work with the ancestors and the Exus can help them to become more elevated and ultimately attain reunification with the Divine Light. Conversely, they consider using "intranquil spirits" for malevolent work to be doubly evil; not only do you damage your target, but also you further ensnare the spirit in its chains.

While the sanity of the spirits is not something that we have generally the power to damage, there is an issue of consent when it comes to smaller spirits, or at least those who are smaller than gods. Sometimes they are called without their consent by magicians or inexperienced spirit-workers who don't understand that their work depends on amiable relationships and alliances with the Otherworlds, not brute force with unhappy eventual enemies. Can an animal spirit say yes to being pulled into a human body? Should a dead person be dragged in to be interrogated by a living loved one? Should a creature from another world be yanked through just because we want it at our party? What about deceiving a spirit? Telling a dead person that X is his long-dead enemy and must be stopped before he can hurt anyone else can be an extremely effective spell, but is it fair to the spirit? We're used to thinking about the moral ramifications of our magic as it relates to ourselves and our targets, but what about the spirits that get used as messengers, servants, and attack dogs? If we want to have a cooperative relationship with spirits greater than we are, we must extend the same consideration to those spirits that we have the possibility of manipulating.

SEX, MARRIAGE, AND HORSING

Being able to see my gods in a public rite is a rare and beautiful thing. It reminds me how amazing they are, why I'm doing this religion thing in the first place. There's something about looking into a pair of real human eyes that have a deity behind them . . . they pull you in and lock onto you. Nothing exists, for that moment, except for the deity and their Presence and Words. You go away different. When I see Frey in the flesh, I understand why, in the ancient Ing rites, women would come out to fling themselves before the man who was chosen as Ing, in hopes that he would bless them with his body and seed. When I see Odin in the flesh, I understand why he could move an entire people to seize weapons and go to war. I'm moved in a way that I can't be when the gods are just voices and vague presences, or even clear, strong ones. My mortal brain needs that physical body connection. It's incredibly powerful.

—Ari, Pagan spirit-worker

One of the ways in which god-possession by ancient European deities is vastly different from the Afro-Caribbean faiths is that a few of the European deities want sexual offerings along with their food, drink, and gifts. In ancient times, sexual offerings were given to deities along with food and drink, and considered much the same in terms of importance. One might remember the Dionysian revels, or Ing/Frey riding through the villages with women throwing themselves at him because to do it with him would bring wealth and fertility.

Obviously, this will vary from deity to deity. Offering sex to Athena would be a profound insult—she'd rather have fancy embroidered cloaks—but we have found that a certain percentage of deities really appreciate the offering, and a very small number will actively seek it out. This can create problems if the issue is not anticipated and dealt with smoothly. While some deities do seem to have the ability to charm a random stranger into sexual activity with them—sometimes totally uncharacteristically—there can be repercussions with the person's real life the next morning. (In fact, this problem comes up in quite a few myths.)

However, we have found this fact to be nearly entirely true in our experience with embodied deities: gods don't sexually approach people who are not interested in them. (The exception seems to be the rare trickster gods who like to make people uncomfortable, and they're a special problem.) Generally a deity will pick out the one person in the audience who is entirely ready to swoon at their feet, even if none of us mortals saw that. One would assume that if there was no one in the audience who was willing, they wouldn't bother.

Of course, some deities understand safe sex and some don't. This seems to be a problem mostly on the basis of how connected to the modern world they are; some are quite aware of the situation, others don't understand it, and yet others understand but don't care. When it comes to divinities who want sexual offerings, one good solution is to have an extra "ritual role"—that of someone who considers themselves to be a sacred prostitute or the like, and who is willing to interpose themselves between the god or goddess and the audience and offer themselves sexually, and is trained in how to deal with safe-sex issues when faced with a god riding in a human body, as well as the astral and or spiritual shaking-up that we've found is often a repercussion of sex with a god or goddess. If the folk suspect that they are dealing with a deity who would want a sexual offering, assigning someone in this role as one of the deity's attendants is a good idea. An even better idea, if you are lucky to have one around, is someone who is already a dedicated god-spouse of the deity in question; they will probably volunteer immediately upon hearing about it, assuming that they trust your group and your horse.

DIVINE AND MORTAL MARRIAGE

The phenomenon of god-spouses is found in many cultures, including those of the Afro-Caribbean deities. As Pagan polytheism grows and the gods get a stronger connection to this world, more and more people are being claimed as god-spouses—the mortal husband, wife, or concubine of a deity. While an in-depth study of this phenomenon would be too tangential to go into thoroughly, suffice it to say that most deities generally want a ritual, often a public one, in order to officially marry their human spouses, and many are not satisfied unless they are allowed to consummate the wedding as well. (This is very different from Afro-Caribbean spirits, who don't physically consummate weddings.) This means that horsing a deity for their wedding can—though not always, depending on the deity and the horse—end with physical intimacy.

Being a horse for a god-spouse wedding is a difficult thing. The horse knows that their body will be used not just as a sacrifice to the masses, but as an irreplaceable part of one single person's very special day. Any intimacy that will go on will not be shared or experienced by them, and they must strive to create professional boundaries between themselves and the god-spouse. In general, we've found that it's healthier for both parties to keep a good separation, unless they are already lovers. Transference issues can crop up that can interfere, and the horse needs to be humble and impersonal about the whole process.

One of the things about such a ritual that often differentiates it from other such rituals is that for once, there is guaranteed to be someone present who is possibly closer to the deity than the horse is. This means that it is the responsibility of the god-spouse to mediate between the two, getting the horse's list of needs and clearing it with the divine spouse. The god-spouse must be aware that while the horse is donating the body to the effort, he is no actual part of it, and the spouse's feelings for the god must not spill over onto the horse. The general advice of god-spouses who have gone through this is to simultaneously keep the lines of communication with the horse open and mostly concentrating on putting together the details of the ceremony rather than worrying about the horsing issues. If the horse is doing his job, he won't be there anyway. When it comes to the wedding, gods who are marrying their spouses tend to put the horse entirely in the trunk.

In actuality, the issue of sex with gods rarely comes up. I mention it only because on the rare occasions that it does happen, many modern Pagans are taken aback. Remember that the gods have a different outlook on the world than we do, and forcing Them to act like mortals is an exercise in futility. On the other hand, They will adapt to our rules over time, as the Afro-Caribbean lwa and orishas have, as long as They are given sufficient space to be themselves and spread their energy. This is a period of rediscovery and reintegration, and there are bound to be a few missteps. That's why structure and boundaries are good, as long as we remember that we cannot control the power of the gods. That's why they're gods. It's also important to keep in mind the reason why they are coming back in force in this very present way: the world needs them, desperately. We need them, too, more than we could ever imagine.

One of the most amazing experiences that I ever had was when a god whom I love and adore and revere, to whom I was being an attendant, chose to grace me with his attentions as part of a ritual. He took my hand and we went off into another room, and he did things to my astral body that would not have been possible without sexually touching my physical body with another physical body. That experience changed and healed me in many ways; in a very real sense, it made me what I am today. Yes, I can imagine the squirming that people are doing right now, reading this—but please try to understand that it was not a sexual encounter with the other guy; it was, quite literally, being touched by a god. I was amazed how, later, when I looked at the horse collapsed on the sofa and being plied with fluids, how I felt nothing toward him that I felt toward the god he had carried. He was an entirely different human being, and one whom I never would have chosen for a sexual encounter. I had no trouble feeling that. I've never yet had that sort of thing happen again to me, but I would not turn it down. To me, it was offering the most intimate thing I had—my body and my sexuality. Surely he was worthy of that gift! You may not understand or approve, but I don't care. It changed my world. My gods can be here, in the world of the body, and they value our bodies. It made me value my body more than I had, knowing that once, a god desired it—and my soul, too. I am so much greater for that encounter.

—Ari, Pagan spirit-worker

Possessory work is about service to the gods. It is not about oneself, one's ego, or one's craving for position and drama. It is a very humbling thing to be utilized as a tool in such a manner. At the same time, never am I closer to the god I most adore—Odin—than when he rides within me, in the vehicle of my flesh. It is a profound mystery, a sacred thing, and one that leaves me immensely awed each and every time it occurs.

—Galina Krasskova, Heathen spirit-worker

11
The Ride
Preparation, Aftercare, and Harmful Possessions

PREPARING THE HORSE FOR POSSESSION

Although there is no one way to "induce" a possession—it seems that the best and fullest possessions come when the spirit in question informs one ahead of time, whether a moment or days ahead, that they are coming—there are techniques that can help, especially when there is a public devotional possession scheduled for a particular ceremony. First, the horse should do a good deal of devotional work and develop some kind of relationship with the god or wight in question. If the horse can't carry on a meaningful conversation with them, it's unlikely that they will have enough connection to be ridden by them, and even if the wight does manage it (because many of them are bigger and more powerful than we are and can push their way in, if you have the right wiring), it's better to have it be an act of devotion than violation.

Even with those gods with whom I have a close and established relationship, I am almost always required to begin making formal devotional observations a week or more in advance; this helps me become familiar with their energy and creates a structured atmosphere for the work to go forward in. Sometimes this is easy because I care for and love the deity a great deal, and sometimes it is a challenge because they are unfamiliar or even unfriendly. I feel that creating a formal, purposeful space around horsing contracts keeps me safe and helps the deity shape the way in which they desire to be known.

—Silence Maestas, Pagan spirit-worker

I keep altars to all the gods who use my body, even though some of them are small things on shelves. It's important. I need to be able to kneel before them and quietly speak with Them, meditate on Them, open myself to Them, before taking Them into my body. This is partly because I need to know about any special thing that They might want before They show up and find it missing, and partly because it strengthens my bond with Them.

—Gudrun, seidhkona

As to helping the actual psychic mechanics of the horsing, being in a state of quiet, meditative Openness, however one wishes to achieve that (perhaps using one of the other seven paths), is a good way to start. Cleansing the body/vessel is important as well. For group ritual horsing, our group has a "prep team" that treats the horse as a votive object—cleansing them, dressing them, singing to them, preparing them for the spirit to enter. It also encourages an objectified feeling that helps with egotism—it reinforces to the horse that it's not about them. Afterward, the prep team becomes the aftercare team, making sure that the horse has water, food if they want it, a warm blanket, the chance to get out of and away from ritual garb, and however much space that they need to recover from the event.

I horsed Anpu twice, both times for someone else. The first time was really something of a trial run, because I was expected to horse him later at a big ritual, so we decided to have me horse him for a lesser ritual well ahead of time so that we could see how it would be when the big ritual rolled around. Anpu was not a good fit for my head. On top of that, we knew in advance that the ritual I was going to be in the second time would be very physically demanding. Being ridden by Anpu was the first time that I used sacred costumes and makeup to assist in the experience. In preparation for the Anpu ride, I also followed a purifying diet for a week ahead of time. In order to successfully take Anpu, I had the help of another shaman drumming, and even then he didn't seat himself entirely until the person he was coming to see was in the presence of my body. That ride was quite long, several hours, and I was completely cut off for the entire time. As soon as he left, my ground crew got me out of the sacred costume, and forcibly fed me foods that were not part of the purifying diet. As soon as I was able to walk around, I was taken down to a local lake and dunked. Because it was such a difficult ride to get started, taking drastic measures afterward helped to completely separate me from Anpu so that I could have my body completely back to myself.

—Wintersong Tashlin, Pagan spirit-worker

Ideally, the horse should get a good night's sleep for at least a few nights prior to the possession, and definitely the night before. Eating lots of protein the night before can be helpful, as it can lessen burnout and exhaustion afterward, although this may vary with the individual's blood sugar behavior. Vitamins are a good thing, as having a deity inhabit one's flesh eats up energy reserves and can have a dramatic effect on one's health. It plays havoc with the immune system, and there can be other temporary side effects as well, depending on the level of compatibility with the deity in question, the length of the possession, and the depth of the possession.

Sometimes the possession can be helped by the horse having spent some days beforehand observing specific taboos related to the deity that they will be accommodating. For example, this might mean celibacy for someone preparing to carry a virgin goddess, or physical workouts for someone who is getting ready to carry an athletic warrior-god. It might mean food taboos geared to the deity in question, or wearing certain colors. If the horse has developed a decent relationship with the deity, they will often let them know what would be most useful and welcoming for them.

As the Afro-Caribbean folk have known for a long time, having someone drumming during the rite helps a great deal. In their case, there are special (secret and oath-bound) drumbeats for each orisha and loa that help to call them and keep them present. Raven has been told by the gods that there are such drumbeats for every deity, but that the ones of the Northern Tradition gods are lost. He has recovered one of them, and intends to discover more. However, even just a simple steady drumbeat can help the god to stay present and the horse to stay relaxed and in trance.

And as with all things spirit-related, plan for what will happen if it doesn't work, or the god doesn't show up. We strongly discourage horses from going out and pretending that they are possessed, even if they think that the congregation won't know. Some of them will, and anyway it's disrespectful to the wight in question, and might even make them angry with you. Better to have an alternate ritual planned, or perhaps the horse can go out and tell the congregation that they are speaking as a symbol of deity X, and what is said to them will be heard by deity X. (Which can reasonably be said to be true, considering that it's likely that deity X will hear them if they were to address a wooden statue of same; it's the horse becoming a votive object rather than a container.) Honesty is more important than pleasing the masses, especially when it's an issue that can come back to bite you in the ass.

HAUNTED COSTUMES

One thing that we've found really helps a horse achieve a possession is what we affectionately call "haunted costumes," or ceremonial clothing that belongs only to that deity and is donned only to horse them. It can be as simple as a piece of jewelry or as elaborate as a full-scale costume. Anyone who has seen the initiatory rites of Korean mudang shamans will be impressed by the ceremonies utilizing dozens of ceremonial costumes, donned one after the other by the spirit-worker, to see which spirits enter into them and become their helpers. After a while—sometimes even after the first time—the costume gets enough magic on it to be used as a gateway for that deity to enter, which helps all but the most recalcitrant, head-blind, or blocked-up horses. It should go without saying, of course, that the ceremonial costume must not be used for any other purpose, including non-possessory ceremonial use by unwitting volunteers.

Sometimes a ceremonial deity-costume can make itself haunted. Raven's Pagan church has, many times, created costumes for ritual participants to wear while speaking the parts of deities. These were not instances of god-possession, only sacred theater. Sometimes, after a particular costume had been worn in this way several times, someone with a slightly more "open head" would put it on, and start to feel like the deity wanted to come in, right now. One ritual participant stumbled in the middle of a ceremony while wearing a costume that the group didn't realize had become a magnet for that deity, and lost a few seconds of consciousness, during which her body continued with the invocation. When something like this happens, there's no going back for that piece of clothing. It is now a sacred artifact of that deity, and should be reverently put away and used only to invoke them, with the full knowledge that they may choose to take the body on which it hangs if they find it suitable.

Among northern African–diaspora religions, pieces of costumes are left by or on the altars so that the lwa or orishas might dress themselves should they choose a horse and arrive. Formal dressing of a horse in order to please the oncoming deity is rare, especially in traditions like Vodou, where the possessions might come fast and furious and leave just as quickly. Candomblé and (to an extent) Umbanda are exceptions to this rule; there may be pauses during the ritual to dress the horse in an appropriate outfit, and beaded masks may be used to help induce a possession. Santeria rituals also pause to dress the horse, but only after the signs of trance possession have already begun—glazed eyes, uncontrolled movements, and so forth. In both Umbanda and Candomblé, there is also the tradition of the "steel point," usually a specially consecrated ceremonial dagger, which is held pointing upward by the horse while swaying and chanting in order to create a kind of "lightning rod" for the spirits to enter. While this is not a costume per se, it is a prop used in the same way: a magnet for the spirits and an objectifier for the horse.

Probably the most effective costume pieces are masks. Because they are faces, and they temporarily obliterate the face of the horse, they are excellent at being a container/door for that spirit's energy. There's also that a mask goes over the head, which is where most possessions come in.

ABORTING A POSSESSION

Especially during the aftermath, when the deity has gone, people may experience a plethora of reactions, from tears to giggling to laughter. Some people want to be left completely alone, whereas others may need human contact. It varies, as does what each horse will require in preparation, though the one common factor is that the experience tends to unlock emotional fetters to some degree. On a psychic level, some deities will leave a person wide open, while others may leave a certain muting in Their wake. I have a fairly strong gift of empathy, but after I horse Odin, that gift is blessedly muted in me for a while. This was disturbing at first until I realized that he uses every part of my mental wiring when he's in me, and the contrast when he's gone makes the gift seem far more muted.

—Galina Krasskova, Heathen spirit-worker

If a horse (or anyone, for that matter) feels a god-possession coming on and just saying no isn't working, there are things that can be done to snap themselves out of that early trance state that opens one for being ridden. The idea is to change your consciousness so that it is firmly grounded in your body and the real world and not doing anything repetitive or hypnotic. These techniques can also be used for anyone who feels that something is trying to "move in on" their consciousness, whether it is positive or negative.

1. Cold water, a lot of it, especially on the back of your neck. Step into a cold shower, as cold as you can stand it. This one has never failed me. Follow it up by eating and drinking something, which will ground you back into your body.
2. Drink a glass of cold salt water. You may not be able to get it all down; swallow as much as you can stand. You may vomit. That's all right; vomiting will bring you back quickly into your body and close off the channel. The salt is grounding, and salt water is the best way to get a lot of it down your gullet at once. (If it's an ocean deity who's trying to get in, this is contraindicated.) Follow it up with clear, cold water, and food if you haven't vomited and can stomach it.
3. Eat something extremely hot and spicy, like a swig of hot sauce or a spoonful of black pepper. Please have lots of water on hand to wash it down or rinse your mouth. (If it's a deity who likes this sort of thing, like a fire deity, this is contraindicated.)
4. Worst case, if nothing else is working: Tell a friend to cause you abrupt physical pain—slap you, pull your hair, whack you on the rear end with a wooden spoon, whatever you think you can take. Avoid injurious things, please; pick someone who knows how to cause noninjurious pain. The pain should be fast and sharp, and you shouldn't see it coming. Doing it yourself is not recommended; self-inflicted pain can actually have a hypnotic effect on some people.
5. After you've successfully slammed the door shut, do some

mundane activity that requires all your concentration, yet is not monotonous or repetitive. An example is doing your taxes, or baking something from scratch with a difficult recipe. It should be complex enough to require your full attention, with many changes of activity. Don't play music or sing while you're doing it; have a friend talk to you instead, or put on talk radio. Don't do anything rhythmic, like pace or drum or tap your fingers or jog; move around randomly. One particularly effective thing is to have someone talk to you about something that makes you angry, or at least something you feel very strongly about. The subject should have nothing to do with spirituality, god-possession, or anything ruled by that deity.

These techniques are useful for bringing the individual back to their body . . . but there is always a possibility that they will not work for getting the spirit out. That's not going to happen with deities—if they're here, they're here, and if they're gone, they're gone. It's unlikely that they can be driven off with the aforementioned techniques, although they may give up in a huff from being unwelcome—but it might be the case for smaller spirits that can "hide" in the back of someone's being. The only way to deal with that, assuming that the horse does not have patron deities or guardian spirits who can evict it (and this is a very good argument for having such things), is for a spirit-worker to look it over and make sure that it is clear. If it isn't, the spirit needs evicting, and that's the sort of thing that a professional spirit-worker, shaman, or other trained individual needs to take care of.

Frankly, if the minor spirit is sticking in there like glue, there's a good possibility that some semiconscious or unconscious part of the individual's own psyche is in league with it and is letting it stay. If that's the case, you have a problem on your hands; while some professional techniques can forcibly remove an aided interloper, it's easiest if the individual does some work on themselves to find out what disgruntled personality aspect is sabotaging their wholeness, and takes care of it.

Then the spirit will often get pushed out, or at least will be easier for a spirit-worker to remove. However, these professional spirit-work techniques are beyond the scope of this book, just as a book on a health condition wouldn't have directions for the patient to perform their own surgery. If there is doubt about a spirit-infestation, please find someone knowledgeable and experienced to help.

AFTERCARE FOR THE HORSE

> *Deities leave like they arrive. They may flow out in a steady stream or hop out very suddenly. My aura and body awareness shrink to normal; during horsing I feel like I'm at the very back of a movie theater and after it ends I feel firmly up in the front of my awareness. My body remembers itself, feeling one part at a time to see if it recalls where everything was left. Ideally this process is smooth and short; ideally there is no leftover trace of divine energy, and ideally all my pieces have been put back where they belong. It doesn't always happen that way. Sometimes I feel like my aura has been shredded and my body feels heavy and awkward; my awareness may not snap cleanly back into place, so I have to mentally flail around to fit inside my body while I try to keep my emotions from unraveling . . . Food helps a great deal, as do supplements like Emergen-C. I may be left with feelings of deep peace and divine blessing, or feel energized; alternatively I may feel scared, alone, and "stretched."*
>
> **—Silence Maestas, Pagan spirit-worker**

While you are making arrangements for the ride, make sure you have plans for aftercare. In Vodou aftercare is generally minimal: horses are given water and, if necessary, encouraged to lie down for a few minutes. Most often they are up and dancing and singing again within a few minutes. However, we need to keep in mind that lwa possessions are generally intense but of comparatively short duration. We also need to remember that they are happening in a culture where possession is taken as commonplace, with spirits that have a long history of possessing their devotees and do it with a minimum of fuss and strain. If you are dealing with a spirit or deity whose possession rituals have been forgotten for centuries or millennia, and with horses who have not been brought up among people who regularly get ridden, you will need to take precautions to ensure the health and continued well-being of your horses.

We have found that most horses are thirsty after a ride; make sure that somebody is on hand with water. It is also useful to have food on hand for when the horse returns to their body. Some say that a small quantity of meat will help them to get back to themselves. Others swear by bread with a pinch of salt; the salt helps to ground while the bread is solid enough to provide an anchor but not so solid as to cause nausea or indigestion. If the deity drank a great deal of alcohol, they might or might not take it along when they leave; if this happens, be ready to deal with a drunk or violently ill horse.

Having a support team on hand to help a horse readjust will be very helpful. One important role that the support team can fill is making sure that helpful bystanders don't barge in to offer "assistance." Most horses are going to need some peace and quiet after a ride; playing Twenty Questions with well-meaning but clueless people is neither peaceful nor quiet. A group of people who know the horse, know the kind of aftercare needed, and know when to provide help and when to provide solitude, will do far more to make the post-possession comedown as quick and painless as possible. We'll discuss more of this in the section on the ritual crew, and how they should behave.

Part of the horse's aftercare is making sure that the horse gets plenty of sleep that night—some horses are completely wiped and will only want to lie down, and some are hyped on adrenaline and might push themselves further than it might be wise to do; being ridden has a distancing effect on the body-spirit connection and it might be awhile before the horse is grounded enough in its body to gauge its actual physical state. While there's no way to force a recalcitrant horse to rest, encouraging them to relax a bit instead of leaping up to dance again can help them get further back into their bodies.

> *Usually I feel physically better after a possession. Once I get grounded into my body, I usually find physical pain that I may have been experiencing prior to the possession having gone away. Very rarely, the possession itself may leave me aching, sore, and headachy, like having a hangover. But that is easily remedied by eating protein, taking a cleansing bath, and getting a good night's sleep.*
>
> **—Galina Krasskova, Heathen spirit-worker**

The next day, if a horse needs to talk the experience through, let them. Horses who black out are sometimes disturbed by the feeling of "missing time" and may want people to tell them about what was done with their body while they were out cold. Others would rather not know. Still others may find the experience too intense to put words to, and don't want to talk about it.

A horse should ideally be reasonably good at checking themselves over astrally, and making sure that everything is back in place after the possession, and that the ride hasn't created any problems or blockages. With most full-on god-possession, this is unlikely; the huge energies of a deity can even blast open existing blockages. However, there is always the possibility that things don't go well for whatever reason, and horses should know how to check themselves over. It is also the ideal that if your group is working with god-possession in any way, you should have access to someone who knows how to fix such problems should they arise. Even at its smoothest, possession can be dangerous, and there is always a chance of the horse getting damaged. Having someone who not only is a healer but also is experienced in dealing with astral injuries (and in working with the psychic "wiring" of natural horses), can make the difference between permanent damage and just a few scars.

POSSESSION AND GENDER

There's no way to talk about possession thoroughly without bringing in the issue of gender. First, both the authors would like to make it quite clear (as you've probably gleaned from Kenaz's gender-neutral pronouns) that we both see the world as having far more than two genders, and when we talk about "gender," we're talking about a spectrum and not a binary. This is because when you start looking at a demographic of naturally wired horses, you're going to see more than two genders represented. When it comes to the two ends of the spectrum—men and women—we've not seen any difference in numbers in most modern groups. There seem to be equal numbers in possession-wiring when it comes to either; some cultures do claim that one or the other is better at it, but considering that some claim that the more "open" gender is male and some female, we feel that this is probably a matter of cultural biases regarding "proper" behavior for people in those roles.

However, historically, there was a definite gender bias in favor of women. If you base your data only on historical reports, it appears that females have a greater predisposition to trance possession than men. This is particularly true of involuntary negative possessions: the Shriekers of Tsarist Russia and Ukraine, the nuns of seventeeth-century Loudun, France, and the possessed women convulsing on factory floors in modern-day Malaysia[1] give some idea of the scope of this tendency. We also find a preponderance of female horses in cultures where possession is an accepted part of ritual. In the Hellenic world both the oracles and the Maenads were overwhelmingly female. In East Africa the Zaar cult is largely the province of women, while in ancient northern Europe the practice of *seidh* was seen as *ergi* (unmanly) and hence confined almost exclusively to women (and gender-crossing men).

In the past, psychologists considered this proof that women were more emotional and given to delusion and mass hysteria than men (whose brains were hardwired for rationality, logic, and all those things lacking in the "weaker sex"). In Malaysia it is believed that women have less *semangat* (life force) and are thus more easily overwhelmed by spirits.[2] Today, many scholars seek to understand these possessions in terms of feminist rebellion against an oppressive patriarchy. According to this line of thinking, women convince themselves that they are "possessed" because they are incapable of gaining the power, status, or attention they need on their own. By taking on a "sacred" role, they are able to say and do things that would otherwise be forbidden to them based on their sex. Possession thus serves the feminist cause as a dual act of rebellion and tool of empowerment.

While many of these "answers" range from condescending to downright sexist, the underlying data remains interesting—historically, while men can become possessed, they appear to be at somewhat of a disadvantage, if only culturally; although there are cultures where possession is entirely or nearly exclusive to women, cultures in which only men become possessed are very rare indeed. In cultures where religious control is in the hands of men, this likely only served to push possession even farther out to society's fringes.

Within Haitian Vodou, possessions are largely gender-neutral. Extremely masculine spirits like Ogou and Ghede will possess men and women alike, as will hyperfeminine spirits like Erzulie Freda and La Sirene. (In practice, Kenaz has noted that the men who are regularly possessed by Freda and her cousins tend to be somewhere between "metrosexual" and flamboyantly gay, and that very few straight and conventionally "butch" men are regular horses for Freda. This is not the case when dealing with masculine spirits, who appear happy to possess manly men and femme-y women alike.) When the spirit comes, they are honored according to their gender, not the horse's gender. Freda will be treated as female whether she comes in a woman or a man, and Ogou will be honored as male no matter what body he wears for the occasion.

For many Haitian women, initiation into Vodou is both a spiritual responsibility and a smart career move. In cementing her relationship with her lwa and learning how to work with them effectively, a woman can establish herself in a relatively lucrative profession, as well as attaining a great deal of cultural capital and social power. The same holds true for those whose sexual orientation or gender identity is non-standard. Unlike Haiti's Protestant and Catholic churches, Vodouisants generally have less of an issue with gay men and lesbians. Indeed, many Haitians believe that butch lesbians are favored by Danto, while Freda is partial to gay men. Many of the lwa have almost comically exaggerated gender presentations. The rum-swilling, cigar-chomping Ogou is a most manly man indeed, while Freda's penchant for perfume, jewelry, and teary displays of emotion can become nearly as stylized as a drag performance. (It may be worth noting that Danto, the "poor sister" of the Ezilis, is by necessity as well as temperament a strong, independent woman who can do a man's work; her wealthy sibling Freda need not concern herself with such matters and is free to indulge in whatever displays of femininity she likes. In Haiti, the ability to live according to one's gender or orientation is a luxury, not an inalienable right.)

On the other hand, many of the African-derived spirits are androgynous, or have "paths" or "roads" (aspects) that are androgynous, hermaphroditic, or engage in same-sex romances. Among the lwa, Legba, Ayido Wedo, and many of the Gedes combine male and female; others may be masculine or feminine, but when they choose a "child" of the opposite gender, they masculinize or feminize them, and often not just during horsing. Among the orishas of Santeria, Candomblé, and Umbanda, Ellegua, Obatala, and Olokun are androgynous and can appear as male, female, or both; Pomba Gira is the archetypal drag queen and prefers gay men or male-to-female transsexuals; and traditionally gendered orishas such as Yemaya, Oshun, and Ogun can feminize or masculinize their followers.[3] The possession experience itself is often cast in sexual terms, with the spirit as penetrative and the horse as the penetrated one, regardless of the gender of either; as we have mentioned beforehand, it is not uncommon for spirits to take mortal spouses who are often (although not always) their horses, and thus the ambivalent referencing of goddesses as husbands and men as wives.[4]

Whether gender diversity (and the attendant issue of diversity in sexual preference) is accepted in any given African-diaspora religious group varies widely. In his book *Queering Creole Spiritual Traditions: LGBT Participation in African-Inspired Traditions in the Americas,* Randy Conner describes how difficult it was to get any kind of interviews with transgender practitioners of Vodou, Santeria, Candomblé, and other African-derived faiths, while his interviews with other practitioners were rife with prejudicial comments against them.[5] Because the practice of cross-gender possession—generally agreed to be enforced by the spirits regardless of how the human practitioners feel about it—has tended to give these faiths a reputation for "queer" behavior in the outside world, many religious leaders in these groups are very defensive about the presence of queer or gender-transgressive individuals, and try to downplay the issue.[6]

In Africa, while there is evidence that cross-gender practices were once more common, centuries of Christian missionaries and widespread Islam have repressed most of these traditions, and the individuals who were chosen for them.[7] Homophobic African-derived groups tend to use the current repressed situation in the "home country" as justification for rejecting nonheterosexual and nontraditionally gendered people; some will not allow them at all or require their initiates to swear to act heterosexual and normally gendered at all times, while others will tolerate them but not allow them into certain societies, such as those of the oath-bound drum brotherhoods. Still others welcome them with open arms, and openly state that such individuals are more likely to be horses or to be chosen by the spirits. In some countries, such as Cuba and Haiti, there are groups that are made up entirely of queer and transgender individuals, although this may be a matter of ghettoization.

There is no question that in strongly Christian or Islamic countries, people with nontraditional sexual preferences or gender expressions are definitely more likely to turn to the polytheistic religions of tribal peoples, which are less likely to demonize them. This is echoed in modern Neo-Paganism, where it has been noted that there is a higher percentage of LGBT individuals present than in any other umbrella faith. The same is true for African-diaspora faiths, especially in Catholic countries, which creates even more tension for practitioners who dislike their religions being cast as "queer" by clueless onlookers. Subsistence African tribal customs have also bequeathed a tradition of placing enormous importance on childbearing and fertility, which underlies some of the anti-queer prejudice in these communities. This is similar to the fertility-religion customs inherited by modern Neo-Paganism, including the rigid dual-gendered heterosexual and procreative Godhead in some Pagan and Wiccan groups. Indeed, Conner reports having "encountered a similar prejudice within some neopagan and Wiccan communities."[8]

We've already commented rather negatively on the fact that the modern strains of Neo-Paganism have no cultural context for possession, but there is one fascinating positive aspect to this fact. We've been able to watch the gods and spirits come through a demographic that isn't expecting possession, and this allows us to see what sort of people the gods and spirits actually pick first for their "divine limo drivers." This has been especially interesting in the matter of gender. While we've seen plenty of men and plenty of women, there is definitely a much higher percentage of people who could be considered "in between" male and female—significantly higher than the population percentage on the street, that is. In fact, in some groups it's stunningly high, and a phenomenon to be looked into more seriously.

When dealing with spirit-workers as a demographic (shamans, vitkis, mudangs, etc.), it is wise to expect that a not insignificant percentage of them will be third-gendered in some way—perhaps fully transsexual, perhaps merely very feminine men or very masculine women, perhaps anywhere on that wide and varied spectrum in between. The reasons why this happens to spirit-workers all over the world are complex enough to require a whole separate book, but suffice it to say that if you are somewhere in between, it is both easier and harder to horse deities of either gender. Mostly easier, especially if you are flexible enough in your astral gender and your comfort with different gender presentations, because many gods ask that the horse be only masculine or feminine to a certain extent (and that extent will vary from deity to deity), and do not require a factory-equipped male or female body. Occasionally it will be harder, because the minority of deities who absolutely require a factory-equipped male or female body will not take a third-gendered horse. Then again, men and women are barred from horsing at least half of that latter category anyway, so on balance it is definitely a gain.

Both of us have discovered that after changing our bodies (in opposite directions; Raven is female-to-male and Kenaz is male-to-female), some gods and spirits became reluctant to horse us further; Kenaz discovered that after estrogen therapy, macho Ogou wasn't as interested ans Ezili Freda became more so. As someone who has been both male and female, and still lives somewhere in the middle, Raven is more able to comfortably horse gods of various genders, assuming that they are appropriate to the inside of his head and to his patron goddess. Generally, they require that he be astrally shifted to their gender first, before they enter; for example, even though his body is currently "male of center," his patron goddess, Hela, can ride him with no problem if he shapeshifts astrally to a female form first. If you are a single-gendered spirit-worker and you want to horse gods and goddesses of the opposite gender, you might want to work with a third-gender spirit-worker on the technique of astral shifting, and then shifting back afterward so as not to walk around with vague uncomfortable feelings. If necessary, a deity of the opposite sex can come in anyway, but they may temporarily reshape things in ways that don't clear up for some time after the ride, unless you're aware and able to put them back. Considering that an unconscious wrongly fitted astral gender can affect one's sexual functioning, it's a technique worth learning for a horse.

The issue around publicly carrying a deity of the opposite sex (or one not so close to your own physical body, if we're talking about a third-gender person) is that it is sometimes jarring to ritual-goers who don't get what is going on. Afro-Caribbean religions vary in their treatment of gender-deviant individuals, depending perhaps on how Catholic they are, but usually there is a great deal of tolerance and understanding of the fact that when a spirit grabs you, the body wears its clothing and acts in the way that it wants, regardless of its physical gender. One Candomblé practitioner related the story of how an American tourist was brought to a celebration of Oshun at the home of a male priest of that golden love goddess. The priest was preparing to be ridden later in the evening, and was already dressed in a beautiful gown with a yellow silk shawl and a lot of jewelry and cosmetics and curled hair. The tourist pointed, laughed, made rude comments, and was quickly hushed by his escorts. However, when Oshun herself arrived, he continued to make rude commentary, unable to accept that the center of all this ceremony was an effeminate man in a dress and mascara. Oshun supposedly laid a curse on him, and he contracted a venereal disease soon afterward.

Being as the gods and spirits will choose as horses whomever they wish, and they are often offended when people complain about their choices, we do not believe that it is in the best interest of the Neo-Pagan demographic to choose their horses as if they were casting for a movie, and were making sure that they looked the part, and that especially includes gender. While a Maiden goddess is not likely to choose an old man for a horse, it's still possible, if he has her energy within him. And yes, it may be that some people—like the American tourist at the Candomblé event—will be made uncomfortable by seeing the gods in bodies that don't look like the traditional forms of that god—but if we are trying to create a cultural context that supports safe ritual possession, we had better create one that encourages people to accept the reality of a tiny little woman being ridden by a big warrior god, or a burly guy wearing a ballgown for a love goddess, because the gods choose whom they will and they don't much care about our visual hang-ups. Indeed, one could also point out that doing so will train people to look for other cues for possession—divinely sized auras, specific behaviors, and so forth—and to be less hung up themselves on the exterior "look" of a spiritual experience—or, perhaps, anything else.

There's also that fact that the high percentage of third-gender horses isn't likely to stop soon, either. This needs to become ordinary and accepted, and that's something that we can do while we're creating culture in this way. At bottom, if we don't respect the preferences of the gods when it comes to designing ritual structure, they'll come in whatever way they want anyway—often to our chagrin—or not come at all.

REAL POSSESSIONS . . . FRAUDULENT SPIRITS

Dissociated personalities or those who constantly want to escape their lives, or don't live their lives, or don't take responsibility for themselves and the changes that are needed in their lives—these people tend to let in anything whether it is a deity or not. If it is happening spontaneously—that is, without prior work, dedicated preparation, and a ritual setting—the person should look for good godparents or find someone who knows what is happening so that the individual can be checked out. If the entity is a positive being—for example, an orisha, loa, deity, or master spirit—then the person should be trained. Initiations might be in order. If the entity is negative, cleansing or de-possession might be needed. No individual should be allowed to remain ignorant of what is happening.

> *If someone is getting possessed without ritualized arrangements and without predetermined potential for possession, the observers should pray. Pray to the benevolent and elevated egun, the orishas, the ancestors, to their chosen deities, or other divine beings to come and help and to remove the possessing entity. If the people are Neo-Pagan, they can still pray to benevolent spirits and deities. Then they need to get in touch with experienced people and ask for teaching. Afterward, friends need to continue to check on the person who was possessed.*
>
> **—Olorisha Lilith ThreeFeathers**

In the Western world, possession has long been synonymous with "demonic possession." Today we have begun to recognize that not all possessions are harmful. However, we must be careful not to make the mistake that every possession is desirable and every spirit has the horse's best interest at heart. Exorcism is not a Christian invention; nor is the idea that some denizens of the spirit world can and will hurt you if given the chance. Putting a FOR RENT sign on your head and letting in any wandering spirit is at least as ill-advised as loaning your credit cards or car keys to any random stranger who asks for them.

Priests and shamans have long recognized that the world of spirit contains entities that are ill-disposed toward human beings. They have also discovered that some of these spirits are highly intelligent and quite capable of masquerading as angels of light, spirit guides, deceased ancestors, and what-have-you. Sooner or later, most spirit-workers will encounter something that means to do them harm. If they are especially unlucky, they will run into one of the spirit world's smarter nasties—and if they allow said nasty to gain control of their body and their psyche, they are going to find themselves in the proverbial World of Hurt.

It's good to learn from your own mistakes—but it's far less painful to learn from someone else's. Hence we have provided here some examples of harmful possessions, as well as a few things you can do to avoid becoming someone else's educational experience.

DEMONIC POSSESSIONS

The word *demon* makes many people uncomfortable. It smacks of the most intolerant forms of Christianity, of a mind-set that says, "You either serve God (in the way I tell you to serve him) or you serve Satan." There is definitely some truth to the old saw that demons are merely your enemy's gods. On the other hand, there's also some truth to the adage "If it has feathers, a bill, webbed feet, and quacks, you might as well call it a duck." The concept of malevolent spirits goes back to before the dawn of recorded history . . . as does the idea that these spirits would try to infest human beings.

In ancient Sumeria, there were two sorts of doctors: the *asu,* who dealt with herbal remedies and the bandaging of wounds, and the *ashipu,* who dealt with illnesses caused by evil spirits or gods.[9] During the reign of Rameses III, a Syrian princess named Bent-enth-reshet was "possessed of an evil spirit" that departed only when a statue of Chons (the moon-god Khonsu) was brought to her.[10] In India the *Atharva-Veda,* a collection of spells and mantras compiled ca. 2200–1500 BCE, included this charm against possession by the *rakshas* (also known as *rakshasas*):

1. O (amulet) of ten kinds of wood, release this man from the demon (rakshas) and the fit (grâhi) which has seized upon (gagrâha) his joints! Do thou, moreover, O plant, lead him forth to the world of the living!
2. He has come, he has gone forth, he has joined the community of the living. And he has become the father of sons, and the most happy of men!
3. This person has come to his senses, he has come to the cities of the living. For he (now) has a hundred physicians, and also a thousand herbs.[11]

Although the Roman Catholic rite of exorcism has received the lion's share of the press (thanks largely to William Peter Blatty's book *The Exorcist* and the subsequent film), exorcism is found in many other religious traditions. Shaykh Mu<u>h</u>ammad <u>T</u>aahir 'Abdul-Mu<u>h</u>sin, a Cairo exorcist, describes the methods Islamic exorcists use to drive out *jinnee* (spirits) who have taken up residence in unwilling clients:

> In the beginning, we ask the possessed if he has been treated by a physician. If he has already been treated by a doctor, we address the jinnee, saying, "Fear Allah!" I speak to it in the same way that I speak to a human. If he is in a state of convulsion, I speak directly to the jinnee. Otherwise, I recite over him some Qur'ânic verses.[12]

Medieval Jews spoke of the *dybbuks,* wandering spirits that attach themselves to living people and control their behavior. To heal someone who has been possessed by a dybbuk, a quorum of ten people gather around the possessed person and recite Psalm 91 ("He who dwells in the shelter of the Most High will rest in the shadow of the Almighty . . .") three times; the rabbi then blows the *shofar* (a ram's horn) in a certain way to "shake loose" the possessing spirit. Once this is done, they communicate with the dybbuk and perform rites to heal both it and the possessed person.[13]

Even (or especially) cultures in which possession plays a regular role recognize the difference between desired and undesired possessions. Tibetan Bon Buddhists credit Shenrab Miwoche with bringing not only spiritual paths to enlightenment, but also *sel-ba,* rites of exorcism by which human beings might free themselves from demonic influences. (To gain this knowledge, Miwoche first had to battle with and overcome the black magician and incarnate demon-prince Khyabpa Lag-ring).[14] In Vodou, uncontrolled possessions by a *djab* (untamed, wild spirit) will be met with a *lave tet* (ceremonial head-washing), prayers to St. Michael (the archangel who cast Satan out of heaven), or other rituals.

Given that this belief in uncontrolled possessions and malevolent (or at least harmful) spirits is found throughout history and around the world, it behooves us to take it seriously. And once we accept that it exists, we arrive at the next important question: How do we avoid it?

WHEN BAD POSSESSIONS HAPPEN TO GOOD PEOPLE

A quick glimpse through the available literature suggests that there are a few things that make an individual particularly susceptible to negative possessions. Mental health professionals and social scientists might say that these are factors that predispose one to the hysterical symptoms commonly associated with possession. We might agree, and add the warning that these same factors can make one more susceptible to genuine negative possessions as well.

Unaddressed Mental Illness

When we try to separate "mental illness" from "possession," we must not forget that the two are not mutually exclusive. Says Rabbi Gershon Winkler, author of *Dybbuk:* "The dybbuk is drawn to someone who is in the state where their soul and their body are not fully connected with each other because of severe melancholy, psychosis, stuff like that—where you're not integrated."[15] While schizophrenia, dissociative identity disorder, and other mental disorders can mimic the classic signs of demonic possession, they can also predispose the individual to spiritual invasion. At worst, the combination of these two conditions can cause a vicious spiral, as the possession exacerbates the illness and vice versa.

This doesn't necessarily mean you should avoid possession work if you are living with mental illness. Some of the best spirit-workers started out with unusual brains, and in some traditions spirit-workers can undergo "shaman sickness," which can be either (or both) a long and life-threatening illness from which the shaman recovers or a period of profound psychic disintegration and upheaval (from which they also recover, or they wouldn't be able to do their jobs). But it does mean that you should be doing something about your illness—be it therapy, medication, or whatever else is required to manage your condition.

Emotional Turmoil, Particularly Repressed Emotional Turmoil Connected to Sexuality

When twenty-one-year-old Bano, a maid in Mumbai, India, was given in an arranged marriage to her cousin, she began screaming obscenities in foreign languages and breaking dishes. The twenty-seven-year-old Zaitun began evidencing signs of possession after her marriage to a violent addict; twenty-one-year-old Saida became possessed within three months of her marriage.[16] In 1860 realist author Aleksei Feofilaktovich Pisemskii noted a connection between sexual assault and spousal abuse and the phenomenon of *klikushestvo* (possession by shrieking demons) in Russian peasant women.[17]

If sexual violence can play a role in these possession incidents, so, too, can sexual repression. In 1320–1322, St. Nicola of Tolentino exorcised the Cistercian nuns of Santa Lucia in Pian di Pieca near San Ginesio, Italy. In 1491, the nuns of the Augustinian convent at Quesnoy le Conte in Cambrai, in the Spanish Netherlands, were attacked by demons that (according to contemporary accounts) caused the sisters to run amok in the fields like dogs, to fly in the air like birds, to scamper up trees like cats, to prophesy the future, and to reveal secrets.[18] In 1633 several nuns at the Convent of St. Ursuline in Loudun, France, began shrieking obscenities and writhing in agony after seductive dreams that featured Father Urbain Grandier, an attractive young priest: these possessions continued even after Grandier was tortured and burned at the stake in 1634. These events have been memorialized several times, most notably in Aldous Huxley's *The Devils of Loudun* and Ken Russell's film *The Devils* (1971).

As with mental illness, a history of sexual abuse or sexual trauma does not necessarily disqualify you from working with possession, but as with mental illness, it is something that you will need to address beforehand. You should be well aware of your boundaries and your comfort levels: most important, you should have a sympathetic and caring support network that will be able to help you deal with any issues that may arise during this work. Frankly, the best judges of whether you are too fragile to bear trance-possession are the gods and major spirits. If they choose you (and if it is verified by other knowledgeable people), then your various mental problems will not be too much of a burden to manage. If they are not actively choosing you, there's probably a reason.

Contagion

There are many accounts of people who encountered a possessed person and soon thereafter became possessed themselves. In 1895 Vasilisa

Alekseeva of Ashepkovo, a small village in central Russia, began evidencing symptoms of *klikushestvo* (spirit-possession) after arguing with a neighbor: by 1898 fifteen people who had seen Vasilisa's spells had become possessed themselves.[19] The various accounts of possession in monasteries and nunneries suggest a similar pattern; after one or two people became possessed, others followed in rapid succession.

Not only people can transmit this disease; there are many accounts of infected areas. Cemeteries are particularly notorious for this, as are "haunted houses" and other places where paranormal activity has been noted. The first take-away lesson from this is to approach possessed people and supposedly haunted places with caution and appropriate shielding—and don't hold a possession ritual in a haunted place or with people who are showing signs of negative possession. The second take-away is to make sure that you purify the participants and the area before you begin your ceremony.

Invitation

For our purposes, this is the most important cause of harmful possessions. Inviting a spirit to come into your life gives that spirit a much greater degree of power over you than they might have had otherwise. In the case of a spirit who wishes to abuse that power, you may find that driving it out is more difficult than inviting it in. Numerous possessions (including the one that inspired *The Exorcist*) have been attributed to misuse of a Ouija board or séances. When you're talking about dropping all your shields and inviting someone into your head, the issue becomes far more pressing.

Kenaz learned firsthand what kind of damage these things can do after a demon-summoning went awry. In hir* own words:

> *It wasn't bad enough that B____ ripped me off for a few hundred dollars (no small sum of money for a college student). He*

*"Hir" is a gender-neutral pronoun.

had to gloat about it, too. And so, being that I fancied myself a super Chaos Mage at the time, I decided I was going to teach him a lesson that he wouldn't soon forget. Accordingly I got out my copy of the Goetia (a.k.a. "The Lesser Key of Solomon" or "The Book of Evil Spirits"), created a triangle of evocation using three black candles, and called on Furcas, described therein as a Knight of Hell and commander over twenty legions of demons. I had worked with Furcas before when I was learning Tarot; I assumed he would be amenable to destroying one of my foes, and since I had been able to call on him once with no ill effects I assumed I would be able to do so again.

He came quickly enough, before I was done with the first incantation. I noted the same things I had felt years earlier: a drop in temperature, a pronounced feeling of someone or something staring from the triangle, and a faint but unforgettable reptilian smell. I gave him a simple command: Fuck B_____ Up. He seemed amenable to that, and departed. I left my apartment, allowing the taper candles to burn out. (Yes, this was a fire hazard. As you might have guessed, I was given to stupid and self-destructive behavior in those days.) When I returned, I discovered that one of the holders had exploded, spilling wax over my table and over the sigil. This was a major sign that the containment had been breached and the demon was no longer under my control. The triangle of evocation is intended to draw a boundary between the spirit being evoked and the magician, so that there is no contact between the magician's psyche and the entity's psyche, but alas, at the time I chalked it up to mere coincidence and shoddy candleholders.

It soon became clear that Furcas was fulfilling his end of the bargain. B_____ was a guitar player; soon after the evocation, all his equipment (which was worth far more than the money he owed me) was stolen. On his way to get a new guitar, he encountered several teenagers who took his money and broke a couple of his ribs as a thank-you note. Right before this happened, his longtime girlfriend left him. He also got a look in his eyes that I've come to recognize in others who are suffering from a spiritual infestation, a look that I can only describe as "hollow." When you stared into his eyes, it was like looking at a husk: there was movement and animation, but there was no vitality or light. It was as if something was eating him from the inside—because, well, something was.

Unfortunately, Furcas wasn't content with wrecking B_____'s life. At about this same time people started noticing certain . . . changes . . . in my personality. I became fascinated with Richard "the Night Stalker" Ramirez, going so far as to hang a picture of him in my bedroom. My old friends began avoiding me, as I became increasingly bitter and condescending toward people whom I saw as "idiots" (that is to say, most of humanity). My sense of humor, which has always been a bit coarse, became positively twisted: I found stuff like Faces of Death unutterably funny. I remember noticing a profound sense of dissociation; when I looked in a mirror, the face staring back at me looked unfamiliar. In particular, I remember that my eyes didn't look hollow, but rather unnaturally bright. (Others commented on this effect as well.) One day this dissociation lifted; by this time B_____ had a new guitar and new girlfriend, so it could be that Furcas got bored or was driven away by Something Else that was either looking out for my welfare or which had other uses planned for me. Completely recovering from the experience took years; I was never able to heal some of the friendships I lost. If the infestation had persisted, I have no doubt that I would have wound up manacled in a courtroom, giggling maniacally as I chanted "Hail Satan" to reporters.

To further complicate matters, your new spirit friends may not be who they say they are. Mediums have long recognized the dangers posed by "lying spirits." Spirits are not necessarily more trustworthy than human beings; in fact, many of them are even less so. Garnet, a Wiccan priestess, describes the havoc wrought by one of these tricksters that insinuated its way into a coven:

> *My former High Priestess wrote fanfic based on the original* Star Trek, *with her own characters thrown in. One day Sulu just began talking to her and being able to speak and act through her. At first, he was a lot like the Sulu we saw in the show . . . gallant and responsible. But, as time went on, she began rewriting his stories to match a rather different version of Sulu, one who had been ritually and sexually abused as a boy, had a multiple personality, and was generally not a nice man at all. At first, she kept all this a secret from us, but "Sulu" began creeping into her Craft practice more and more. He not only took over her personal life, but over her Craft life, as well. If she was somewhat emotionally manipulative, he was incredibly emotionally manipulative. She insisted that those of us who remained in the group had to interact with him and help him solve his problems, so we quit concentrating on other business and were forced to either concentrate on her or on him to the exclusion of everything else. This went on for several years, while the whole feel of the coven got progressively darker and darker, until all that was there was hate and anger and fear.*
>
> *I left the group in the spring of 2004, and I was one of the last holdouts because it had been ingrained in me to be ultra-loyal over the 15+ years I'd been involved with them. The final straw came when I realized that not only was my HPS and "Sulu" emotionally manipulative, but that he was taking energy from people. It was the hardest thing I'd ever done to finally leave . . . but I felt if I didn't that they were going to destroy me. When I was around him or her, my thinking would get clouded and I would also feel drained afterward. I know that she, at least, was more than capable of attacking people with her energy (having observed it more than once), and he was even more powerful in that regard.*

I have no doubt at all that he has basically taken over her to a wide extent and started by draining her, before he turned to her coven. When we had a lot of people in the coven the energy drain wasn't so noticeable, but when it finally was just him and her High Priest, plus me and another girl, it became palpable. I am now with another coven and we asked our spiritual contacts about this, and were told that she was in contact with the "wrong sort of entity." My feeling is that she provided this entity with a way into our reality so that he could steal energy. He would often take over her and do and say things (generally nasty stuff), and she would claim afterward that she had no memory of it. I believe, at this point, that the only way to rid her of him would be some sort of "exorcism"—but not only would she refuse to cooperate, but it might send her over the deep end. I feel this entity has become too intertwined with her that you can't really safely separate them anymore.

It's important to note that these possessions (which might more accurately be called "infestations") were not of the spectacular pea-soup vomit and levitation variety. Rather, they were a gradual but unmistakable change for the worse in a person's character. While some minor "bleed-through" is not uncommon after possession work (that is, someone who horses Mars may feel more energetic and short-tempered for a few hours or days afterward due to residual divine energy), major changes in the horse's personality (especially major changes for the worse) are a sign that something has gone seriously wrong. If you see this happening within your group, stop what you are doing immediately and seek competent spiritual help.

No one who is inexperienced should presume that everything will be all right after a possession seems to end. I have seen people who assumed they understood what was happening, but they didn't. I've seen untrained people after they had called in an entity that they thought was a certain type of being, but what came through was something entirely different: it was a negative entity. Before the possession, that person had a good life, marriage, relationships. But the individual allowed that negative entity inside and it did not leave. In all honesty, the individual may not have wanted it to leave. Since the entity stayed, the person's life blew up: divorced because of unpredictable behavior, refused to speak to long-term friends, and even left the children with the grandparents to go out drinking and partying every night. The change was like the "road to ruin" in those bad fundamentalist pamphlets.

It's not a game. It is a spiritual calling. People need to be careful. If a person wants to be an oracle, he or she needs to do the work to become an oracle. If a person wants to be a medium, training and working diligently is the way to go. Trance-state work should be studied along with a variety of spiritual development tools as part of an ongoing training process. Spirit-possession and god-possession can be transformative—no, it should be life-changing in a positive way.

—Olorisha Lilith ThreeFeathers

If this is happening to you, find a qualified medium who knows about different forms of possession and the manifestation of those possessions, and also different kinds of spirits and what their possessions are like. Get their opinion as to what is happening. In my experience, it is unwise to assume that all possessions are real, that the possessing spirit is who it says it is, or that it is positive and helpful just because that is what you asked for. These types of relationships take a lot of work to consistently work well. Be cautious; don't do it just because you can. Get training from someone who has experience, or get initiated into a tradition that practices possession. It is important to have a network of knowledge and a spiritual framework of support in order to remain protected.

—Olorisha Omi Lasa Joy Wedmedyk

DO-IT-YOURSELF EXORCISM

After reading this chapter, you may have decided that one of your friends or acquaintances is possessed, and with the aid of a few appropriate holy symbols and the best intentions, you plan to cast out this intruder once and for all. Here's a word of advice, in boldface and capital letters for emphasis: **DON'T.**

If your friend is suffering from a mental illness that mimics some of the symptoms of possession, your efforts will be worse than useless. While an exorcism ceremony may temporarily alleviate some of the symptoms, it will do nothing for the underlying condition. At best you will be placing a bandage on an open wound. At worst you will reinforce their idea that they are possessed and exacerbate the behavior you were trying to control. If your friend is actually possessed by something malevolent, on the other hand, your "exorcism" may be putting yourself and anyone who assists you in serious danger. As noted above, possessions can be contagious. If you don't have spiritual backup, you may find yourself infected by the same negativity that has claimed your friend.

Exorcism is serious business. If this book is your first introduction to trance-possession, you are not qualified to attempt it. If you have not eliminated all other possibilities (ranging from schizophrenia to substance abuse to "we thought they were acting strange, but it turned out we misinterpreted their behavior"), you should not even be thinking of exorcism. Just as you would not try to do brain surgery or pilot a fighter jet after reading a book or two, you should leave exorcism to experienced spirit-workers who know what they are doing.

PART FIVE

The Community

Kenaz's Story

June 2006

The fet is almost over, which is good. Kathy and I have been doing all the spins, libations, and greetings for every spirit. About a third of the way into the proceedings we discovered that this is an awful lot of work. By now we're running on fumes and determination and a dim hope that things will be over soon.

Look on the bright side, I think as Firesong, our *houngenikon* (leader of the songs for the lwa), sings loudly for Danto. *At least you're not leading the chante lwa.*

I finish saluting the directions, then head for the *tambouye.* Our drummers don't have a lot of experience with Haitian polyrhythms, but have captured the hot, herky-jerky syncopated spirit of Ezili Danto's song. I pour some red wine before them, then *viré.*

On the last turn I stumble.

The drummers are playing louder now; Firesong is calling out over them, her voice is slithering through the drumbeats like a rattlesnake, the edges sharp as a knife, the edges, the edges . . . I move toward the cornmeal vévé that marks the barn's center. In a peristyle this is where the *poteau-mitan,* the center pole between heaven and earth, would stand.

Another viré, more wine on the floor.

Kathy sprinkles Florida Water; the sharp citrus tang cuts through the dust and lingering undertone of moldering hay. The crowd is singing now, but I can't understand the words.

The altar now. We're in front of the altar, this is the last salute. I'm not even dizzy, Danto's lamp is burning bright and clear just like I'm running, bright and clear, not tired any more, I have my second wind.

I guess Danto isn't coming tonight. I pour out the last of the wine. Before it hits the ground I hear myself screaming. I awaken across the room. My throat is sore and my mouth tastes of perfume.

Raven's Tale

May 2004

It was at the beginning of our Beltane gathering that I got the word, but I chose to ignore it. Beltane is a stressful time for us, running a weekend-long event for anyone who shows up. I am generally in charge of programming, and though my job is done at the end of each day when the rituals and workshops are finished, I'm usually dead beat and ready to collapse. Besides, there was a field full of people back there on my farm, many of them strangers, and my group didn't, at that time, think that doing anything as socially difficult as god-possession during a public event with strangers present was a Good Idea at all. Actually, we all agreed that it was a Bad Idea. Yeah, okay, the Umbandistas had done it, but that was different. They had a structure, a team, and expectations of how it would go. They were experienced. Their "tourists" were in the minority, and usually well prepped by House people.

Still, the signals were there, if I hadn't been deliberately ignoring them. *I am coming.* I did the evening farm chores, and my assistant commented that I kept drifting off into trance in the middle of sentences. *I am coming.* I tried to eat a late snack, but nothing would stay down. *I am coming.* Screw you, whoever you are, I thought. I'm going to bed. And I did, crawling in next to my already unconscious wife. It was still there, like a tickle, like a Presence standing over me, but I told It "Another time," and did deep breathing until I fell asleep . . .

. . . and woke up again by the fire in the back ritual field. I was sitting in the big thronelike wicker chair with something laid across my lap—a large knife—and I was wearing furs, my wife's boots, and not much else. And it was cold, so cold—I was immediately taken with a bad case of the shivers. Someone threw a woolen cloak around me. Someone else said in a concerned voice, "Are you back?" I nodded, croaked something out. "He's back!" and water was passed to me, then hot tea made over the fire. My assistant helped me up to the house, got me out of the furs and boots, helped me wash off the permanent marker with which that god had ritually marked my face, and got me into bed again, for the second time. The clock read four hours later than the first time I tried it.

I was furious, and ashamed. I had been yanked out, slipped a mickey, and used without my consent—at a public gathering, in front of all those people! Damn, what had they seen? What did they think? That was the part that really worried me. I already understood that I was a god-slave, and nonconsensual use was part of my lot to some extent . . . but innocent folk at a Beltane gathering hadn't agreed to host a god. The lesson came home to me over the next day, as I got over my sulking and actually listened. It also came out of the mouths of the other elders of my group, among whom I was not the only horse, nor the only god-slave. "If you get tapped again," they said, "tell us! We'll figure out something to do. Even at a public event!" They had quickly picked up on what was going on, and circled the god discreetly at a distance, in order to deal with any difficulties between deity and congregation.

The next day, people told me everything that had happened. I had them tell it to me over and over, from different perspectives, so that I could fool myself into believing that I had a memory of it. Missing time makes me feel crazy, and it's comforting to have even a pretend memory of a real event. Most of the strangers were still clueless (and claimed to have had a wonderful time at the event), no one was hurt, and a few people had truly intense experiences from small interactions with that wandering god. One person was upset by her interaction, but my staff talked to her the next day and she understood. If we'd had preparation, staff with knowledge and training, and a ritual space, even that one minor problem might have been dealt with sooner. (I won't say that it wouldn't have happened, because it had the feeling of inevitability to it. Sometimes people just have to deal with their issues, and assuming that a god will be tactful about their feelings on the matter is just asking for too much coddling on the part of the Universe.)

That second day, a woman friend came to me to talk about her interaction with the god, which was the longest and most intense, taking up half the time of the visit. She revealed to me that He had come to her twice before in other bodies, that He was her lover. That she was intensely grateful to have had this wonderful experience with Him under the Beltane stars. Her words, and the look in her eyes, brought me right out of any self-pity that I might have had.

That second night, I made a deal with the gods: *If you will give me warning, if you will let me know well enough in advance who you are and what you need, so that we may properly honor you, I will not fight this again, even if it means doing it in public where strangers can see and perhaps think that it is just me, gone mad or trying to get attention or doing any number of other stupid things.* After I made that promise, they have always held to my bargain, and I think that was the lesson that god brought to me.

That week, my core group met to discuss how we would set up a structure for public god-possession at Pagan events. It was clear that we couldn't put this off any longer, and it hasn't failed us yet.

12
Keeping the Community Safe

IT IS FAR LESS PAINFUL TO LEARN from the mistakes of others than to repeat their errors. With that in mind, Kenaz (with input from SheDragon, an occultist and Neo-Pagan) gives you one of hir more spectacular foul-ups—a fet lwa that quickly became more than the participants and clergy bargained for.

Kenaz and hir partner, Kathy, had been holding workshops on Vodou for several years at a large Pagan festival. For the 2006 festival, they decided to hold a fet that was dedicated to Legba but (like other Vodou parties) saluted and honored many of the other lwa. Kenaz and Kathy were careful to bill this as a "Vodou-inspired ritual" rather than an actual fet lwa—a distinction that did not, unfortunately, make it into the program. While a few drummers would be present, they were not trained in the rhythms used in a typical Vodou ceremony. No one there was an *asogwe* initiate who knew the sacred *langaj* (language) used to call down the lwa. Most important, the audience was not skilled in (or even experienced with) horsing the lwa or any other spirits. Accordingly, they assumed that the ritual would cause few if any possessions, and that any lwa that arrived would come into Kathy or Kenaz, both of whom are initiates in Vodou with experience in dealing with possessions.

Lesson 1: *If you're working with spirits that are given to possessing people, assume that they will and take appropriate precautions.*

This is especially true when you are dealing with groups of people who have dabbled in "psychic stuff," possibly increasingly their sensitivity—and thus their attractiveness to spirits—without being trained in how to handle these situations. (We don't know why more spirits tend to be attracted to people who have a regular history of working with magic for long periods of time; it may be that it makes changes to the psychic "wiring," but we can't say for sure. However, anecdotal evidence does seem to point in that direction.)

Though calling the event a "Vodou-inspired ritual" rather than a fet, Kenaz took pains to make it as authentic as possible. Kenaz drew a vévé for Legba before the table that served as the altar. Firesong, the houngenikon, prepared a sheet of traditional Haitian songs dedicated to the lwa who would be saluted. To add that extra touch, Kathy and Kenaz also prepared the oil lamps that are used in a Vodou fet to call on the lwa.

Lesson 2: *If you call on the spirits, don't be surprised when they arrive . . . even if you are certain that you haven't called them in exactly the right way.*

The ceremony commenced; the opening salutes to Legba, Loko, and Ayizan were without incident. Next came the salute to Damballah, the great white serpent who straddles heaven and earth. Kathy is a bride of Damballah, while Kenaz is very close to Him and has been ridden by Him on a couple of occasions. Kenaz felt the energy levels, and thought it likely that Damballah would show up. As Firesong began the song to Damballah, Kenaz noticed Kathy beginning to stumble and showing the signs of an oncoming ride. Kenaz ran over toward her, hoping to facilitate the possession, but was suddenly distracted by a loud hissing noise. In SheDragon's words:

> *I was participating in the dancing and as much of the songs as I could manage, when I found myself starting to trance, and my*

limbs starting to numb. I could feel the port/base of my skull starting to tingle and feel as if the flesh was being pressed together. I came to a dead halt, and my chin lifted upward, and my arms lifted a bit. I began to lean back, and back further still—my spine wanted to form a bridge. I found my eyes rolling back, and a distinct breathing change—heavy, rhythmic, firm. In that moment, I found myself thinking, "Yes, I will not resist you."

The Being or Beast came in, and dropped me to the floor like a stone. My perception of being became constantly in The Now. There was no consideration of action—just constant fluid movement. I could see, but only sporadically—it was like looking through a View Master:

click
there's the floor
click
there's a pair of legs
click
there are steps.

The rush of having what seemed like an endless supply of physical energy was intoxicating. I raced about on my belly, hissing and snapping my teeth at the air. I chased someone. I felt immense, white-hot rage. That person was cornered, and I hissed a hostile message in that person's ear. I fought slightly, barely managing to pull myself out of biting range: my salivary glands were filling at an immense rate. I hissed and spat, and began to rush forward again.

When Damballah comes in possession, He never speaks. Upon hearing SheDragon hissing "You have offended me," Kenaz suspected that sie* was dealing with a drama queen who was faking a possession for attention. Taking a look over at Kathy (who was at this point writhing

*"Sie" is a gender-neutral pronoun.

on the floor in that twilight space between the lwa's descent and its full-on takeover of the horse's body), Kenaz used a technique that is designed to drive out a spirit. Sie thought this would either calm SheDragon down or make her fraud obvious. However, the "imaginary spirit" was offended by Kenaz's efforts, and threw Kenaz into the bleachers with an electric jolt. Kenaz felt consciousness slipping away, and worried that sie was going to get possessed as well. Kenaz remembered saying jokingly, "So what are we going to do if the only two people here who know how to control a possession get possessed themselves?"

Lesson 3: *When holding a possession ritual, keep multiple spotters on hand.*

SheDragon continues:

> *The Rider came on harder still, and I moved. Like soap on wet tile, I dashed forward, sideways, up on two arms become crocodile rolls. I was on the defensive suddenly—moving faster—overwhelmed. I started to rear up, only to escape again. I was eventually subdued. I was frightened, and the Rider made a few attempts to get me out of the grasp of the priest(s?).*

Within a few seconds Kenaz recovered and returned to the task at hand—trying to control the wild spirit. Seeing a sheet nearby that would normally be thrown over Damballah when he arrives, Kenaz repurposed it—putting it over SheDragon's head and cutting off her line of vision. This worked, as her body slumped and the spirit left. Meanwhile Kathy was recovering; Damballah had apparently passed through her, found the other entity distasteful or found that no one was paying him the appropriate attention, and then left.

They took care of SheDragon using the same standards of care that are used at a Haitian fet. Somebody gave her water; Firesong recommended that she leave the area if she felt another possession coming on. (At fets given by Kenaz and Kathy's société, it's not uncommon for people who have had a rough ride to go upstairs or into a neutral area until they regain a feeling of control.) Besides, Kenaz had seen SheDragon at numerous events and knew she was connected with a Pagan group that occasionally did ritual god-possession, and accordingly assumed that she had prior experience with possessions and would know what to do. Only later would they discover that this was the first time SheDragon had ever been hit with a full-on possession.

Lesson 4: *Don't assume a horse has prior experience in possession unless you know otherwise.*

The fet continued; the remainder of the party appeared uneventful. One other audience member got taken in an unplanned possession by La Sirene, but she thought that it was wonderful, and had no problems afterward. Another audience member reported feeling an altered state coming on; he had seen possession before but never experienced it, and didn't want it to happen there, so he went outside and shook it off, and then rejoined the fet with no difficulty. Meanwhile, Kenaz and Kathy had no idea that SheDragon was in need of more than a bottle of water and a suggestion that she go out for a walk. In her words:

> *It took me about six months after the incident to get the help I needed to heal properly. While I don't regret what happened to me in retrospect, I really did not like being "shattered" inside for six months afterward. I had injuries to my heart chakras, down to my root (which was inflamed, causing a few medical issues). I respect the group that held the fet, but to be honest, I found that the advice I received after asking "If this happens again (getting ridden during the fet), what do I do?" was poor. The Singer suggested I go outside if the spirit came back, and this sounded like a bad plan.*

Lesson 5: *The standard of care appropriate for experienced horses may not be appropriate for someone who has no experience with possession.*

Raven was meanwhile at the same gathering and considering whether he wanted to go to the fet. His friends assumed he would go—"Kenaz and Kathy are holding a Vodou thing! And you're a horse! Of course you're going to go!" But it was late, and there was a chronic illness and a busy schedule to deal with, and he just wasn't sure. So he went outside to sit and did a divination to ask his patron gods and spirits the following questions:

Will this ritual exhaust me?
If I go, am I likely to get ridden?
Is there any god or spirit who is counting on me to be there and give them a body?
What's the best thing I can do here?

The answers came quickly and clearly: *A) Yes. B) Absolutely. C) No, but if you show up, they'll consider it consent. D) Skip the fet, go to bed, and get some sleep. You'll be needed in the morning.* Raven took their advice, and the next morning SheDragon pulled him aside to talk to her about the experience the night before. He recommended that she get some divination on the matter from an objective third party, and let him know if things didn't get better. That eventual divination suggested that although the possession was real, the spirit was neither god nor lwa, just a random wandering entity that happened to be attracted to the ritual and magic work being done at the gathering. It had been feeding, and somehow got sucked into the rite. Raven eventually did some heavy shamanic work on SheDragon to clean up the mess left when someone gets forcibly entered without preparation. He takes this to mean that although the spirits gave Kenaz and Kathy enough rope to hang themselves, they also bothered to arrange for a bit of backup just in case, an ending that should give everyone hope.

Most fets are held in peristyles and areas that have been used for Vodou ceremonies for years or decades. Nearly all of the remainder are held in rented halls and rooms that have had very little or no ritual use prior to that time. This fet, however, was held in the middle of a Pagan festival, in a site that had seen hundreds of rituals calling down

Everybody from Anubis to Zeus to the Unseelie Court in between. Some of these rites had happened literally earlier in the day, or the day before. Kenaz and Kathy prepared the space using precautions that were adequate for a normal Vodou service—but they had not taken into account the power of the land on which we were going to be holding that service, or the other spiritual activities that were going on around us. Because Vodou has a reputation for power and effectiveness (one that is admittedly well deserved), they assumed that the standard preparations would be sufficient. They forgot that they were not dealing with a standard ceremony, a standard location, or a standard population.

Lesson 6: *Before you do any rite involving possession in a strange place, especially one that has been used at any time in the past week for energy-raising purposes, take precautions.*

Talk to the land-spirits, check around for any hungry loiterers, and ward, ward, ward. And have someone around for people to talk to the next day, someone who might have the skill to fix something that goes wrong.

Lesson 7: *Check with the gods and spirits before doing any ritual where They might be present. They may know better than you do about the possibilities, and be better able to advise.*

SheDragon was fortunate in that while she sustained some damage from her rough ride, it was eventually cleared up. You may not be so lucky. We don't plan on making the same mistakes twice—and after you've read this, there's no reason for you to make them once.

The next year, the same rite was done at the same Pagan gathering . . . with some major changes. First, the space was cleaned, cleared, and warded by the staff . . . of whom there were several more people than the prior year, including some experienced folk who "worked clear" and were adept at catching possessed people who were about to hit the floor. Divination was done to see what else might be needed, and the best suggestion seemed to be a "clear tent," a place outside the building where people could go if they needed to get away from the rite—to rid themselves of the last of a spirit's energy, to avoid an unwanted possession, to freak out and be calmed, to eat and drink and ground. Raven decided to run the tent, and SheDragon offered to help. It was an open pavilion just outside the back door of the building, with blankets and pillows, food and drink, and ritual tools. Raven and SheDragon cleared, cleansed, and warded it separately, and manned it for the entirety of the three-hour fet.

The clear tent turned out to be a great success, and prevented any problems from developing. Of the half-dozen people who used it, half just needed space to calm down, ground, and eat a little after possessions, and then returned to the rite. Two had trouble coming back to their bodies after the lwa had left them—especially after days of sleep deprivation, forgetting to eat, doing sweatlodges, and going to multiple rituals—and were gently brought back into themselves and sent off to bed. One individual did start to act strangely in the ritual and was dragged off to the clear tent. It turned out that he had a small guardian spirit who had inhabited him since his troubled childhood, although he had long since forgotten the matter. When one of the lwa, in another body, noticed it and called it forth, it became frightened and took over his body, trying to flee. The clear tent workers couldn't fix this problem, as it had too long a history, but he was sent off to bed, warned not to attend any more triggering events, and told to get some professional spirit-worker help in the future. This specific sort of problem will be dealt with later in this chapter, under Spectators with Baggage.

COMMUNITY SAFETY

What do people see when they come to a possession ritual, and what do they think? Obviously this depends heavily on the demographic, the audience, the cultural context, and the specific spirits in attendance. We are most worried about those Neo-Pagans who are dabbling in possession without really understanding what it can do to the watching masses. Let's start by conjecturing what they see: first, assuming for no psychic vision at all, they see an ordinary person, possibly dressed strangely, acting oddly (and perhaps awkwardly), and being the center of attention. They see other members of the ritual staff being deferential, or protective, or awed, or just extremely attentive, to this attention hog. If they don't believe in possession—or even in the gods, for that matter—it may just seem silly to them. If they have self-protective mental and spiritual boundaries that block out most divine energy, they may not get the instinctive response that so many have to the presence of Spirit. Such folks are going to be bored, or not impressed, and will probably feel like they are wasting their time.

Other folks may be frightened, especially if this is their first experience seeing ritual possession, and its reality is driven home to them. For some, actually perceiving the riding spirits can be just as troublesome as not perceiving them. They may find the idea of possession violating in general (especially if they themselves have personal issues of trauma around boundaries) and even if a horse is just fine, they may project those emotions onto the entire situation, and feel that it is inherently dangerous to the horse and anyone in proximity. They may find the idea of the gods being right there, in front of them, instead of at a safe and perhaps theoretical distance, to be unnerving. The strong presence of Something That Much Bigger Than You can scare those who aren't used to it, or whose identity is strongly based on being the biggest and most competent person in their worlds. They may be frightened by the strong feelings that a deity can inspire in someone. They may be uncomfortable because they don't know what is expected of them in this situation.

In cultural contexts where everyone understands the situation, and appropriate behavior has been modeled for them since they were children, these problems are much less likely to come up. Even Western-educated indigenous people who have lost faith in religion will still tend to respect the native rituals, or at least not be frightened or appalled by them; they'll either not go or go politely as a social more. It's those of us with no context who will be having the most problems, although we assure you that cultural context can be built up more quickly than you think.

For the bored or appalled unbelievers, the best line of defense is to educate them on what these sorts of rites are supposed to be about, and what those who run them believe, and then allow them to decide whether this is something that they want to take part in. Rather than concentrating on "But it's real!" it's better to point out that one of the beautiful things about Neo-Paganism is its great diversity, with many different sects and traditions; that most traditions do not practice possession at this time; and that there is no shame in deciding that this is not your thing. There are groups who work skyclad and those who don't; there are apolitical groups and those who build their rituals around civil disobedience; there are ones that are high-ceremony formal and those who are earthy and loose; there are polytheist, pantheist, and archetypist groups. Casting ritual possession as just one more religious practice about which one can have preferences, and choose to attend a ritual or join a group on the basis of those preferences, generally removes the pressure to believe in something that isn't yet speaking to that person, and makes her more comfortable. A group leader can also gently point out that even if one doesn't believe that the body they are treating as if it held a god is actually so blessed, things said sincerely to the horse will still be heard by that deity, who knows and listens and cares.

For the frightened onlooker, communicating the fact that the group has as many safeguards in place as possible can help them feel better about possible repercussions. Stressing that this group has done this before, that you all do this as an act of deep devotion and not just a piece of cool religious theater (which should be your attitude anyway), and that you are aware of the ways in which it can be done badly and strive not to fall into those traps can also help. The group communicator can also stress that it is normal to have all sorts of strange feelings during and after a possession, and be willing to talk about their own experiences. Knowing that "this is normal and expected" can settle someone down a lot, even if they still aren't fond of the sensation. It's like knowing that going out in the rain will get you wet. Also, having a staff that are good at modeling correct behavior, helping awkward first-timers to adapt to it without being pushy, and showing their genuine comfort with and joy in the situation can reduce fears as well.

> *It definitely causes problems with the relationships of people around you because when the god speaks through you, they may or may not accept that it's the god, because it's your mouth that is saying hurtful things to them, things that are arriving with such force that they can't defend against them. They'll either say, "Well, this god stuff wasn't real anyway, you just made that up so that you can say these nasty things to me," or "You colluded with that nasty god, and that nasty god said these nasty things to me, and you're an asshole for letting it happen. Why didn't you stop it?" And then, there are certain truths that as a human being you don't necessarily want to know, and the god will come out and tell them to someone who needs to hear them and you'll say, "Oh, no, I didn't want to hear that!" It can be emotionally quite painful, as well as physically quite wearing.*
>
> **—Lydia Helasdottir, Pagan spirit-worker**

> *In terms of etiquette for witnessing: do not interrupt a possession. It can cause damage to the horse to have the process broken off abruptly before the deity is fully seated. This is another area where a competent team of trained handlers is incredibly helpful. Most deities, when they come down, like to do work. If a horse is seemingly wandering around aimlessly for too long, handlers should be cautious. Some people have a hard time getting out of possession, not just getting into it. There are techniques to help bring a person back, and it's best if the horse, early on in this work, can condition him- or herself to respond to specific stimuli. For me, calling my name, touching me while calling my name (just touching or eating won't always do it because some deities will put me*

extremely far under so they can eat and drink and touch while in my body), and removing ritual regalia often help.

Know that when that deity is physically present, you are standing on holy ground.

Be respectful. If you can't be respectful, either leave or be silent. Those present during the possession should not be frustrated by a horse's lack of ability for elaboration afterward. After the deity departs, many horses will have no memory of what happened, or at best only the vaguest of memories. Ask the average horse "What did deity X mean when she said this?" and you'll likely get the answer: "Beats the hell out of me, she said it, I didn't!"

Sometimes those witnessing a possession may project certain feelings onto the horse after the possession is over. This is quite common, for it can be difficult to separate the physical person's image from the deity that temporarily inhabited it. The horse should be aware of this possibility and make sure to be up-front about it. Attachment, romantic feelings, etc. can all be evoked by the presence of a god or goddess. It's important to be aware of this fact because those feelings really have nothing to do with the horse (him- or herself) and if someone expresses such feelings to the horse after a possession, the horse should be direct and point out that it's likely transference. This is a time to set and maintain gentle but firm boundaries. I prefer not to interact with those present during a possession too much immediately after in order to counteract such perfectly natural effects.

—Galina Krasskova, Heathen spirit-worker

If you're an observer of a possession rite, be open to something different, and hold the energy of the space as it is happening.

—Olorisha Omi Lasa Joy Wedmedyk

The danger isn't just on the human side of things, of course. Any public possession ritual puts both the horse and the entire congregation in direct contact with the Divine, and direct contact with the gods is always dangerous. If angered, the gods are capable of doing you gross spiritual and bodily harm. Depending on the deity, it can also be easier than you expect to anger them. This is something that many inexperienced spirit-workers and magicians forget. In the Neo-Pagan demographic, there is a general view that the gods are all Good, and would never harm anyone, and that their patience is never-ending, even with jerks. In African-diaspora faiths, and in existent Paleo-Pagan religions (and, for that matter, ancient European pagan cultures), the assumptions were very different. Gods and spirits could get pissed off and cause damage, and the tales all tell of how lack of knowledge of the rules didn't count for anything. In fact, one interviewed horse commented that "if what you've got on the line is guaranteed never to get angry, offended, or feels that someone has done something worthy of retribution, you've probably got an archetype on the phone, not a deity."

As any houngan or mambo will tell you, spirits will sometimes take out their anger at an individual on the entire community—especially the one who is responsible for running the ritual at the time and ought to have screened and prepared better. The actions of one drunken jackass can lead to bad luck, ill health, and all-around bad energy for everyone present at the ritual, not just the jackass. Do not hesitate to disinvite or immediately remove someone who behaves inappropriately. At least in the beginning, and when doing a ritual in a new place, the group may find it best to treat possession rituals as "invitation-only" affairs open only to those whom they know and trust.

Do everything in your power to keep your spirit guests happy. Be aware of and honor their quirks, and have a backup plan in case things start going wrong (and if you have any experience with public ritual, you know that they generally do). Slavish groveling and quaking fear are unnecessary; honest caution and good service will generally be more than sufficient. The gods are for the most part neither wantonly cruel nor stupidly bloodthirsty. Good worshippers are hard to come by, never mind good horses or clergy. They would rather reserve the smiting for those who deserve it, or those who might profit from a liberal application of boot to backside. You can actually sum up the first rule in one phrase: *The best way to deal with the gods safely is to avoid acting like an idiot in their presence.*

> *Yes, gods can come angry. A Lukumi friend of mine once attended a ritual where the patron Spirit of the house showed up and angrily called for his machete, chastised a follower who had been disobeying certain spiritual taboos and behaving in general like an ass, and whipped him with said machete. My first experience with a totally amnesiac possession occurred with a very angry goddess—in my case, the Morrigan. While it hasn't happened often—in fact, only three times have I horsed a truly enraged goddess—it can and does occur. While experiences such as this can test the mettle of anyone involved, and while it's very difficult not to become emotionally invested as no one wants to see the gods they serve angry (or be the one who's used to speaking harsh words), it's still important to maintain the thread of trust and respect. I have never once experienced or witnessed a possession that did not have beneficial results, including the experience with the Morrigan.*
>
> **—Galina Krasskova, Heathen spirit-worker**

KEEPING THE COMMUNITY SANE

> *The most amazing experience I've had with possessory work occurred Lammas 2006. I was invited to horse Gerda at a public ritual while another spirit-worker was horsing her husband Frey. This was the first time I really understood what a valuable service to the community public horsing is. It really hit me that for the majority of people, this is the only time they will interact face-to-face with a deity or see two deities interacting with each other. It's not like being a shaman or spirit worker, where the gods are an almost constant presence. After that rite, I had people telling me what a*

profoundly moving experience it had been and what a tremendous impact it had on them. Prior to that, I'd always done possessory work because this was what the gods required of me. It was a service to the gods. It never, ever occurred to me to consider the impact it might have on the people present. I'd never looked at it from the human perspective. It was, in a word, mind-blowing.

—Galina Krasskova, Heathen spirit-worker

Then again, there's that second issue: Can you look into the eyes of a god and remain sane? Even as there's part of me that yearns for it, would throw myself into it, there's a part that screams and wants to run away. They are so much bigger than me, they remind me how small I really am in the big view. Even if what I'm seeing when I gaze into the god behind those human eyes is only one finger of their being, it's enough to overwhelm me. I can see how I would promise them anything, even if I shouldn't, even if it's not in my best interest. Religion isn't safe, and neither are the gods. We can't expect that of them. We can only expect them to be what they are. The presence of a god disrupts everything—people's lives, assumptions, energy. Everything that you put into nice neat little boxes, their presence overturns. Some groups simply may not be ready for that, and it's a wise leader who acknowledges it.

—Ari, Pagan spirit-worker

The gods are real.
They do not owe us anything.
They may demand things of us.
They have every right to demand things of us.
They are not all loving cosmic nursemaids.
They are bigger than we are.
They are stronger than we are.
They cannot be controlled by us.

Those who horse do not do it for their own ego gratification. It is a path of service and devotion and often something that the gods demand of their folk. Through possession, one has the opportunity to meet a goddess or god face-to-face, through the medium of the horse's flesh. It unites the worlds, bringing the numinous tremendens into temporal time and space as safely as possible. But do not ever forget that it is a god you are dealing with and while they are utilizing the vehicle of a person's flesh, that does not in any way limit their power.

—Galina Krasskova, Heathen spirit-worker

Possession is a communal experience—the spirit comes down for the benefit of the people. The key word here is "benefit"; everyone involved should be getting something out of the process. This doesn't mean that everyone is suddenly going to become healthy, wealthy, and wise, but in some ways their lives should be better now by virtue of their direct contact with the Divine. They may find these encounters challenging, even painful, but there should be some real, tangible value for the community.

If possession-related craziness and general drama are affecting your group negatively, you need to figure out what has gone wrong. Are people refusing to hear what the gods are telling them—or are they calling human beings on dubious claims? What about the spirit's track record? Do their predictions generally come true? Have they given any kind of help to anyone, or otherwise provided evidence that they are who they say they are? Please note that it is not irreverent or blasphemous to ask these questions and expect considered answers from your horses and clergy, and if they try to tell you otherwise, that's a warning sign.

Being in the vicinity of a possession can trigger stuff you didn't know you had. The release is generally cathartic and ultimately beneficial, but it can be intense and painful while it's happening. This does not mean you are going crazy, nor is your reaction inappropriate. Make sure you have people on hand who can provide emotional and spiritual aftercare, and keep an eye on the audience before, during, and after the possession. If you see anybody who is getting into deep emotional waters, step in and offer assistance at the first opportunity. A sympathetic ear and a little bit of immediate attention will be far less effort than cleaning up a mess after the fact.

Sometimes when the presence of a deity makes things worse rather than better, the problem is entirely with the people involved. If a majority of folk reacted badly because they were not prepared for what the ritual would feel like, this problem rests squarely on the clergy who were responsible for bringing the unready into a dangerous situation. Safe ritual structure starts beforehand, with education of the congregants and some thought for their emotional safety. A possession ritual that ends in a whole lot of upset people is likely going to put a damper on any future attempts at same. It's also bad juju to structure things so poorly that you end up making a bunch of people's first real touching-deity experience into a bad memory that they'd rather not repeat.

This sort of thing, unfortunately, is most likely to happen spontaneously, when a deity graces a rite with their presence to a level that no one expects, and the populace freaks out. Another common cause is an over-enthusiastic and inexperienced ritual-worker who invites the clueless to a ceremony involving god-possession and doesn't think to really explain to them beforehand what will happen, or how they should properly act. For example, let's imagine that a Norse ritual is to be run, and the god Odin is to be invoked into a willing horse. Divination has been done and the omens checked, and Odin is pleased with the idea, the time and place, and the offered flesh. The priest or priestess running the rite has bothered to check and see what sorts of physical offerings—food, drink, and so forth—Odin likes, perhaps by research and inference, perhaps by contacting other groups who have brought him through.

However, it does not occur to our over-hasty priestess to think about the fact that Odin has many *heiti,* or titles, that describe his various aspects. Calling him as Odin Grimnir the Berserker or as Ygg the Hanged Man will be very different from calling him as the benevolent All-Father or the gender-deviant Jalkr. If you don't specify, you'll get whatever he sees fit, which may not be what the priest or priestess had in mind, especially if they are looking to give the congregation feelings of reverence and devotion, and not merely terror. Our hapless ritual-worker also neglects to tell those who come much at all about what Odin is like personally, or at least no more than a few threadbare tales, and little about how a possession experience might affect bystanders. Thus they are not able to decide how much involvement they want with the ritual. Should they not come at all? Should they come, but stay in the background and not approach the god? Approach the god briefly in order to make an offering? Attempt a conversation? Be an attendant? In order to preserve people's mental safety, it's best to give them as much foreknowledge as possible so that they can make informed choices and take care of themselves.

In spite of this, some people may still be strongly affected and need counseling or at least a listening and sympathetic ear afterward. Still, it may make the difference between them remembering it as a powerful and cathartic if difficult thing and a frightening experience that they would rather not endure again. Being in the same room (or ritual field) with a deity affects how you view that deity, and the gods in general. It has an impact on the faith of everyone who brushes up against that Presence. While the interaction between a deity and a human is in the end up to them, both the ritual-designer and the horse have a certain amount of responsibility for cushioning that impact and helping it to be as positive as possible under the circumstances.

It's never gone badly in the sense that I came to physiological harm. I have had deities do or say things while riding me that I would have preferred that they not do or say, and I have paid the price later with people who didn't entirely grasp the god-possession concept.

—Wintersong Tashlin, Pagan spirit-worker

CONSENT AND THE COMMUNITY

To the spirits, your presence at a ritual that involves possession—or even, in some cases, one that does not—may constitute implied consent to be possessed. This may be problematic, particularly if you don't want to get ridden. There are a number of precautions that you can take to guard against this. You can pray and ask that you not be bothered. If you are taking on some ritual responsibilities that ought not to be shirked, that can be used as a bargaining point. You can block the possibility of incoming spirits by putting a "blocking" whammy on a piece of cloth and wrapping it around your head. (For those who use runes, Raven finds that the simple rune Isa—a single vertical line—is good to draw on the back of your head with marker.) Of course, blocking things in this way can also cut you off somewhat from the energy of the ritual, and any messages that might come in other than spoken ways, but you may feel that this is worth it, especially if you've been assigned a job to do. You can also use other blocking or binding magics, such as black string tied around you. All of these, of course, assume that you do not have any prior agreements to be ridden. They work much better for people who are not regular horses and are trying to avoid accidental possession; the best defense of a regular horse is to have a good relationship with their patron deity and be fully forewarned about any impending rides.

However, one of the most effective ways of avoiding difficulty for the community at large may be to set boundaries beforehand. It is perfectly appropriate to say, "We are providing you with a horse, and will welcome you as best we can, but in return we ask that you abide by the following rules." If the deity in question does not wish to abide by those rules, they simply won't show up. Some Gnostic magical groups, for example, have very strict boundaries around divine possession. In their rites, the deity is allowed to come down through a particular chosen priest or priestess, but may do nothing more than beam their energy out over the crowd. They may not speak, or perhaps speak only once, and they may not get up and walk around. However, the rituals do not try to predict which god or goddess will show up; they allow the possibility of surprise and wonder. Those who work with these groups point out that those gods who are not comfortable with these boundaries simply won't show up. Obviously, it must be good enough for some of them, because they never lack for deities to come and beam their energy out.

Keep in mind that the community always has the right to say no. If a deity demands something that you are unable or unwilling to give, you may respectfully decline. In fact, you should do so. Do not ever agree to anything that you are not prepared to give, or it will go very badly for you when you have to break that deal. Your happy "smile and nod" response will be taken as an affirmation, and even though you may forget your promise, you can rest assured that the spirit world will not. You also have the right to leave the ritual if things are getting too intense for you, and again it's better to do so than to stay and let your traumatized energy disrupt the rite for others.

Whatever you do, remember this: By showing up at a possession ritual, you have agreed to interact with the Divine in some way. This is a major undertaking, and one that can have enormous repercussions in every aspect of your life. Understand that you are putting yourself in the spiritual line of fire. You are asking for the gods to take a direct and personal interest in you. You may think you are heading off for an entertaining afternoon with friends, but They may have other plans. If you're not ready for this, find something else to do. Otherwise, consider your attendance consent for a Close Encounter of the Divine Kind.

Regarding the controversy of whether to put limits on the gods: When you do public ritual, and you set rules as the price of entry for a deity, with the implication that if they don't like the rules, they shouldn't come, you aren't really setting limits on them. If they want to come and possess a person, they're going to do it anyway whether you like it or not, because human beings in general are not powerful enough to stop that from happening. But the effort involved for a deity to come and possess someone who isn't open and actively seeking it is huge, and not worth it. It's painful for deities to manifest down here; that we know. It's not a walk in the park. They have to make quite an effort to get this dense.

And anyway, most gods want to come down where they are wanted and honored, or at least where they have jobs to do. They don't come down without a purpose for all that effort, and if you can set things up so that they get the honor and ability to work that they desire, it will be worth it to them to come by appointment rather than randomly. The one exception might be trickster gods like Loki, where all bets are off, but they're a separate problem. Most gods would rather be welcomed than fought off. Wouldn't most people, as well?

—Lydia Helasdottir, Pagan spirit-worker

SPECTATORS WITH BAGGAGE: WHEN WATCHERS HAVE SPIRIT-PARTNERS

Vodouisants (and followers of many other traditions) believe that we are all surrounded by spirits—and that some of those spirits take a direct, personal interest in us. Whether or not we believe in them is of no consequence; they believe in us. If you have worked with magic, you have probably made the acquaintance of one or more of these spirit beings; indeed, the "archetype" or "egregore" you work with may very well be a spirit being. And if you are attending a possession ceremony—especially the sort of possession rite where multiple people may become possessed and it's not unheard of for it to happen to audience members—that being may try to take control of your body.

Because modern occultism is largely a free-form affair, it's difficult to say exactly what sort of spirits practitioners might attract during their magical career. In a community where Celtic Native American shamans share sweatlodges with Asatru Kabbalists, we can expect all kinds of spiritual crossover. This makes giving hard-and-fast guidelines for dealing with this situation difficult. Instead, we can point to a few examples of systems or practices that involve spirit contact and offer some pointers on ways you might deal with an unexpected appearance by somebody's spirit guide.

Dabbling with Demons, Flirting with the Fae

Many ceremonial magicians work with grimoires and other texts that promise contact with "evil spirits." Some consider this a sign of their Nietzschean disregard for consensus morality; others justify it by saying the true magician must both plumb the depths and climb to the heights; and still others believe they are using those "demonic sigils" as spooky trappings for elaborate psychodramas—useful and harmless exercises in consciousness reprogramming and entertainment that play upon medieval superstitions without actually believing them. These practices are not necessarily "dangerous"—in fact, they are eminently safe and balanced if used properly and with the appropriate precautions. The problem is not with the Goetic demons, but with those magicians who cannot be bothered to follow instructions.

When rituals call for a "triangle of evocation," they do so for a reason. The entity that you are calling upon is not to be allowed into your psychic space; rather, it is constrained within a place outside your body. From there you may speak with the being, order it to do things, and interact with it while protecting yourself from dangers. The creators of these rituals recognized the dangers of allowing certain entities unfettered access to your psyche. Unfortunately, many who perform these ceremonies today do not recognize these risks. They skip the boring parts like the opening prayers; they forget to draw the protective circles and geometric figures that keep their consciousness separate from that which they have called; they neglect the purifications and banishings that close the ritual.

As a result, many DIY Diabolists have attracted the attention of beings that might not have their best interests at heart. If you've summoned entities using books like the *Goetia* and various *Necronomicons,* you may want to take some time for purifications, fumigations, and general banishings before attending a possession ritual. This is true even if you've never noticed any untoward effects from your workings. You should also keep in mind that spirits don't necessarily work on a human time scale and might wait years or decades, then act when you least expect it. Anecdotal evidence compiled from various cultures suggests these negative entities often seek to possess or take control of their targets—and a possession ritual might prove the perfect opportunity for a patient demonic spirit to make its move.

Still others work with entities that are more benign but nonetheless extremely powerful; more than a few psychonauts have burned their fingers playing with Enochian magic. Still others have been exposed to the various strains of "Faery" magic and have become acquainted with the Good Folk, with all the beauty and terror that entails. Psychic contact with these spirits may not be nearly so corrosive as an unprotected encounter with the demonic, but that doesn't mean that possession by a fairy or Enochian angel can't cause serious damage.

The sheer amounts of energy raised by an Enochian, elemental, or other powerful spirit can cause major psychic short circuits and damage, while the Fae are notorious for separating people from their bodies, then failing to bring them back.

If you have been working with these (or other) spirits, you will need to establish appropriate boundaries before attending a possession ritual. Let them know ahead of time that your attendance is not an invitation for them to take control of your body. If this advice is not heeded, then you may have a very serious problem. Your spirit guide is out of control and you need to consider severing your ties and protecting yourself from your "ally." At the very least, you need to think about what level of control you have in your interactions with the spirit. If it is taking you over at possession rituals, how often is it pulling your strings in daily life?

Those leading the ceremony should treat an unexpected possession by a spirit guide or spirit companion like any other unexpected possession. The arriving spirit should be gently but firmly escorted out of the premises. Someone should take notes of the spirit's behavior: what it said, how it acted, any specific requests it made, etc. It may be that the spirit guide had some important reason for making an appearance; you may have to address that issue, or possibly arrange a ceremony where the guide can come through in a more appropriate setting.

Carefully warding the area of a rite can cut down on possession by outside random spirits looking for a place to party; however, it will not keep out a spirit whose right to enter is tied to an audience member. In other words, if someone walks in with an indwelling spirit, or a spirit trailing after them whom they have formally given the right to mess with their lives in some way, it will pass your wards. (In the event that your wards are formatted in such a way as to keep out such spirits, they would also exclude the human beings who carry them or the relationship to them. This might manifest in those people feeling extremely uncomfortable entering the rite.)

Another possibility is that if a new audience member has a possession relationship with their patron deity, then that deity might try to show up in a multiple-possession rite. Generally deities don't trespass on each other's territory, so if this happens, see how other embodied gods or spirits are reacting to the gatecrasher. If they seem all right with it, shrug and assume that they allowed that guest to enter. And remember: No one is capable of discerning and punishing a faked attention-getting "possession" like an actual riding spirit in the same room.

Community Preparation for God-Possession

First, ask the right questions. A short period of time before the public ritual—perhaps a week—do a divination to make sure that everything is going to go all right, and that there is no important information from the gods that hasn't gotten through yet. If there is any uncertainty in the group about the ritual, you might want to have two separate people do this, each with witnesses, and compare results.

Questions for Pre-Ritual Reading

1. **Should we be doing this possession ritual at all?** Continue on to number 2 only if the answer is clearly a yes. If it's a no, ask further: Why should we stop? Is this the wrong time? When would be a better time? Does the deity not wish this after all? Is it merely that there is something unacceptable that must be fixed and then all will be well to go ahead, or is this a complete no-go?
2. **Have we chosen the right people for the positions?** Assuming for a sortilege-type divination method, lay down one card or rune or whatever for each of the ritual positions. There should at least be answers for the horse(s), the attendants, the priest or priestess, and general staff. If all looks good, continue to number 3. If there are problems, ask: If this person is not appropriate, what sort of qualities should we look for in a replacement? Is there someone suitable in our group or should we look elsewhere?
3. **Is there anything that these folks need to keep in mind?** Deal another row under the first one for any specific instructions for your staff.
4. **How will things go with the audience or congregation? What should we change or make allowances for?**
5. **Is the ritual going in the right direction?** Are there changes that we should make?
6. **Most important, what does the deity or spirit desire or expect?** Are our offerings acceptable? Are they happy with what we have planned? Are they willing to stay within our expressed boundaries?
7. **Is there anything else that we need to know?**

Should the answer to the first question come back as "no" or "not yet," you may want to research another question: Why do we want to hold this ritual? Possession is a sacred event, which should be approached with reverence. If you want to hold this ritual because you crave novelty, or because you want to prove your credibility as Serious Magicians and Priests, you are setting yourself up for serious trouble. At best your gods are going to ignore you; at worst they will arrive and give you a dressing-down that you will never forget. Another bad reason is because "Joe really wants to talk to god X for personal reasons." Someone's desperate need to commune with their god, while admirable, is not a good reason to put an entire community at risk. It would be better if Joe found a spirit-worker who works with that deity and can arrange a personal one-on-one conversation.

Second, the group needs to do some research, and by "research" we don't mean consulting the *Happy Shiny Book of 101 Gods and Goddesses for All Occasions* or its ilk; we're talking about primary sources and academic literature. If possible, you should try studying the legends, sagas, and primary sources in their own language: if not, try to find the best possible translations. Look for works put out by universities in addition to (or instead of) works put out by popular publishers, and don't limit yourselves to a study of the gods: explore the lives of the people who worshipped them. Anthropology, archaeology, and history can teach you a great deal about the cultures in which these deities were honored and provide insights into the standards they set and the expectations they have for their worshippers.

This admittedly will make for some turgid reading. Academic texts are notoriously long on verbiage and short on readability; if you're used to "adaptations" or "retellings" of stories about your deities, you may discover that the unabridged originals are far more difficult to follow and far less engaging. But after you grit your teeth and slog through this material, you will have a much better grasp of what your gods are really like. There's a difference between giving lip service to "the Hunter God" and understanding what he meant to a people whose hunters were the only thing between them and starvation. Hellenic culture bore little resemblance to *Clash of the Titans* or the *Hercules* movies; most worshippers of the Northern Gods were merchants and farmers, not steroid-bulging Conanesque barbarians. Understanding the world in which they were worshipped and the similarities and differences between that world and your own will help you to experience them as individuals, not just interchangeable window dressing.

There are a few things for folks witnessing a possession to keep in mind. The most important things to note are the wants, likes, and dislikes of the deity in question. This is especially important for those of us in traditions that lack a long-standing practice and structure for ritual possession. It's best if handlers or attendants can record what a given deity likes for the future. Most deities like to have some sense of continuity and continuation. Write it down. You'll get some leeway the first and second time a god or goddess shows up, but by the fourth and fifth time, you may get a pissed-off deity. I, for one, would not want to be there when Odin shows up, asks for a drink, and there's no alcohol, for instance!

—Galina Krasskova, Heathen spirit-worker

I'd like to speak a word here about the usefulness of research in setting up the ritual contexts. I started out doing all the research and preparation for the people, not for the gods. Justifying possession (which was going to happen to me anyway) to my new religious community was something that had to be done with tact and sensitivity. Turning in ritual specs with voluminous documentation both helped my credibility and prepared onlookers for what was going to happen, giving them a sense of appropriate behavior. What I didn't expect was that in the process of my exhaustive research, I turned up a few new things that were actually useful for my own practice—offerings I hadn't thought of, and so forth. The gods talk to me, but they don't always tell me everything, or hold my hand.

—Gudrun, seidhkona

But this sort of research will take us only so far. The available primary sources are fragmentary at best, nonexistent at worst. A good bit of what remains comes from converts and missionaries, and a good bit more comes from academics and historians who have often misinterpreted their findings to support their own preconceptions. To compensate for this lack, you may want to go straight to the source—ask your gods how they wish to be served. The transmissions and suggestions received from divine sources have become known in many circles as Unsubstantiated Personal Gnosis or Unverified Personal Gnosis—or, for short, UPG. This term is less loaded than words like *epiphany, prophecy,* and *revelation.* It recognizes the experience as a personal one—and it also acknowledges that we will not accept it blindly without further supporting evidence. However, sometimes this will be the only evidence that you can find on a particular deity, and it's better to go with that than nothing at all.

The exercises provided in chapter 8 may help you to achieve this god-contact. You should also speak to others within your greater religious community and see what insights they have gleaned from their work with your gods. Some folks are now referring to the concept of Peer-Corroborated Personal Gnosis, or PCPG. PCPG happens when you discover that others have independently arrived at UPGs that resemble your own. If several different groups have come to the conclusion that one deity likes obsidian daggers or that another favors champagne, for example, it provides further confirmation that your personal UPG is more than just an idle whim—and suggests that you might be wise to have those things on hand should you choose to call on those deities. (Whether you should share the specific details of your possession work within your community is another topic altogether, and one that we will discuss soon.)

Just as important as making sure what you should have on hand is making sure what you should *not* have in the general vicinity. In Vodou the congregation puts out all cigarettes and closes all open containers of alcohol during the salute for Damballah, since the great serpent does not like alcohol or tobacco; a woman who is menstruating or anyone who has an open wound cannot participate in his salute since he also does not like the smell of blood. You should also keep in mind that not all gods get along. In Lukumi, Oya and Yemanja are never allowed to appear together, nor are Ogun and Chango. Were they to arrive at the same time, their long-running conflicts would flare into open warfare and the service would become a battlefield, complete with civilian casualties. Similar conflicts exist in other religions: Ares and Hephaistos have come to blows over Aphrodite, while only the most foolhardy will call Loki and Heimdall or Set and Horus to the same event.

Third, plan your ritual carefully. When you first see a Vodou fet, you might think it an unstructured whirlwind of dancing and singing, punctuated with what appear to be epileptic seizures. In fact, all this chaos is governed by an underlying set of rules and regulations, the *regleman* (regimen). The regleman governs the order in which the spirits are saluted; the rhythms used to salute them; the songs, libations, perfumes, and colors that are used in their salute; and the details of each salute. It helps to focus the energy and provides a structure within which the congregation and officiants can respond to possessions quickly, appropriately, and safely.

While your ritual should have a definite beginning, middle, and end, it should also include room for the unexpected. If some deities choose not to arrive (and they may not: we can invite them to the party, but we cannot ensure their attendance), there should be a Plan B in place that will allow you to hold a reverent and respectful ritual that does not culminate in possession. (Whatever you do, don't play-act a possession just because you don't want to disappoint the audience, no matter how tempting it might be.)

At the same time, you should have plans in place for ending the ride should it prove to be more than the horse can handle; you should also be prepared to deal with possessions (including ending them) among members of the audience. Simply calling the horse by their name is often enough to shake them back to self-awareness; we have found that calling a magical practitioner by their birth name can be particularly effective, if you know it. Asking the horse a work-related question can be useful as well: asking a computer professional a question about network administration or a writer a question about their novel in progress can cause their mental state to shift quickly from one receptive to possession to one firmly grounded in the material world. If that fails, cooling the horse's head by pouring water on it can end a possession. (But be careful with this one, since it can also *encourage* a possession by a water spirit or a deity of a cool nature!) Another extremely effective technique is throwing a sheet or a bag over the horse's head and cutting off their field of vision. When you do any of this, be prepared for the horse to slump limp or possibly go fully unconscious for a few seconds; if you are dealing with a large or heavy person, make sure you have people around to prevent a fall and attendant injuries. Check back to Aborting a Possession, page 206, for more ideas about bringing someone fully out of trance.

Fourth, know your audience. Probably the most important decision that you can make is whether or not to keep this ritual a small one, attended only by carefully vetted "inner circle" people who all "get it," or open it to a larger congregation in a public ritual. When you invite the gods to a ritual, they will expect *everyone* to be on good behavior. A disrespectful drunk or self-absorbed drama queen might not just call down the wrath of the gods on their own head but all cause long-term problems for the whole crowd. There is also a very real danger of someone who is not prepared becoming unnerved by what they see; many people assume that seeing the gods will be great fun, until they actually find themselves in the presence of deity . . . and then there are those who will attend and report to all who will listen that you are all nutty cultists who think that you get possessed by the gods. When you're working with people you know, people who have proved themselves trustworthy and willing to do the required work, you can weed out the flakes and sensation-seekers beforehand. Mambo Vye Zo's group, Sosyete du Marche, has taken this approach; their fets are open only to members and trusted people. As she explains:

Education on what constitutes an authentic possession is part and parcel of being a member of this house. Because we are not a public sosyete, we don't have the problem of strangers who are not familiar with our ritual protocol attending our fets. We adhere to a strict policy of privacy, and a rather tough entry program, that deters most wannabes from coming to the door in the first place. We educate everyone in the house on correct behavior in service and on the value of not faking possessions. We regard our services as religion, not parties or dances. As such, we have concentrated on worship as the primary focus of our gatherings. By studying the liturgy and memorizing the prayers, songs, and drumbeats, we've given more than enough to our members to learn, apply, and master.

As we do not offer public ceremonies, we don't have the issue of strangers coming in and acting out. The folks who come here are full-time house members, who are exposed to our regular service, with all its codes and structures and morals. They've been through our classes; some of them have traveled to Haiti with us, so they have a firsthand knowledge of structure and decorum in ritual. We are trying to work Vodou in the old-fashioned method. Our Haitian contacts are older houngans and mambos, who do things the "old" way. Courtesy is mandatory. Family comes first. And histrionics, in any form, are not tolerated.

But while closed rituals have their advantages, they also come with dangers. It's easy for a closed house to become a back-patting society where no one wishes to offend his or her friends and colleagues. Dubious possessions (and dubious behavior in general) can go untested and unquestioned because everyone is afraid of hurt feelings. If your group goes with closed and private possession ceremonies, make sure that they are constructive and useful to the development of the group and of the individuals who are part of the group. This doesn't mean that they need to be easy, or that there will never be any unpleasantness;

indeed, we'd argue that sooner or later *any* kind of productive spiritual work is going to force people to own their shit and deal with their shadows. But there's a big difference between being challenging and being counterproductive.

TIPS FOR PAGAN EVENT STAFF

Running a big Pagan festival is always a challenge, especially when you have people from a myriad of traditions who all need the space—physically and psychically—to get their rituals' needs met. Sometimes those needs clash; sometimes they just can't be met due to the limitations of the space, no matter how well meaning everyone is. And, hey, religion is difficult enough without bringing the actual gods and spirits down among you in physical bodies, right? Yet as we illustrated in the vignette at the beginning of this book, they may choose to show up anyway, even if there are no rules or ritual context with which to greet them. And then what do you do?

Let's say that this year your festival is hosting a ritual that will feature possession. Given modern Paganism's aggressive eclecticism, there are any number of ways in which your event could become the arena for a god-visit: summoning the Delphic Oracle, holding a bembe for the orishas, performing a trance dance inspired by Balinese Hinduism, and so forth. You may not know much about the gods or spirits being honored—but that's fine, because you don't need to. The ultimate responsibility for the ritual's success or failure rests with the people who are holding it. However, there are some things you can do to ensure that things go smoothly for everyone concerned.

Make Sure You Know and Trust the People Holding This Ritual

They are dealing with the psychic equivalent of high-tension wires or powerful explosives. If they are incompetent, careless, or disrespectful, they may injure not only themselves but also those attending the ritual or those in the general vicinity. Don't assume the celebrants know what they are doing just because they are initiated in Tradition X or Y, or because they sounded impressive in an e-mail or on the phone. In this situation there is no substitute for direct, personal, face-to-face experience. Ideally, they should be interviewed by people you trust who have extensive knowledge of possession rituals and the deities and spirits that they are calling up.

Check to Make Sure That They Have Enough Staff

Are there people who will run the ritual, drum, lead singing, ward the boundaries, attend on the god(s), attend on the horse(s), fetch and carry, run interference, and counsel worried onlookers? Ideally, these should all (or mostly) be different people, and none of them should also be the horse. Check to make sure that the ritual staff have enough trained people so that when and if a possession occurs, they can maintain distance between the horse and rubberneckers. In our culture, spirit-possession is still a novelty. As a result, attendees may let curiosity override their sense of boundaries and propriety and surge forward for a closer look at this strange event. This can quickly make things uncomfortable for the horse and attendants, not to mention the spirits. If you don't have experience with possession states, stay out of the way and let people who know what they are doing handle the situation.

Make Sure That Ritual Participants Have What They Need to Call, Welcome, and Honor the Spirits Involved

Many gods will get short-tempered if they arrive and discover that nobody has thought to bring their favorite items. As a result, there should be less tolerance for chaos, improvisation, and "winging it" than you might find at a standard ritual . . . but at the same time, they need to have the graceful, experienced flexibility required when dealing with powerful entities that may not wish to stick to a human script. You can help here by checking with the organizers to make sure the space is ready for preparation at the appointed time, that the participants are allowed the undisturbed time they need for setup, and that everything they requested for the ceremony (and which you agreed to provide) is on hand and properly prepared. If attendees are supposed to show up with something special—specific kinds of clothing or offerings—find out when you put together the blurb for the program, and list it then, along with a ritual organizer contact for answering questions.

Check with Them to Make Sure That They Are Able to Clean and Ward the Space Properly

If you can, find out what went on in that space for the last couple of days and let them know. Don't schedule more than one ritual in the same space that involves possession, opening doors to Otherworlds (even metaphorically; sometimes they don't consider that invitation a metaphor), or serious invocation of deities without doing a cleansing of the space between rituals.

Treat Possession Like the Sacred Experience It Is, and Make Sure That Everyone Attending Shows the Same Reverence

If you see crowd members acting inappropriately, ask them to get with the program or find something else to occupy their time. ("Acting inappropriately" is an umbrella term that can cover anything from smirking disrespect to stumbling drunkenness—and when in doubt you're wisest to take a hard line on this one.) Those called on their misbehavior may think you're being a big fascist meanie, but you're actually doing them an enormous favor. If they don't like being chided by the support staff, just imagine how they will feel when they have Ogou or the Morrigan shrieking at them—or worse.

Interlopers

Just because you don't have a possession ritual planned doesn't mean that you won't have a visit from unexpected spiritual guests. Many

Pagan events feature fire circles with drummers and dancing—a combination that can trigger possession in those who are susceptible. It is entirely possible that your "trance dance" will result in a trance possession. To that end: When you see someone stumbling or acting disoriented, break the trance. You can do this by pulling them aside, calling out their name, asking them if they are all right, or otherwise distracting them. If you do this quickly enough, you might be able to stop the possession before it starts—and if at all possible, you *should* stop it. (Of course, you should also ascertain that you are dealing with a trance and not dehydration, exhaustion, or some other physical condition.)

Experts

Should you be fortunate enough to have on hand someone who works with possession (i.e., a horse or a priest or priestess of a possession tradition), you should call on their services. Let them call on their bag of tricks for appeasing or ejecting a wayward spirit. (If no one else is on hand, you can use some of the techniques mentioned in the section in chapter 11 called Aborting a Possession, although that is, by definition, for beginners and not comprehensive.) Actually, it's a good idea to make previous arrangements with such an individual (or a couple of them, from different traditions) who will be present at the event and able to help if needed. If you have an "expert" or two on staff, one of their jobs perhaps ought to be explaining the nature of possession to people who see one—whether unplanned and unwelcome or carefully contexted as part of a ritual—and who are troubled or curious. You might even want to schedule a workshop on possession at the beginning of the weekend (and strongly suggest that people who want to attend any possession ritual should see it first) or at the end, to explain things. If there's not room to do that, at least have someone on hand who will publicly answer questions and reassure people that this, too, is a normal if unusual part of religious devotion.

If You Are Unable to Stop the Possession, Maneuver the Horse Away from the Crowd

You will likely have a number of curious people crowding around the entranced person, speculating on what is going on and offering "helpful" suggestions. Move them aside politely but firmly. Once you get the horse in a relatively secluded area, you can try reasoning with or talking to the spirit. If you don't know what sort of deity you've got, address them as "My Lord" or "My Lady" (guess the gender from the way that the horse is acting, not the horse's gender) or at the least, something neutral like "Honored Guest" or "Sacred One." You may feel silly, or worried that this is just a drama queen acting out and that calling them "Sacred One" will just feed their ego, but it's better to err on the side of assuming for an actual possession until you can get the situation under control. If it turns out to be fake, you can berate them later. If you are able to get a positive identification on the possessing entity, try to find a priest or priestess or devotee of that tradition. They may be able to tell you something about the deity's likes and dislikes. Should that quest prove unfruitful, speak to the spirit yourself. Explain that you are not presently equipped to handle their visit; ask that they return at another time when you are prepared to provide a fitting reception.

Fakers

If you see an egregiously phony possession that endangers other people—an assault on a fellow attendee, grossly inappropriate sexual contact, or similar nonsense—end the show by any means necessary. If that means pouring ice water over the offender, wrapping them in blankets and throwing them to the ground, or doing something else that may prove uncomfortable or humiliating to the faux horse, so be it. If, by contrast, your fakers limit themselves to behavior that is melodramatic but not dangerous, you'll do best to ignore them and to encourage others to do the same. Any kind of attention you provide, positive or negative, will only serve to feed a faker. Treat their antics as though they were beneath contempt or even notice; this will prove more effective (and more painful) than any kind of public denunciation.

Knowledge

Your health and medical safety staff should have at least some knowledge of what possession is, and how to handle the horse once it's over. (Being med staff at a Pagan gathering is, and should be, different from being med staff at a secular event. This is one of the religious issues that sometimes come up when dealing with Pagan religions. A special workshop, pre-gathering, for the staff and especially the health workers, might be in order.) It's not their job to stop the possession, but it is their job to step in if it's been discovered to be something other than a possession—a bad drug trip, or someone off their medication (sometimes referred to as a bad *lack-of-drug* trip), or mental illness, or dehydration, or exhaustion, or any number of other things of mundane origin. One should also consider it their job to provide aftercare for inadvertent horses, but only if they know what to do. Have them read the chapters on aftercare for horses in this book, and keep curious onlookers away from the exhausted and possibly claustrophobic horse afterward.

Prayer

It might behoove the staff, as a whole, to get together and have a group prayer-and-invocation ritual before the event, where you beseech all the gods and spirits to please refrain from possessing anyone without warning, or showing up in a way that will cause serious disruption of the event, or coming in such a way that you cannot give them the honor that they deserve. Remember that you're asking, not ordering or demanding or banishing. They hear and appreciate, and we've found that they will generally do as asked. You might want to let it be known that the staff, as a group, has done this. It will cut down on temptation for fakers.

13
Recognizing Fakes and Frauds

FRAUDULENT GODS: FAKING SPIRIT-POSSESSION

Probably the first and most anxiety-producing issue that the conundrum of spirit-possession brings up among those who are first hearing about it is the fear that someone could pretend to be possessed by a deity and thus gain power and influence over a gullible group. In fact, when certain well-known Pagans have publicly referred to it as "dangerous," it is this—rather than any danger associated with the gods themselves—that they are referring to. The idea brings up understandably terrifying visions of some charismatic and unscrupulous high priest or priestess convincing a troupe of naive newbies that every pronouncement and whim is actually mandated by a god, and should be obeyed as such, simply by conveniently dropping into a fake trance and acting the part of Isis or Odin or whomever.

Indeed, when Raven wrote a chapter on god-possession among Norse-Germanic practitioners and posted it to his website, one of the first criticisms that worried readers expressed was that this information could be used as a how-to for faking god-possession in the Pagan community. This was why, these readers explained, this information was a high-level secret in their tradition, and why god-possession was only "performed" in private among trained and trusted members. Protecting the masses from each other, rather than from the spirits, seems to be the first line of concern—and to be fair, it is a legitimate problem. This chapter will discuss what to do with people who are deliberately and knowingly pretending to be possessed, rather than those who are simply enthusiastically deluding themselves into believing it.

The first thing to keep in mind is that the people who are most likely to fake god-possession are people who do not actually believe wholly in the gods to begin with. As we have discussed in chapter 3, Cosmologies, the phenomenon of god-possession is a strongly polytheistic one. Natural horses soon learn the personal nature of deities; they also learn that their deities can be offended. Among those who are natural horses, a frequent comment about anyone repeatedly faking deity-possession is, as Ari says:

> *You think that the gods don't notice when they are invoked in this way, even without the proper intent and result? What people who fake possessions don't understand is that they are playing with fire. If you pretend to be possessed by deity X, well, you're placing yourself directly in the path of two extremely dangerous results. First, deity X could become offended and smite you. This will happen even if you don't believe in any of this—trust me, belief is not required in order to receive a smiting, although if you don't believe in the gods, you probably won't believe this. Second, deity X might take your actions as offering yourself to actually be their servant, and they might just show up and claim you. I've seen this happen at least once. Among some pantheons, mimicking a god for the public is lawfully offering yourself to that god, and they might just show up and make it a reality—and then you won't be able to back out, ever, because you put the sign on your forehead. If you're really stupid-unlucky, you'll get both claimed and smited. Those who don't believe in gods should stay far away from*

anything to do with them, for their own safety. The Universe is perfectly capable of avenging itself in the most appropriate way.

While every possession—and every deity and spirit—is different, many Neo-Pagans have been compiling accounts of the externally visible hallmarks of a real god-possession experience, and comparing them in order to find common ground. The following is a basic list of things to look for if you can't psychically see the immense change in aura and astral body that a possession creates. If your situation is violating these rules, there may well be something fishy going on.

1. The deity does not advocate for the horse. God X doesn't start telling the folks listening how great Joe (whose body they are borrowing) is, or why they should listen to Joe. The deity usually treats the body as if it is their own, and doesn't refer to the horse much at all. They may have an inner dialogue going with the horse, but that's between them, and onlookers never see or hear it. In general, an overemphasis on issues pertinent to the horse, vendettas, favored politics, and so on, is a huge warning sign. If the "deity" starts lashing out over an issue personal to the horse, it's worth taking a second look.
2. If the deity does refer to the horse, they will very rarely refer to them by name. More likely they'll say "this one" or something like that. This is because being called by name can actually shake many horses out of the possession and call them back to themselves (a useful trick for helping someone ground afterward if they're having difficulties coming all the way back). In some Afro-Caribbean religions, the orisha or lwa may not recognize themselves as being in a horse, although we've never had this happen with European deities.
3. Beware overstressing of the archetype of the deity: most possessions are unique. If it's nothing but a carbon copy of lore or what you would read in a book, but it never gets "high," never gets

personal, or beyond the assumed archetype, it's worth questioning. In most possessions, the deity gets personal. It goes beyond and yet doesn't feel distant. They are right there with you.

4. Don't be bothered by a lack of supernatural manifestations. That doesn't mean that it's not a true possession. Not all possessions are going to involve healing or divination. Some of the most powerful do not. The gods, after all, are not there to do parlor tricks.
5. The support staff will get a better understanding with repeated possessions. If the same god or goddess goes into the same person on more than one occasion, it becomes easier to see the pattern. Sometimes, a deity will refer to something they've said in a previous possession, even if that possession occurred in another horse.

Heathen spirit-worker Galina Krasskova writes:

A Lukumi friend of mine offered this advice: Take the first possession at face value . . . there's just not empirical evidence beyond that. Note, however, that in subsequent ones, the crisis situation of possession (by the same deity) tends to produce the same symptoms in the horse. This is a tell. The way that the individual horse reacts to that specific crisis, that particular deity, will be through certain signals, movements, and gestures, which indicate that the horse is about to be possessed. The horse (him- or herself) may not be aware of this. When I was possessed by a goddess at a public gathering recently, one of my handlers, also a horse, noted that as she was settling herself in me, she kept making a specific hand gesture—I've no idea what it was—and he noted it's exactly the same gesture that his patron goddess and god will make when one of them is trying to ride him and he's resisting . . . But most important, as a person witnessing, trust what it is you see and feel more than anything else. How do you feel about what it is you're witnessing? It should have emotional impact; you should feel something.

AMATEUR FAKERS: DRAMA QUEENS

The most common sort of faked possession comes from people who are insecure drama queens. These folks desperately want to be seen as important, and believe that this will gain them status and attention. And it usually does, at least at first. Part of what will discourage this, or nip it quickly in the bud, is if the elders of the group already have a policy on god-possession in place, including how they will react if someone suddenly "comes down with it," as drama queen fakers usually stage it. In Vodou the reglamen and folk custom provide a structure in which possessions can take place, as well as a means for dealing with sudden involuntary possessions. If your group does not have the luxury of a long tradition, you are going to have to improvise. It helps if the group already has a policy about the way in which public ritual god-possession can happen, and that it excludes sudden appearances (see the appendix on Asphodel Public Ritual). This policy should have been formally (and perhaps ritually) stated to both the group *and the gods,* so that the likelihood of a sudden possession is very small to begin with.

The elders need to agree that they will all react calmly and purposefully, and that the first order of business will be to respectfully request that the deity come again another time when they can be properly honored, if they are present. If the individual comes to the elders with a story of being possessed, this can be checked out discreetly without making them feel special, which will discourage the attention-seekers. A dispassionate divination procedure can be most helpful in these matters. It is far easier to fool individuals than to fool the runes or yarrow stalks. There is also less potential for drama in saying, "The tarot says that you should ignore this 'possession' and concentrate on something else" than in accusing someone of deceit.

THE PROFESSIONALS: CON ARTISTS

In a full-on possession ritual, the horse literally *is* the god, goddess, or spirit in question. Their words should be treated with utmost respect and seriousness, their suggestions should be given enormous weight and, barring very good reasons to the contrary, their orders obeyed. This provides great incentive for a con artist to master the fine art of faking possessions for fun and profit.

Fortunately, most drama queens are pretty transparent even to people who don't have the Sight. The attention-addicts and smarmy wankers claiming "I am Pan and you must sleep with me" generally manage only to make themselves look silly. The real problems are the smart parasites, the ones who make a career or a serious hobby out of using vulnerable people for fun and profit. A newcomer who doesn't have or hasn't developed psychic discernment is easy pickings, and will need to approach a supposed horse with considerable caution.

One of the problems is that while a deity does not advocate for the horse, they might well give advice like "Respect your Elders and your leaders," or "Sometimes you have to follow orders even when you don't understand them," or "You must be willing to make sacrifices for important things." Innocuous statements like these can indeed be faked to browbeat members into submission and stifle dissent, and a master manipulator is likely to use this kind of behavior when confronted with skepticism or challenges to their authority. Fraudsters are often very skilled at presenting themselves as tireless servants to the Greater Good, and wrapping themselves in the mantle of one Cause or another. A smart fraudster won't say, "I, Thor, demand that you give your car to my horse." Instead, they might have "Thor" make comments about how some people were giving their all to Saving the World, and it would be nice if others would do their part and chip in. It's not a clumsy "you must do this," but rather a very powerful encouragement to do whatever benefits the "horse."

Again, divination can be your best friend in these situations. If you are regularly getting one message from the "horse" and another message from your divinations, you need to examine the possessions. You need to look not just at the purported horse but at the group as well. What are the participants in these rituals getting for their time and trouble? Are they becoming better people? Are they gaining more self-awareness and finding themselves more able to cope with the various stressors of day-to-day life? If it seems like everybody involved in the circle is miserable and barely functional, and that the god-visitations cause the group more anguish than any feelings of divine connection, perhaps it might be time for a moratorium on such things, and the "horses" closely scrutinized. A leader who is relying on faked possessions to maintain control will invariably evidence other inappropriate behaviors. However, just because a group or leader is dysfunctional does not mean that the possessions are faked. (Anyone who has ever been involved in Vodou knows that the lwa will happily show up in some extremely chaotic and unhealthy situations.) However, if a group appears to be by and large sound, productive, and functional, it's overwhelmingly likely that the possessions are genuine.

God-visitations are often traumatic, life-changing events; be suspicious if the possession rituals seem too "comfortable" or "regularly scheduled," say, for every week. God-possession is physically and psychically rough on a horse and it isn't safe for them to do it too often, so a "horse" who is eager to leap into any excuse for such a situation and seems to have few ill effects is suspect, as is someone who claims to be able to horse any deity. Also, god-speak rarely involves inoffensive platitudes. Gods are much more given to simple words or phrases that get under your skin and resonate in your bones. If they never have anything of any real value to say when they arrive—if you never see any kind of actual tangible impact from their visits other than a general unspecified sense of goodwill—then you must question whether you are actually speaking with them at all. While many gods may spread feelings of goodwill, most will have specific encounters with at least some people that will leave an impact.

When it comes to supernatural manifestations, many Afro-Caribbean and Asian religions test their horses by expecting them to perform strenuous and dangerous acts such as drinking hot sauce, eating fire, walking on glass, and sticking spikes through their faces. Frankly, when one is dealing with average modern Westerners, there's good reason to be *more* suspicious of someone who regularly has spectacular possessions complete with such theatricalities. Sure, some people who are possessed by lwa eat fire—but so do some circus performers. A good cold reader might well give you "irrefutable evidence" that they were possessed, especially if you desperately wanted to believe them. It's not difficult to learn a few pretty impressive-looking tricks and present them as supernatural "proof."

Once again, it gets back to the *impact* that the god-visit has on the congregation. Ideally, it should garner something more than "Wow! Did you see that, dude!" There should be a feeling that you have been in the presence of the Divine, a spiritual shock and awe that warms you to your core and chills you to the bone. The reaction should be closer to the frisson you get upon entering a massive and magnificent temple, not the excitement of seeing a spectacular stage show. The only other immediate safeguard is having elders with the Sight and/or with close enough connections to that deity to check with the Source.

FRAUD—
AND FRAUDULENT CLAIMS OF FRAUD

When you hear people talking about fraudulent possessions, remember to consider both sources. In Vodou it's not at all uncommon for a houngan or mambo to claim of the competition, "She has no lwa; she just fakes it for stupid people." It's as easy to reject a possession just because you dislike the horse as it is to accept one just because you consider the horse a friend. Erring on the side of skepticism can be as bad as an excess of gullibility, in some cases. Remember also that the gods do not necessarily choose their horses on the basis of moral character or friendliness, a decision that makes many moralistic humans shake their head. In the long run, it's safer to be discreet and careful about coming down on a possibly faked possession than it is to offend a god or goddess.

So what do you do if you visit a group and see a suspicious possession? If you're a guest in someone else's house, be polite. We strongly advise against publicly challenging the possession without an exceptionally good reason (like stopping the "horse" from assaulting an onlooker or something equally dramatic). If you're dealing with an actual possession, you may well wind up dealing with a very offended deity. And if you're dealing with a fraud, it's going to be your word against theirs, and their followers are likely to trust them over you. Treat the "deity" with due respect while you are there, and then, when you are alone, check your suspicions via divination and see what the Universe has to say.

PEER CONSENSUS

Among Korean shamans, when the novice shaman has completed their training, they are brought to a gathering of elders for testing in a private ritual. A good example of this ritual can be seen in the documentary film *An Initiation Kut for a Korean Shaman* (1991), made by Diana Lee and Laurel Kendall. The elders bring a rack of ceremonial costumes that have been used by hundreds of spirit-vessels and are imbued with their presence, and spend the entirety of a day dressing and undressing the novice in every costume. If particular spirits have chosen to ally with that novice, they will enter when their garb is donned. This is known to be an especially grueling test, with the novice being possessed several times in one day; it is said that it takes weeks to recover from it. However, it serves an excellent purpose: the would-be shaman demonstrates their ability to carry the spirits in front of the scrutinizing second-sighted eyes of a whole quorum of elders who have the same abilities, and there is no way that a faker could get by.

If you do have the Sight, god-possession is hard to miss. The human body standing before you no longer has a human aura. Some gods shine so brightly that it's been described as trying to stare at something too bright to bear with the eyes. Some (especially some death-gods) are like black holes. Some gods have auras that expand out ten feet or more in a radius around the body that they are wearing. Some of the really older and less human-personal gods have auras so large that they may take in an entire field or woods, which may look at first glance as if the body is simply standing around with no aura at all, until you look further and notice how huge the situation is. Those who can't See have described the sensation of being near someone who is god-possessed as "standing right next to an electric fence turned way up." Some particularly talented spirit-workers have described how they looked at the horse and their Sight "telescoped out" to see the figure of that god "through" the physical body.

If you are an elder of a group and your group is not having any god-possession or the like, our advice is not to go courting it. If the gods want it to happen for you, they will make it happen, perhaps by sending in a new person who is a natural horse. This is not some new fancy technique like energy healing or tossing around Zen watermelons that all the novices ought to learn, and all the rituals become centered on. Be grateful that you don't have to deal with this, and go about your normal routines.

However, if god-possession has reared its controversial head in your group and you are one (or more) of its elders, your first job is to get more up-close information. The best suggestion is to make a couple of field trips to see what actual god-possession looks like. One field trip might be to a reputable house of some Afro-Caribbean religion (do call well ahead and explain the nature of your information-seeking if you want to have any chance to get invited to a serious rite and be able to "interview" people before and after), and if possible to a ritual by a Pagan group that is reputably known to do such things. Check out your impressions of both experiences. The styles of possession preferred by the orisha or the lwa are very different compared to those of most Western deities, but there should still be that feeling of trailing in the wake of something much bigger, more powerful, and more impacting than just a theatrical performance. (We also respectfully suggest that you pray or make offerings, the night before, to whatever deity or spirit(s) you might be seeing during the next day's ritual, and you may get a more direct experience.)

If even after multiple observances outside your own group, you and the other elders are not sure that you could tell a faked possession from a real one—and there's no shame in saying that, just as there's no shame in saying that you can't tell a gold necklace from a gold-plated one from a distance—enlist folks from other groups to come and help you with that, if needed. The farther away they are in personal relationship to your group, the better, as they will have a more demonstrable (to the group) lack of bias. If you're not sure whether a member is really able to open that far to a deity, you can have them come and check. Another possibility is a series of divinations on the subject, perhaps done separately by different people and compared. Still another measuring stick is having someone with the Sight who does a lot of energy healing to take a look at the "horse's" astral body; as we've discussed in chapters 10 and 11 regarding the health of the horse, such things can leave definite temporary or even permanent marks there that cannot be faked.

If a possession occurs in your group, or if a member says that it did or will, and the various evidence is all checked out, and it becomes clear that the "horse" had no rider, you may take any number of approaches. For a student, novice, or newcomer, a gentle but firm conversation will often do the trick. Remind them that faked possessions are bad form and that the spirits find them insulting. Rather than being confrontational and outright accusing them of lying, it is more tactful to tell them that you are assuming for overenthusiasm and imaginatively mistaking the depth of the experience, rather than willful lying. There is no shame in this; as we saw in previous chapters, even experts and practitioners disagree on the boundaries between aspecting and shadowing and full-on possession. Pointing out that ultimately the gods are the final arbiters on the subject, and suggesting that they back off and pray more to the deity in question rather than attempt to do anything public, will help them to avoid embarrassing themselves in the future.

If you're dealing with an elder, things can become a bit more complicated. You can state your concerns to the pseudo-horse or to your fellow members, but there's no guarantee you will get a positive response. If the consensus is the "horse's" word against yours, you may ultimately find yourself forced to dissociate yourself from your group rather than support fraudulent spiritual activities.

As we've stated, getting a useful policy in place for your group before anything difficult happens is a good idea. While we might advise against "we don't allow this sort of thing here" as a blanket policy, especially if the issue has already begun to arise, there are acceptable versions of this that still have tight boundaries yet leave room for the gods. One such example is, "A deity may bless us with their presence through borrowing the member of one of our elders only if they tell us in advance (preferably more than one of us, separately) in ways that are verifiable through divination, so that we might make the correct arrangements and properly honor them. Any deity who does not do this cannot reasonably expect proper honoring from us, and we ask that it not happen." This policy has worked quite well for several groups that we know of. Another variation is, "You may bless us with your presence once we have all the right things and people in place, but not until then." This would, however, come with an unspoken (or even better, spoken) promise to work on that.

And if you're thinking about faking a possession for your own benefit, here's one word of advice: Don't. Obviously, if you don't really believe in any of this, we can't force you to understand the danger . . . but you *really* don't want to be play-acting Odin when Odin shows up in a cranky mood (perhaps in another horse), and you certainly don't want a reputation as a faker and a drama queen. In our experience, deities have ways of outing egregious fakers: often they will cause the phony "horse" to slip up or harm themselves. Public humiliation hurts, especially when it's combined with some spectacularly nasty public injury.

MISTAKEN POSSESSIONS: WHEN OVERENTHUSIASM ABOUNDS

Noxious as they may be, fraudulent spirits or phony horses are easy enough to deal with. Dealing with sincere, well-intentioned people who mistakenly believe they are horses is a bit more complicated. As someone who has witnessed (or actually experienced) a full-on ride, you will have no problem recognizing it, as Mambo Vye Zo of Sosyete du Marche, a Haitian société in Pennsylvania, says:

> *I feel that having seen members who have had genuine possession states has actually set most folks back a piece. There's a big difference between saying you're possessed, and then watching the mambo be pale and withdrawn for an hour after being ridden by the lwa. They see the physical effort involved, they see the physical signs in the person afterward. All this brings home the point that while desired, possession is a lot of work, some of which isn't always pleasant. I can honestly say that no one in Sosyete du Marche would ever fake a possession—the reality is too scary to do so.*

This, of course, presupposes that a prospective horse has had a chance to witness genuine possession states. Someone who has not may become easily confused. It's hard to tell exactly where co-consciousness ends and a full takeover of the horse's body begins. There are no clearly demarcated boundaries delineating shadowing, aspecting, and full-on trance possession. Indeed, some might ask if it's necessary to draw those lines. One might argue that we are splitting hairs and playing semantic games here: As long as the gods are present, why do we need to classify the exact extent of their involvement?

Our postmodern culture places a great deal of importance on the individual's experience and "personal truth." Many will tell you that there's no One Truth, that everybody is entitled to hir own opinion, and that "facts" are all relative anyway. We aren't advocating a return to dogmatism or intellectual fascism, and we know all too well that any effort to define possession will result in people using that definition as a club to beat their competitors or enemies. ("They aren't really doing possession because they don't X, Y, and Z. We, on the other hand, do *real* possession rituals.") However, we'd also like to point out the dangers inherent in an approach that states "Possession is whatever the horse says it is."

For thousands of years, shamanism was something that only a few specially chosen and rigorously trained people could do. This doesn't mean that it was a "privilege"—indeed, many prospective shamans did everything they could to avoid the profession and became shamans only when they had no other choice. Today, anyone who can afford to buy a few books and attend a couple of workshops can become a self-proclaimed shaman. That doesn't mean that they have actually made contact with the spirit world, or that they know how to fulfill the roles of traditional shamans. (Indeed, more than a few shamans have found themselves cleaning up messes left by well-intentioned rattle-shakers who thought that mastering a couple of techniques qualified them to perform psychic healings and exorcisms.)

Given the increasing interest in possession, it's a given that we will start seeing "Possession Workshops" that teach interested newcomers how they too can become horses over a long weekend. Possession is not something that can be taught in a workshop or two—indeed, we would argue that, like perfect pitch, it's an innate talent that one has or does not have. What these students are going to learn is basic aspecting (something that most people can pick up with practice) . . . or, worse, basic acting skills. After the workshop, they will then be told that they are now "horses" and set free to act as deities for their audience back home, along with a certificate that proves that they are full-on trance mediums, despite what anyone with experience in actual spirit-possession may think.

Shadowing, aspecting, and the like provide a telephone line between the congregation and the deity. Like any phone call, aspecting and shadowing can be marred by static and interference. Subconscious and conscious preconceptions and wishes can get in the way of the actual message. (That's not to say that someone skilled in channeling can't minimize that static and provide a very clear message, but that ability is also an innate talent and not something that can be taught.) Possession, on the other hand, is a direct experience with deity. There's nothing standing between the congregants and their gods, nothing that could interfere with that message.

If you mistake aspecting for possession, will you also mistake your subconscious (or not so subconscious) desires for a message from the gods? It's not difficult to do—and it's even easier if you are receiving reinforcement from your group. Once you start presenting yourself as a horse, and have other people telling you that you're a horse, it's hard to say "Wait, maybe this isn't complete possession after all." On the other hand, it's quite easy to say "These messages are coming from the gods, with no interference whatsoever from me. Therefore we must treat them as messages from the gods." And down this way lies madness . . . or at best lots of time wasted spent chasing delusions.

Questioning a dubious possession from a group member can be painful and lead to all kinds of hurt feelings. If someone who has generally been proved truthful says they are possessed, why should we doubt them? We don't have access to their interior states; we have no way of knowing for certain that they maintained control over their body and ego during the purported ride. But difficult as it may be, we *need* to make certain that our possessions are actually happening and that our horses are truly horsing rather than aspecting, shadowing, or play-acting.

So how do you know that your experience was a genuine possession? If you have to ask, it probably wasn't. That doesn't mean that it wasn't a powerful, valuable encounter with deity—but it wasn't the experience we're discussing in this book. If this makes you feel that your gods think less of you, remember that possession is emphatically (and indeed by definition) *not* about the horse. We could say, "Not everybody needs to be a horse," but it would probably be more fitting to say, "Not every religious community needs horses." Once you get past the novelty, having the ability to temporarily carry a deity or spirit is no more or less special than having the rhythm required to be a good drummer or the sense of pitch required to sing on key.

And how do you know that your group's "horse" is actually experiencing possession rather than aspecting or self-delusion? This one is trickier. Yes, when in the presence of a deity there's generally a feeling of enormous energy, far greater than that generated by aspecting or channeling . . . but this is a subjective definition, and not everyone is sensitive to energy. One person's "overwhelming power" can be another's "moderate levels of chi." Mambo Tamara offers this suggestion: "Real possessions don't just tell us whatever we wanted to hear. I have yet to have any spirit tell me exactly what I wanted to hear, even if it was most of it or things were confirmed. There's always something, some phrase or some nuance or some event, that comes out of left field that causes me to leave my normally skeptical harbor. There is such a thing as a healthy sense of skepticism in these things, too."

As previously stated, be wary of possessions that seem too much like the archetype. One of the main reasons for possession is a direct personal encounter with a deity . . . and any personal encounter with someone you've admired for years but never met is likely to hold a few surprises. If your "horse" spouts typical platitudes and generally acts like the Hollywood blockbuster version of the deity, you may be talking to the horse's preconceptions of the deity rather than the deity him- or herself.

Mambo Vye Zo describes how Sosyete du Marche trains its members:

I think educating your people is a big part of the work. We've talked at length about the lwa, about their characteristics and their flaws. We have an enormous library of books, films, tapes, and recordings for our people to peruse and study. And we've said it's not necessary to have possession in service. Desired, yes, but only as a vehicle of communion for the community. We've talked endlessly about Vodou being community, about it being for everyone, and that possession is not an opportunity to do personal therapy in public. By taking these steps, I feel we've placed possession back into its proper context.

In practice, you will likely find mistaken possessions more common than fraudulent ones. Those who are given to faking possessions for melodramatic effect will typically misbehave in other situations as well; giving them the boot before the possession ritual begins will save you the public embarrassment of dealing with a faker when the ceremony is in full swing. As we advised earlier, when in doubt, you'll generally do well to attribute inauthentic possessions to overenthusiasm rather than willful chicanery.

Yes, I've seen so-called possessions where the individual was just aspecting and didn't know the difference. It's not that this is a bad thing, so long as we call it for what it is. Aspecting—bringing the energy of the deity through while acting as the deity—is good for a lot of things. It gives people a ritual focus, and if they speak to the person who is aspecting that god, the god does listen and hear them, even if the reply that comes back may be partially from the human's filter. But let's not call it possession. The ideal of a horse should be to do everything they can to make sure that as little of themselves is present in the experience to get in the way and color things.

—Ari, Pagan spirit-worker

THE PROBLEM OF CONSCIOUSNESS

Here we come to a point that may be one of the most difficult and controversial parts of the all-important question of what is a real possession versus what is faked. In one school of thought, the horse loses all consciousness, all memory of anything that happened during the ride, and—while the spirit is entering and exiting—all motor control. In fact, this is used as a "litmus test" of real possession as opposed to mere self-delusion. In another school of thought, the level of consciousness the horse has during a ride is more variable, although there is at the least a strong sense of dissociation, of being far away and not in control of the body, and a vague confusion over what happened.

It's a difficult thing. On the one hand, both of the authors of this book have had possessions that created total unconsciousness, and also possessions where there was some sort of partial consciousness. We are both convinced that the latter sort were just as real as the former, due largely to our clear and gut-deep awareness of the Presence next to us, taking the steering wheel in our heads while we were relegated to the backseat. Some horses have used the terms (scattered throughout this book) of being "in the backseat" or "in the backseat behind the safety glass"—meaning able to see some things, but not hear or control anything—and "locked in the trunk," meaning unconscious.

On the other hand, some spiritual groups will find the lack-of-consciousness line a good clear one to draw, aiding them in weeding out false possessions, and will not want to compromise that line. Mambo Chita Tann (Tamara Siuda), a Mambo Asogwe and current Nisut-bityt of the Kemetic Orthodox Faith, takes a hard-line approach to use of the word *possession*.

> *For me, and I am aware that people disagree with me on this, but it works where I am: If you remember it, it's not a full possession. With both the lwa and with the Kemetic gods that we occasionally get knocking on the doors of our heads, there is a distinct break in consciousness between "Oh, great, I'm about to get one—" and "Oh ****, floor!" If you can recall anything in between the going and the sudden rush of the floor toward your forehead, then it's not quite a full possession and could be any of those*

> *various in-between states. For me, possession is like pregnancy: it's not something you can be "sort of" or "partially." You either are or you aren't. I don't use the word* possession *to describe anything that isn't full, so I don't have to worry about nuances.*

While both authors have witnessed and experienced possessions that left the horse at least partially conscious, both have noted the profound and unmistakable sense of dissociation that is part and parcel of a genuine horsing experience. If the horse has any recollection of the event, it is typically fragmentary and incoherent, like the memories of a dream an hour after waking. Often this fragmented memory is accompanied by a feeling of standing outside oneself (not surprising, since the horse *is* detached from the physical body during the ride) and a sense of watching the events from somewhere else. Of course, to a psychiatrist, this is simply a classic dissociative state and has nothing to do with spirit-possession, but the likelihood is that this same psychiatrist wouldn't take any state as proof of possession, so the point is moot.

In spite of the firm "full-unconsciousness" line drawn in some African-diaspora religious groups, this belief is not always held completely across the board. Kenaz has also heard elder priests and priestesses claim that someone who is initiated to Asogwe level (the highest rank in Vodou) will never completely lose consciousness during a possession, even though the lwa has complete control of their body. There is a possibility that this emphasis on "losing consciousness" has its roots in etiquette rather than reality. It is considered very bad form to say "you did X" to someone who was possessed by a spirit. Instead, the horse will be told "Ogou did this" or "Ellegua did this." Saying "you did this" implies that you believe the possession was faked—a serious insult. We can imagine anthropologists trying to get an iyalocha or mambo to admit that they were just play-acting, only to be met with increasingly irritated statements like "No, Spirit did this! I don't know anything about it!" This was then duly noted as "subjects claim to be unconscious during these 'possessions.'"

Meanwhile, outsiders who came to the religion took this linguistic courtesy as a sign that the only true possession was one that involved a complete loss of consciousness. They believed that admitting to some vague and broken memories of possession would mean they had "faked it," hence they claimed they too were completely unconscious, while those who were courageous or foolhardy enough to report their experience were dismissed as frauds. Since money frequently changes hands in these traditions, there is plenty of incentive to smear one's competition—and more than one observer has compared the behavior of outsiders in these traditions to an episode of *Survivor,* with white folks squabbling among one another for control of the jungle.

Kenaz has experienced what Raven calls "locked in the trunk" possessions, but has also experienced Vodou possessions that involve an intense feeling of depersonalization and a sense of "looking in from the outside." Kenaz has discussed these possessions with elders in the tradition and was assured that this is not uncommon, so it appears that the question may be more complicated than some would have you believe.

There's also the point that different deities behave differently, and this is something that has been noted across the board by people who have been ridden by spirits as diverse as the lwa, the orishas, and Norse, Greek, and Semitic gods. Some deities, and some entire pantheons of deities, tend to enter a human body in a way that feels mechanically very different from the African-derived spirits. As we have discussed in chapter 7, Spirit and Flesh, many European deities seem to enter more slowly, and may or may not entirely "black out" their mount, depending on their particular proclivities. Whether the horse is relegated to the backseat or the trunk in these cases will vary widely. Some Western deities prefer to have the body to themselves; some are fine with the horse being somewhat conscious so long as they don't interfere; some will even talk to the horse in the backseat while "driving" their body, although this is more rare. Some horses prefer to be unconscious and ask the deity to make them so, while others prefer to be at least partly present at all times, usually for reasons of assuaging personal feelings of control. We've noticed that it's common for a deity to block out the hearing of a horse while the god in question is speaking one-on-one to someone else, because it is private and not for the horse's ears. Certainly for weddings of deities with their mortal spouses, the horse is as a matter of course "stuck in the trunk."

If the gods have come for a specific purpose, either because they are being honored in some ritual sense or because they have a specific message to give to someone, I rarely have any memory of what happened. It may be a full blackout, or it may be that all of the words that people say are gone, like the "mute button" was on in my head. I could see the mouths move, and I can occasionally hear what the god is saying back, but it doesn't stay with me. The words just go away, and it's like I never heard it.

—Fireheart Tashlin, Pagan spirit-worker

Loki was an interesting ride in that I had pretty much no warning beforehand. I was, again, doing divination for a client, only in this instance, one minute I was doing divination, and then I was gone. He didn't take a great deal of control over my body; he was mostly there to speak, but I was totally disregarded. He tossed me in the trunk, quick and dirty, and left me there. He did this two or three times over a span of several months. The Loki rides left me feeling more crazy than they usually do, because of the suddenness of it, and also because of something in Loki's energy.

I only horsed Ba'al once, but it was very intense. I started doing divination for a client whom Ba'al had his eye on, and Ba'al decided that it would be easier to talk to him directly. It took me a lot more work to let go enough to let Ba'al come in, and once he was in, I totally lost all awareness of anything. He left me in pretty bad shape. It was the only time I can remember that I've thrown up immediately after getting my body back. I'm told by the witnesses who were there, including the client, that there was very little, if anything, to be seen of me in the body while he was there. One thing that stands out with him is that he left me with difficulty in talking for time, as he spoke in a voice very different from my own, and it tore up my throat.

—Wintersong Tashlin, Pagan spirit-worker

Some active spirit-workers have noted that possession is different for those who regularly talk with and work with the gods and spirits. Anecdotal evidence suggests that the chronically "god-bothered"—specifically the folks who are full-time spirit-workers, in service to their religious communities and in constant communication with a variety of deities and spirits as allies, helpers, and masters, may have an experience that is more "aware" and "partnered," especially when the deity or spirit is one of "their own," so to speak. By "partnered" we are not referring to partnered control of the body—when you give it over, you give it over—but an experience where the deity establishes a connection, warns them that they are coming, allows them to open properly, moves into them with the grace of two people doing an easy swing-your-partner during a dance, and then may actually communicate with them while riding their body, separately from anything that is happening to the body or the outside world. This does not seem to give spirit-workers any advantage when it comes to the aftereffects of horsing—they end up looking and feeling just as run-over-by-a-truck as anyone else—but if there is generally constant communications with spirits in the rest of their life, it appears that it remains just as constant while the same entities share their flesh.

Of course, not all—or even most—spirit-workers are horses, and horsing is not a test of being a spirit-worker (or shaman, shamanic practitioner, seidhworker, volva, vitki, and too many other cultural names to list here). Real spirit-workers show who they are by their other works, and if they are horses, that is only one of many responsibilities. Generally they will also be very clear as to whether they are natural horses, because the spirits that they work with will already have told them, in no uncertain terms. Those who are horses have sometimes reported having been astrally "altered" by their spirits so as to be more easily possessed, or in some cases less easily possessed by anything except their particular patrons. However, all report that in the cases when they were partially conscious, it was clear that they had been "allowed" to be so by the possessing deity.

When it comes to spirit-work done in private practice as part of community service, as opposed to public ritual work, spirit-possession is sometimes done one on one as part of a reading or professional treatment. An example of this would be someone asking a question about their life path, and the spirit-worker opening to and horsing a deity or spirit who wants to answer that question directly. While this is not uncommon in Eurasian traditions, it is also sometimes done by some Umbanda practitioners, perhaps due to the influence of Spiritism. We have touched on this already, in the list of reasons for possession in chapter 7, Spirit and Flesh: How Possession Works, but its relevance here is that this is the type of possession in which the horse is most likely to be allowed some memory and consciousness of what the possessing entity said and did. According to spirit-workers who will horse gods or spirits for clients—usually because it is their patron deity or allied spirits and the client wants to talk with them more directly—when this is allowed by the spirit, it is to enable the spirit-worker to more effectively counsel the client. In the event of an unconsciousness possession in these cases, the spirit-workers generally assume that the deity wants privacy, including from their horse, and do not attempt counseling afterward.

Just as different gods or goddesses of disparate pantheons may have varied attitudes on, for example, whether or not to take a nonconsenting human as a god-slave (the Netjer place a high value on consent and won't forcibly take someone who refuses, whereas some of the Norse gods seem to take veritable glee in grabbing up anyone it is lawful for them to take and who they would find useful), they may also differ on what boundaries are appropriate for possession. These boundaries seem to be based largely on what was done in the time before the thousand-or-so-year gap of lost worship and lost connection; indeed, when they are asked by their bewildered horses "Why do you do it this way?" the answer seems to be, "Because this is the way we've always done it, of course!" with little attention (or caring) paid to that gap of continuity.

> *The first time that I carried Mimir, the beheaded giant of the Well of Wisdom, he was displeased that I was not willing to lie in the shallows of an actual pond with only my face protruding in order to bring him through. The first time that I carried Freya, she kissed—rather passionately—someone else with her borrowed lips, and I am only glad that it did not go further, because I am sure that it might. She was also offended by my drab clothing, and removed it, draping herself in scarves offered by other folk present. I've had deities arrive and complain that they did not get the right food, or the right drink, or the right sort of respect. In some cases, I negotiated—"I'm sorry, there is no pond here in suburbia, I will make a watery tapestry with a hole in it charged with watery energy and dipped in a pond, and lie under that on the floor, but that's the best that I can physically do." In some cases, I went out and got what they wanted and made sure that it was there the next time.*
>
> **—Gudrun, seidhkona**

In the end, it is the choice of each group as to where to draw the line. Keep in mind, however, that the end goal of all this is to have a closer relationship with the gods and spirits, and that while possession may be the farthest edge of this, it is not the first line by any means. Perhaps the best way to discourage overenthusiastic delusional "possessions" is, first, to make sure that many people in the group have a strong votive connection to the gods that you work with, and second, letting horses—and potential horses—know that any horsing may be challenged (by divination, for example, or experienced outside observers) and that this scrutiny is an accepted part of keeping the community safe and the elders honest. Submitting humbly to this scrutiny, and trusting that the gods can take care of themselves, is part of the appropriate humility of the position of being a divine taxi driver, anyway. The horse need not defend the gods against the people; the gods need no defense and can look out for themselves quite nicely, and if they choose to abandon a community, they will often take their horses with them.

The best defense may well be stressing that humility, making sure that the social "secondary-gain" rewards of being a horse in your group don't amount to much, and reminding everyone that the gods are watching. Deities have ways of taking down someone who is doing something in a deity's name for their own personal gain, rather than in wholehearted devotion to them, even if those motivations are unconscious. Actually, especially if they are unconscious—no one is quite as good as the gods at turning over the compost heaps of our complicated minds and forcing us to smell the rot underneath. A community always has the option of praying—and if it a public prayer, so much the better—that it be shown, as a group, the best ways to honor its gods and to make plain their presence, or the lack thereof.

PART SIX

The Future

14
Touching Gods
The Future of Possession in the Neo-Pagan Community

Possession is the big theological bomb that could split the modern Pagan community. Seriously, it poses a theological conundrum: either it's true, and those are actual spirits—and gods—inhabiting people's bodies, or it's fakery or delusion and they can be utterly discounted. There's no middle ground, or at least none that doesn't require more vague philosophical hairsplitting than reality can stand. In the end, either it's real or it isn't. Either that was Athena who said that stern thing to you, or it was Jane the priestess . . . and only if it was Jane the priestess do you have the right to be offended. Are we modern, skeptical, pretending-to-be rational Pagans ready to have our gods come down right there in the middle of the rite? Maybe we are, maybe we aren't . . . but they don't seem to be willing to wait on our readiness.

—Ari, spirit-worker

God-possession should not be treated as a fad. It is not something that one should decide would be "cool to do" to spice up a sabbat ritual. I do not believe it should be commonplace, nor that everyone should attempt such possession.

—Olorisha Lilith ThreeFeathers

I am initiated to Yemaya, and to the Egun. We take care of each other on an everyday basis, not just because a ritual is approaching. I have a daily practice that involves prayers, offerings, and mutual communication. Their presence in my life is a continual source of strength for me. Our relationship together keeps us all strong and protected. I believe that the health of the unseen world is dependent on the seen world, and vice versa. Possession is one tool used to keep all creation functioning in a whole way.

—Olorisha Omi Lasa Joy Wedmedyk

Union is at the heart of every mystical tradition, and possession is a way to experience a form of passionate union. I work to remove the barriers that separate me from my beloved gods, and in doing so, I become more open to them; this openness is essential for horsing or any other devotional practice. To me, divinity is an immanent force—ourselves and our world aren't separate from the gods, and the gods can't separate themselves from us. Possession illustrates this immanence very well; when they use our bodies, the gods are in the world and of the world in a greater way. Witnessing or experiencing possession emphasizes this connection, and helps build faith. So many Pagans shy away from the "F-word." They say faith is blind, but in reality faith sees something that is hidden to other people; experiencing our gods in this world and more fully understanding that we are never truly separate from them except through our perception—this shapes the way we experience every day. This is faith, and this is union, and it is very real.

—Silence Maestas, spirit-worker

IN HIS BOOK *Ecstatic Religion: An Anthropological Study of Spirit Possession and Shamanism,* I. M. Lewis discusses the social contexts of spirit-possession cults, and the fact that when they reappear as minority religions (as opposed to being the main religious paradigm of some small tribal societies), they tend to appear among the socially downtrodden—often women, lower-class and marginalized men, slaves, and former slaves. (This view ironically echoes the Viking-era prejudice that *seidhr*—Norse oracular mediumship—is "unmanly" and practiced only by women and gay men, a prejudice that has endured to the present day.) Lewis's perspective is, of course, that of the academic trying to find some explanation for the phenomenon that does not actually depend on the existence of spirits. However, it is interesting to note that where possession is spreading among Western Caucasian populations is, indeed, in a minority religion filled with people whose general life views are likely to be unusual as well. Or is it that the gods and spirits seek out this sort of demographic deliberately, because we have less to lose?

At any rate, this book is not the definitive manual on how to handle gods, nor could it be. That would take an encyclopedia. It is simply a vehicle to ease the Neo-Pagan demographic a little more safely and a little less frantically into a situation that is slowly growing from the roots up. Those roots are old, and they go deep, and although they have not seen trees in millennia, the first shoots are starting. Our faith is the fertilizer; our reverence the sunlight . . . but the force that drives them upward comes from the same place as the force that drives the grass, the trees, the shoots of wheat upward every spring. That force was cut down once, but we will not allow it to be stopped again.

Hail to all the Gods and spirits who bless us,
Hail to the Dead who came before us,
Hail to the Universe that birthed us
And to whom we will return in the end.
We praise you with great praise,

We honor all your many names,
We open our hearts and souls to you,
And, sometimes, our bodies.
May you bless us again and again
With the nebulaic intensity of your presences.
Hail to All!

Raven's Tale

Lammas 2006

After the first half of the Lammas ritual that year, I went off to the small cabin in the woods with my assistant, who dressed me solemnly for the part. It was a deal I'd made with Frey, golden sacrificial corn god of fertility and love. Do this thing for me, I said, and I will give you whatever I can give. He asked for a pole with his head and phallus on it, erected in my ritual field, and . . . my body for one day of the year. I was taken aback, not because I was unwilling—I loved Frey with great devotion, and would have given more than that. It was because He is tall and golden and beautiful with a huge phallus, and I am short and fat and balding and graying and, well, not very well endowed. He laughed and told me that no mortal man was endowed well enough for him anyway, so not to worry.

Dressed in the tunic embroidered with gold sheaves of wheat, grain-wreath on my head, bronze torc and amber strings about my throat, I went to the pole we'd made for him of cherry wood (his tree). I put my arms around it, the head high up in the air, the jutting wooden phallus just brushing the wreath on my head. I looked up at the Sun behind his head, and opened as best I could. Someone walked by, quickly, and left an offering just at my elbow. It was a cup of my wife's homebrewed beer, for Frey. I drank it. I never drink and I hate beer, but this went right down, and as it went into me so did he.

I remember there being bright light, everywhere, as my body walked back across the field to sit in the place they had made for him, next to his altar. His wife was there as well, wearing the body of a female horse who had volunteered for the honor, and he greeted her with a kiss. He drank more beer, and I faded out.

Later, I came back to myself walking along the path. He took the beer, and the food he'd eaten, with him; I had no symptoms of ever drinking anything and I was quite hungry. My assistant, who had been Frey's page up until that moment, was now my assistant again and caught me when I stumbled on the path. He got me to the cabin, undressed, redressed, back to the ritual field, and got food into me. The other horse was there as well, laughing with a slightly hysterical edge and being calmed down by her assistant. As we sat there stuffing our faces, a Norse Pagan man came up to us and solemnly thanked us for allowing him to see his gods. He expressed regret that I couldn't horse Thor, his patron.

"Not me," I said, "but maybe someone else, in the future. They are coming."

It rang true as I said it, with the last wisp of Divine force left like a residue in me. The horse beside me nodded, her eyes wide. It was true.

It is true. They are coming. Make ready, for there is no turning back.

Appendix

Asphodel's Ritual Structure for Public God-Possession

While historically I've seldom had the luxury of a ground crew, the first time I worked with a trained team of handlers I was absolutely amazed at the ease with which I went out and came back. They facilitated the whole process, watching over me and taking care of me throughout. It enabled me to release into the process of possession far faster than I otherwise would have and I had far fewer negative aftereffects. They made sure that I was taken care of properly afterward and attended the visiting goddess while she was in me as well. It was wonderful, and those who have the luxury of working with trained handlers are truly blessed.

And as to being a handler, I would say this: your role and duty to the deity, the care you provide to the horse is invaluable. It is such an important role and frankly, takes more training than being a horse, which is really a matter of wiring and gods. If you can't horse but have the opportunity to become a handler, please know that it is such an important role and that those of us horsing benefit immeasurably from your care.

—Galina Krasskova, Heathen spirit-worker

Being an attendant to the god or goddess, when they have arrived, is an honor and a privilege, a hands-on way of serving them and showing my devotion to them. Maybe this is something that modern independently minded people can't understand until they have looked into the eyes of a deity, but . . . that's the way that I feel. I'm not someone who likes to be told what to do, but for a god I will kneel, and give them offerings, and show my love and reverence—and what they give in turn, I do not have the words to express. On a lesser scale, helping with the ritual and the horse is its own sort of honor—you're making it possible to have them come through your efforts. That, and the horses are usually friends of mine and I don't want them abandoned while we all celebrate. Even a vehicle needs maintenance.

—Ari, Pagan spirit-worker

AUTHORS' NOTE

What follows is an edited version of the original article published by the First Kingdom Church of Asphodel. Certain concepts and measures that are already more than adequately covered in other areas of the book have been pared off, but the basic structure remains. This has been thoroughly tested and remains the best and most thorough system for safely doing public open Pagan ritual that involves possession. We highly recommend it for Pagan groups who already have members who are being plagued by possession.

THE PAGAN KINGDOM OF ASPHODEL is a church of devout polytheists. Our policy is that the Gods are wonderful, awe-inspiring, dangerous, and necessary. We believe that it is important to bring divine energy directly down among people who would not otherwise be exposed to it. We believe that being able to see and touch the Gods, in whatever way we can, is a Good Thing. We believe that ritual god-possession, a phenomenon found throughout the world and in almost every ancient culture to some extent, is a tool that can be used—carefully and with great thoughtfulness—to bring this divine energy to a Pagan laity.

When Asphodel formed, one of the central members had experienced god-possession as part of their sacred duties for some time, but it had generally been while alone or spontaneously in small groups. However, our group somehow seemed to become a magnet for unusual pagan practices (and a haven for the "chronically god-bothered," as someone once put it), and we soon gained other folk who also horsed deities. At some point, They began showing up at public rituals. As our rituals are not closed to strangers—we are a church with a congregation, not an initiatory mystery group—we ended up with the problem of deities appearing to and interacting with hordes of clueless newbies, some of whom were not even Pagan but had been dragged along by their partner to "see what this is all about."

There was a twofold dilemma here. First, members of the congregation who did not understand the situation could be upset, disturbed, or just bewildered by someone who suddenly walked into the crowd, perhaps dressed oddly, and began saying strange things to people. It wasn't just that they were behaving oddly, either; some deities would call people by names they hadn't been called by since high school, or say things that only that person knew, or just generally bring up strange feelings simply by being present. While this might be seen as "proof of deity" by some, it was upsetting and disturbing to those who didn't understand what was going on. Additionally, people had no model of how to act in the presence of God/dess.

On the other hand, the deities in question communicated very specific things to us. First, these were European deities who had not been able to appear this way to the people in hundreds or even thousands of years. They wanted this outlet again, very strongly. They felt that it was good and important to be able to appear to the masses in forms that could speak and communicate, for the sake of those who could not hear them any other way. However, they did not want to be disrespected. They had particular things that they wanted to wear, eat, and hold, and they wanted to be treated in specific ways. For some deities, we had barely any information as to what those parameters might be. For others, we had information about offerings that we could not in all practicality give them—large burnt offerings, for example, or human sacrifices.

In the Afro-Caribbean faiths—Voudou, Santeria, Candomblé, Umbanda, Palo Mayombe—god-possession is a regular part of their worship. Unlike European paganism, these faiths have continued in an unbroken line for thousands of years. The loas/orishas/spirits have had a long, slow time to adapt to changing formats and structures, such as the overlay of Catholic saints, the offerings of canned food, and so on. Our gods haven't had this period. They tended to expect what they would have been offered thousands of years ago, and it takes some careful and respectful negotiating to explain the new circumstances.

This means that we pray, a lot, and ask them to please accept our limits. We assure them that within these limits, we will do everything we can to please them. So far this system has worked well, although there is always the chance that a deity will visit and completely ignore our limits once ensconced. We've not actually tried this system with trickster deities yet, although we will likely have to do so in the future.

The first limit is that they have to warn us that they are coming, and allow us to schedule them in. This gives us time to research what that deity likes and have it ready, so we make it clear to them that spontaneity is not in their best interests. (This planning period also gives the horse time to work with them and get used to their energy.)

We ask them what they might like that we might have forgotten or not known about, which sometimes leads to shopping trips with the horse being "shadowed" by the deity, a situation that has their presence riding in the back of the horse's head but not in any sort of control of the body.

Generally, we will make up programs for the ritual, containing not only the time when each thing happens, but also some basic information about what we'll be doing, who is coming, what that god is like, how they should be treated, and how one is expected to behave. We've found that with the exception of those people with uncontrollable authority issues, most folk would rather know what is expected of them than be confused and make mistakes in a new and strange public situation. We are careful in how we word the program, as there may be people present who do not believe in the reality of the gods, or in the possibility of god-possession, and we would rather that they do not feel pressured enough by our assumptions of their belief to feel the need to act out during our ritual. One example of careful wording might be: "Some subjects of Asphodel have requested a ritual in honor of the (origin, type, and name of deity) on Saturday night. During this ritual, one of our folk will be connecting with the essential energy of this god(dess). While s/he is channeling (deity), s/he may choose to interact with participants and bystanders, as we of Asphodel believe strongly in participatory ritual. Please be courteous of this tradition; consider it a blessing of good fortune to be singled out. If you are not comfortable with the level of interaction, please move away politely. If you wish to approach the God(dess), ask the staff and they will arrange it. The rest of the ritual staff will be glad to help you in any way that we can."

Setting up for the ritual includes creating a special space for the deity to be in. This usually consists of some kind of appropriately decorated throne, draped in the god/dess's colors, with a table on each side. One table is decorated as an elaborate altar, with space in front for people to leave offerings. The other table bears whatever food or drink is to be offered to the deity through the horse, and anything else that they might want to use, handle, mess with, pick up, or put down. Some deities use their throne-space as a place to accept audiences, and when they wander among the crowd they want to be unbothered; others seem to prefer that their throne-space is a sanctuary undefiled by any save a servant or two, from which they can look out over the festivities, and when they want to speak to people they will come down. We generally ask them beforehand which is which, and we usually get that information intuitively while setting up the space and the altar.

Another policy is that when the deity gets up and moves around, the entire staff moves with them, unobtrusively fielding people and creating a space around them. The space is permeable—if the deity wishes it, people can approach them—but we make sure that they are never crowded or inundated, unless they make it known to us that this is what they want, and then we make sure the throne-space is kept clear for them.

When the public ritual actually happens, we have a staff with several positions, each trained to cover more than one of them. This staff provides a buffer between the onlookers and the deity, and also makes sure that everyone gets what they want and has a good time, gods and humans alike. While a small, intimate, well-educated group might not need such an elaborate setup, we've discovered by trial and error what is necessary for a large Pagan gathering where not everyone will understand what's going on.

I. THE HORSE

Another of the main complaints against god-possession by some members in the Pagan community is that it could be faked by unscrupulous Pagan leaders and used to gain earthly influence over their fellow Pagans. We are aware of the legitimacy of this worry, and although there is no way to guarantee anything to someone who doesn't know us, we strive to answer that worry with the "one god, one horse" policy. This means that we generally only horse one god per ritual (we've made exceptions, such as gods who are a paired couple, or family members, or who ask strongly to appear at the same ritual) and only one person is allowed to horse each deity, as opposed to Afro-Caribbean faiths where a single god might take over the "heads" of several people present, including unwitting bystanders. Those faiths generally have a context and structure that allows for this; we don't. One of the limits that we ask of the deity who wants to manifest is that they stick to the chosen horse and not go wandering into other bodies. If they are not satisfied with this limit, we generally have to respectfully decline.

Anyone who is allowed to horse gods in Asphodel must be someone that we trust. Ideally it should be someone that our core group has seen horse deities before, and is sure of. We have also been known to help people in other groups who have been told that they must horse a deity, but they don't know how to go about it. We find that our system aids a possible horse in opening up fully and receiving the god/dess, although we generally pray to that deity first to find out if the calling of this stranger is real, or if they're imagining it. If none of us get a verification, through prayer or divination, that this is a real need, then it doesn't happen.

Even with our experienced folk with the Sight standing by, and all signals showing that this is, indeed, a legitimate possession, we realize that not all folks are going to believe that this might not be faked, and we accept that. These rituals are not for everyone, just like any other religious practice. However, even if you disagree with the precept, it is best to be courteous if you choose to attend such a ritual anyway, and to acknowledge that we are at least sincere about our beliefs.

The horse's job during the weeks leading up to the ritual is as follows: Pray to the deity who you will be horsing, and ask what they want. As with the ritual presenters in general, if the horse can't make any kind of contact with that god/dess, then they might not be suitable and another horse should be chosen. Make a connection with that deity; ask if there are certain ways that you should be treating your body in order to make it a better physical vessel. Some gods might want purification rituals, others dietary restrictions, still others various taboos. These restrictions can actually help the horse in preparing for the ride. They create a slow ongoing sense of preparing a ritual space for the deity to come in, and they also work to jolt the horse back into their body when they are broken or discarded after the ride. For example, one horse abstained from meat and sex for a week prior to the ride as a purification; after it was over, the prep team handed him beef jerky as a way to remove the god's foothold and reclaim his own body. If there are particular things that the deity wants, or that the horse needs to go under or come back, the prep team should be apprised of these.

On the day of the ritual, the horse's job is to do whatever they can to maintain an open headspace. This may involve meditation or *utiseta* or prayer or chanting. An experienced horse will know what to do in order to get ready for a ride; some horses (and some deities) require very little preparation, while others may take hours. The horse should be given plenty of time and not rushed; you can't rush the gods and spirits.

Sometimes, no matter what the horse does, the god just doesn't enter fully. In this case, we stress that there is no blame involved. Sometimes things just don't go perfectly. Generally, we go ahead with the ritual anyway, but with the change that the horse announces publicly that s/he is representing the deity, but is not the deity. We have no wish to dupe the audience, especially since the ones who are more aware of such things will be able to tell anyway; a deity's aura is unmistakably not that of a human's. We figure that even if the deity has changed their mind, or something else is interfering, anything said to the horse will still be heard by them, and they will still appreciate the acts of worship and reverence.

2. THE PREP TEAM

Every horse does better with a prep team. While in the end it's a dance between the horse and the god/dess, there are certain experiences that make the entry easier, especially for a nervous horse. One helpful thing is dealing with costuming and makeup. We generally have the horse stand still and be passively dressed in the finery created for that god/dess; this reinforces the knowledge that their body will be offered up as a temporary sacrifice for that deity. To watch yourself being dressed and transformed (which can include not only clothing but also hairdressing and makeup) into a vessel for a greater power, not for any pride in your own appearance, can push the horse into the right receptive headspace.

As an example, for a female horse who was horsing a love goddess, the prep team gave her a ritual bath in perfumed water. They anointed her body with scented oil, dressed her, had her sit quietly and meditate while her hair was arranged, and touched her gently and respectfully in specific ways. For a male horse who was opening to an Egyptian god, we braided his hair into many small braids, and attached beads of specific colors to each one, singing and chanting quietly while it was done. Afterward, dedicated kohl from Egypt was applied as makeup, while reciting a whispered invocation. Decorating the horse should be done with the same attitude as one would prepare an altar for the deity; you are aware that the deity is not present, but you are preparing the sacred space that will be filled with them, and this must be kept in mind.

You should also keep in mind the needs of the horse, however. The horse should be comfortable with the prep team, and trust them. (Generally, we hold that the horse has the right to choose whom they do and do not want on the team.) They should have discussed the preparation with the horse before the ritual, and be clear on what the horse needs to open themselves properly. If they are nervous, the prep team should act calmly and confidently, reminding the horse that this is a sacred duty, and that they wouldn't have been chosen if the deity didn't find them worthy. Beyond the actual dressing (which is for the god/dess, not the horse), some horses like to be touched in a particular way to calm or reassure them; others find any extraneous touch a distraction to their internal process of opening to the deity. The prep team needs to stay with the horse through the whole process, and not abandon them; if the ritual must be delayed because the horse is having difficulty, this is relayed by a prep team member to the HP and the horse is never bothered with issues of time pressure.

Sacred costumes—special clothing that is worn only when horsing a deity—can take on the vibrations of that god/dess, to the point that some pieces should not be handled by any horse who could theoretically horse that god/dess, or it might start happening inadvertently. This can be an extremely useful thing for the horse, but the prep team needs to be careful. Theirs is the job of making sure that every piece is ready and in good working order well before the ritual. If the prep team contains other horses, no horse that has been ridden by that deity before should touch the ritual costume pieces unless they have already spoken to that deity and cleared that they will not be the vessel tonight.

The prep team positions can be held by folks who also hold down other positions, since it is strictly a before-and-after role. In fact, we've found that it's useful to have at least one drummer on hand for the preparing period, and if the page is a team member and right there when the god/dess enters, they can be on hand from the get-go. However, if the deity is meant to enter in the middle of the ritual, the HP and the shills will be focusing on the people and may not be able to be part of the prep team.

After the ride is over, the prep team swings into action again, surrounding the horse at a respectful distance and keeping everyone else away. Horses often feel disoriented and claustrophobic after coming out of a ride; their soul has been squeezed down into a tiny space to make room for something much larger, and even the crowding of someone leaning worriedly into their personal space can make them want to scream and run. The team should stand at a short distance, out of their aura (which may be a bit overexpanded to compensate) with everything that they might need at hand and in view. Unless they ask for it, do not touch the horse. This is very important. Some horses have been known to bolt and run when touched during the confused, irrational after-stage.

Experienced horses who are dealing with deities they've horsed before will usually come out of the blurry phase quickly. In some cases, people can be nonverbal for a while, or confused; having a loose ring of people quietly holding food, water, and blankets in view can help, as they only need to gesture to get something. Most horses feel dehydrated and want water fairly immediately. Do not give them alcohol or other substances; a cigarette may be all right if the horse smokes, the deity doesn't or wouldn't, and the horse is using it to get back into themselves. They may want to get to the bathroom; the presence of a deity can put off bodily urges for a long time. They may want to get the sacred costume off them as fast as they can undress, and the team should be ready to take it off their hands. They may want to wash their faces and hands, or get in the shower to "wash the god off them"; in one case a horse asked to be taken to a nearby pond and dunked in the water. The prep team waits until the horse is entirely back with them and doesn't need any more help.

3. THE PAGE

We used to refer to pages as "handmaidens," or even as "handmaiden, gender-not-specified," but people felt that was too tongue-in-cheek and we settled on "page." The page is an attendant to be on hand for the deity once they appear; they bring them food and drink, fetch things, take things away when the deity is done with them, and so forth. This job was instituted because we discovered that many deities would gesture to someone and inform them that they were to attend Them, or some similar command, and those people were suddenly seized with the urge to do nothing but stand or kneel at attendance, with their entire focus entirely filled with the god/dess before them. Now we automatically provide them with a page, to stave off spontaneous recruitment.

A good page should be courteous and comfortable with unobtrusive service, and be willing to have their entire will seized by the deity, which is what usually happens. Pages often report that they feel glued to the deity's side and totally focused on them, as if nothing else in the universe matters at that moment. It's basking in the shadow of the god/dess, but at the same time it is a position of total subservience, and one that may be somewhat ego-destroying for some people. (For the record, we've never had an instance of a deity mistreating their page. Some practically ignore them, some are commanding and keep them running on small errands, but none has ever been harmed.) If the deity gets up and moves, the page follows Them, making sure to stay always at hand but never underfoot.

If we can find out what sort of servants a god had in ancient times, we will try to select a page on that basis. A goddess like Aphrodite will want female—and femme—attendants; a god like Mars will want guards who can stand at attention. A deity who is known to occasionally request sexual attentions should not be sent a page of the gender that god/dess is known to choose as a sexual partner unless they are comfortable with that, because there is a chance that it might arise.

4. THE STEWARD

The steward holds the boundary between the deity's area and the audience. They generally position themselves several feet away, and anyone who wants an audience with the deity approaches them first. We've generally found that the deity lets the steward know who they want to approach them by making eye contact; if the deity is looking in the direction of the individual who has approached the steward, that usually means that they should be sent through for an audience. If the deity is utterly ignoring them and looking elsewhere, that's usually a sign that they should be politely told to try again later. Sending them through anyway is likely to get them ignored while kneeling at the deity's feet, or brusquely ordered away, which is hard on the worshippers.

The steward needs to be firm and have good boundaries. They need to be able to field the occasional pushy bully or rude drunk or anyone who looks like they want to be deliberately disrespectful and ruin the ritual for others. (Yes, there will always be those people, especially in an open public ritual where you can't be sure what strangers will show up.) This requires the ability to say no very clearly and firmly, and take no nonsense. If the deity rises and moves, the steward moves with them, circling them at the same distance, and interposing themselves between the deity's space and anyone who might be a problem. If there is a large crowd and a deity likely to wander a good bit, there might need to be more than one steward.

On the other hand, the steward ought not to get into an overly self-important headspace, thinking that they are "Protecting The Deity From All Who Would Malign Them." Deities need no protection. The people who the steward is protecting are the ones who they turn away, as some gods will punish those who are jerks in their presence. The steward should stay humble enough to realize that they are only the doorway to the deity's presence, and not the one who gets any say in it. They need to be constantly aware of what the deity is doing, and watching for signals.

The steward is also the boundary between the deity's space and the staff. If, for example, the deity requests something that is not present, but that could be fetched (from inside the house or out of someone's pockets), the page should not get up and run around trying to find it. Pages should never be out of the deity's sight and easy call. Instead, the page goes to the steward and tells them, and the steward calls over a staff person and sends them for the item, thus not disturbing the deity's sacred space with disharmonious details.

5. THE HIGH PRIEST/ESS

The HP (or in some cases, we've referred to them as the emcee) is the one who actually runs the ritual. They get the crowd prepared for the appearance of the deity; they read the invocations; they do all the public speaking to explain what's going on; they wind the crowd down after the deity has left and finish things up. They are the ones that the crowd will look to when they're not looking at the deity, in order to understand what's going on and what to do.

A good HP should be able to speak fluently and articulately, command the attention of a large crowd of people, and do any prepared invocations without too much dependence on printed papers. They should be flexible enough to bend the ritual if the deity suddenly decides to make changes, and they should know how to signal the drummers, make quick eye contact with the steward to know that everything is all right, and roll with the punches. Sometimes god-possession rituals go absolutely according to plan, and sometimes they don't. A well-trained HP will be able to adapt to changing circumstances gracefully, and bring the entire crowd with them.

They also need to be able to project the right kind of reverential attitude, in a way that it will spread to the rest of the crowd. That might be reverent-enthusiastic, or reverent-solemn, or reverent-intense, depending on the nature of the deity. The HP must also walk a fine line between commanding enough attention to direct the audience, and not pulling attention away from the deity in a way that could be interpreted as arrogance or pride.

If the deity wants someone to do specific religious acts for the public, it will probably end up being the HP. This could include kneeling, singing, making offerings, sacrificing something of their own, or in the cases of sacrificed gods, being the one who wields the knife. Like the position of page, this position should not be held by anyone who cannot offer genuine reverential respect for that god/dess. Mere general respect is not enough; they must honestly have a place for that deity in their soul.

6. SHILLS

Shills are a great thing, and we suggest that you have at least one of them in the audience at all times. Being a shill is a good position for group members who want to take part wholeheartedly in the ritual, without having their experience interrupted by staff work, but who still want to help. The shill is briefed beforehand by the HP as to what the ritual will be, and may be given cues to memorize. When the HP calls out an invocation line that requires a response, they are the first to make the response. When the HP tells the crowd to move to a particular area, they are the one who jumps up and leads. When the HP says that people may approach the deity, they are the first one up. If they have nothing in particular to ask of that deity, they should welcome them, preferably with enthusiasm.

The main quality of a shill is that they should be anything but shy. Their job is to model appropriate behavior to the audience, and they need to do it boldly and confidently. The better briefed they are by the HP, the better they will be able to do their job.

7. DRUMMERS

As anyone in the Afro-Caribbean traditions can tell you, god-possession always works better with drumming. In those faiths, the drummers are all trained in the specific rhythm used to call each god into the horses. There is some evidence in research that at least some ancient European cultures had such divine rhythms as well, but unfortunately not a single one has survived. While we are fairly confident that future spirit-drummers will rediscover them through interactions with those gods, right now we have to do the best we can with what we have.

Being a horse is not an easy thing; sometimes the horse is unable to remain submerged and begins to rise, which can interfere with the deity's manifestation. A drumbeat that goes on throughout the entire ritual is an excellent tool for keeping them in trance. Even a single person with a frame drum and a slow, plain beat is remarkably helpful. Of course, if you have skilled drummers who are also spirit-workers, they can do more. They can pray and drum to the deity beforehand, and ask them to give the proper rhythm to bring them into manifestation. They can help the prep team by drumming the god into the horse.

During the ritual, they can energetically direct their drumming toward the deity, in order to feed them.

If there are going to be drummers, they should not be required to do anything except concentrate on the drumming. Ideally there should be at least two, if not more, so that each drummer can manage to eat, drink, or at least relieve themselves without worrying about ruining the atmosphere. They should be given a space to park themselves and their drums, and not have to get up except for bathroom purposes; this means that the staff should bring them food and drink, and keep checking in periodically to make sure that they are taken care of.

8. THE STAFF

The staff is in charge of physical objects. If there are props, they find them and have them ready to hand. They set up the ritual area and the altar; they make sure that food and drink are available to the god/dess, the drummers, and all the people (if you are feeding everyone); they serve food and pass around or collect group items; they hand out programs and tell people where to hang their coats and where to gather. They pull out the corkscrew, the HP's wand, and the extra copy of the script as the person in question is looking around worriedly. Remember that a staff is a thing that you lean on in order to get somewhere; that's their job. The more staff people that you have, the less each has to cope with, and the more present and active they are able to be for the actual ritual.

The other job of the staff is to reassure the audience. They do this by having a calm and unsurprised demeanor, doing what has to be done, and never freaking out. We often like to have one or two staff members who have the additional job of talking to people afterward who have questions. Sometimes these questions are purely curiosity about the ritual phenomenon; others are personal questions coming from someone who may have been deeply moved for good or ill by the ritual, and needs to be talked down from a difficult space. It's good if these particular staff members are knowledgeable in what's going on, have helped with several such rituals, and are good at counseling people.

We've found that this system, with a well-trained group, can be used to safely perform public god-possession rituals for mixed Pagan groups where many of the people have never seen anything like this before, or even groups that are mixed Pagan and non-Pagan. If there are going to be a significant number of non-Pagans present, more care may need to be taken with the program, explaining what this is supposed to be in words that they can understand or at least respect, and emphasizing that this is Our Tradition, and while belief is not required, courteously going along with things (or at least staying quietly in the background and observing) is.

You might well ask why a group would do a public ritual featuring possession at some unknown festival, on unfamiliar territory, with a crowd of strangers. The answer is: Because the spirits asked for it. At some point during Asphodel's development of this structure, some of our members went to an open Pagan Pride Day in a park and witnessed a possession ritual done by another group. We had, to date, only done these things on our own home ground, in controlled space, and we were impressed. Afterward, as they were packing up, we complimented them on their bravery. The horse rolled his eyes and said, "Yeah, like we had a choice!" We all grinned, understanding. It's a hazard of getting your group intimately involved with the gods, as opposed to distantly involved: They ask more of you, and you give it to them, because you become more devoted to them. At the same time, you receive more attention from them, which is worth all the work and taking of risks. Touching the gods for that one moment is an unforgettable experience.

Notes

CHAPTER 1. METAPHYSICS AND HISTORY: A LONG VIEW OF SPIRIT POSSESSION

1. http://dictionary.reference.com/search?q=possession. Accessed March 14, 2006.
2. Gonzalo Fernández de Oviedo, "Devil Worship: Consuming Tobacco to Receive Messages from Nature." In *Shamans Through Time,* Jeremy Narby and Francis Huxley, eds. (New York: Jeremy Tarcher/Penguin, 2004), 12.
3. Ram Charran, "Incest, the Silent Killer." Available at www.swamiram.com/articles/kalb3.php.
4. Frederic Lieberman, "Relationships of Musical and Cultural Contrasts in Java and Bali." Available at http://arts.ucsc.edu/faculty/lieberman/contrasts.html.
5. Denis Diderot and Colleagues, "Shamans Are Imposters Who Claim They Consult the Devil—And Who Are Sometimes Close to the Mark." In *Shamans Through Time,* Narby and Huxley, eds. (New York: Jeremy Tarcher/Penguin, 2004), 32.
6. Quoted in S. N. Chiu, "Historical, Religious, and Medical Perspectives of Possession Phenomenon," *Hong Kong Journal of Psychiatry* 10 (1) (2000): 14–18.
7. T. K. Oesterreich, *Possession: Demoniacal and Other* (New York: Lyle Stuart, 1974), 377.
8. Wilma E. Wake, "Swedenborg and Andrew Jackson Davis." *Studia Swedenborgia* 11 (2) (May 1999). Available at www.baysidechurch.org/studia/studia.cfm?ArticleID=172&VolumeID=42&AuthorID=56&detail=1.

9. "Harriet Beecher Stowe—Only Holding the Pen." Available at www.spirithistory.com/hbstowe.html.
10. Eliah W. Capron, *Modern Spiritualism, Its Facts and Fanaticisms, Its Consistencies and Contradictions* (Boston: Bela Marsh, 1855; reprint, New York, 1976), 338.
11. "Seybert Commission Report: Mr. Fullerton's Introduction." Available at http://ncas.org. ncas.org/seybert/fullerton.html.
12. Ibid.
13. Henry S. Olcott, "People from the Other World" (1874), The Theosophical Society. Available at www.theosophical.org/resources/library/olcott-centenary/ts/otherworld.htm. Accessed May 2, 2007.
14. H. P. Blavatsky, "Are Chelas Mediums?" (1884). Available at www.blavatsky.net/blavatsky/arts/AreChelasMediums.htm. Accessed May 2, 2007.
15. Ibid., "The Key to Theosophy, Section 14" (1889). Available at www.theosociety.org/pasadena/key/key-14.htm. Accessed May 1, 2007.
16. William Q. Judge, "The Ocean of Theosophy: Chapter 5" (1893), The Theosophical Society. Available at www.theosociety.org/pasadena/ocean/oce-hp.htm. Accessed May 1, 2007.
17. Ibid., "The Ocean of Theosophy: Chapter 17" (1893), The Theosophical Society. Available at www.theosociety.org/pasadena/ocean/oce-17.htm. Accessed May 2, 2007.
18. Doug Skinner, "The Immortal Count." *Fortean Times* 146 (May 2001). Available at www.forteantimes.com/articles/146_stgermain.shtml. Accessed May 2, 2007.
19. Kevin Williams, "A Biography of Edgar Cayce." Available at www.near-death.com/experiences/cayce02.html. Accessed May 2, 2007.
20. J. Gordon Melton, "Edgar Cayce and Reincarnation: Past Life Readings as Religious Symbology" (1994). Available at www.ciis.edu/cayce/melton.html. Accessed May 2, 2007.
21. Jack Romano, "The Sleeping Prophet." *Fortean Times* 165 (December 2002). Available at www.forteantimes.com/articles/165_cayce.shtml. Accessed May 2, 2007.
22. "Seth on Wealth and Abundance." From *The Seth Audio Collection,* vol. 1, tape 1, selection 3, excerpt C. Available at www.sethlearningcenter.org/q_wealth_abundance.html. Accessed May 2, 2007.
23. Ramtha's School of Enlightenment, "Greetings from JZ Knight." Available at www.ramtha.com/html/aboutus/about-jz.stm. Accessed May 2, 2007.

24. Ramtha's School of Enlightenment, "About Us" (2006). Available at www.ramtha.com/html/aboutus/aboutus.stm. Accessed May 2, 2007.
25. Kate Connelly, "Medium Wins Channeling Right." *The Guardian*, June 9, 1997. Available at www.rickross.com/reference/ramtha/ramtha6.html. Accessed May 2, 2007.
26. Mircea Eliade, *Shamanism: Archaic Techniques of Ecstasy*, Willard R. Trask, trans. (Princeton, N.J.: Princeton University Press, 1992), 450.

CHAPTER 2.
THE GEOGRAPHY OF SPIRIT-POSSESSION

1. Christina K. Campo-Abdoun, "Zar: Power and Meaning," Center for Arabic Culture. Available at www.cacac.org/Christina_Campo_Abdoun_Zar_Power_And_Meaning.htm. Accessed April 18, 2007.
2. Karol Harding, "The Zar Revisited." *Crescent Moon* (July–August 1996): 9.
3. Ibid., 9–10.
4. Dr. Richard C. Jankowsky, "Black Spirits, White Saints: Sub-Saharan Music, Spirit Possession and the Geo-Cultural Imagination in North Africa." Available at www.diasporas.ac.uk/assets/jankowsky%20sg.pdf. Accessed April 17, 2007.
5. Karen Allen, "LRA Victims Seek Peace with Past" (September 14, 2006), BBC News Africa. Available at http://news.bbc.co.uk/2/hi/africa/5341474.stm. Accessed April 17, 2007.
6. Quoted in Sam Farmar, "Uganda Rebel Leader Breaks Silence" (June 28, 2006), BBC News Africa. Available at http://news.bbc.co.uk/2/hi/programmes/newsnight/5124762.stm. Accessed April 17, 2007.
7. Francesco Brighenti, "Shamanistic Echoes in Rituals of Hindu Devotional Ordeals." Available at www.svabhinava.org/friends/FrancescoBrighenti/ShamanisticEchos-frame.php. Accessed April 18, 2007.
8. "Fairs and Festivals." Available at www.webindia123.com/MADHYA/festivals/festival5.htm. Accessed April 18, 2007.
9. Elizabeth Fuller Collins, "Pierced by Murugan's Lance: Ritual Power and Moral Redemption Among Malaysian Hindus" (1997). Available at www.murugan.org/research/collins.htm. Accessed April 17, 2007.
10. Deguchi Onisaburo, *Divine Signposts* (1904). Available at www.oomoto.jp/enSignpost/. Accessed April 17, 2007.
11. Kawamura Kunimitsu, "The Life of a Shamaness: Scenes from the Shamanism of Northeastern Japan" (1984). Available at www2.kokugakuin.ac.jp/ijcc/wp/cpjr/folkbeliefs/kawamura.html.

12. Häußermann, C. "Shamanism and biomedical approaches in Nepal: Dualism or Synthesis?" *Music Therapy Today* 7 (3) (2006): 514–622. Available at http://musictherapyworld.net/modules/mmmagazine/showarticle.php?articletoshow=178&language=en. Accessed April 17, 2007.
13. Éric Chazot and Jean-Pierre Girolami, "Art and Shamanism in the Himalayas" (2000), Tribal Arts. Available at www.tribalarts.com/feature/himalayas/index.html. Accessed April 17, 2007.
14. Sunthar Visuvalingam and Elizabeth Chalier-Visuvalingam, "Between Veda and Tantra: Pachali Bhairava of Kathmandu (Towards an Acculturation Model of Hindu-Buddhist Relations)" (1992). Available at www.svabhinava.org/vedatantra/vedatantra-frame.html. Accessed April 17, 2007.
15. Elizabeth Chalier-Visuvalingam, "Bhairava and the Goddess: Tradition, Gender and Transgression." In *Wild Goddesses in India and Nepal* (Bern: Peter Lang, 1996), 253–301.
16. Kevin Volk, "Shamanism in Mongolia and Tibet." Available at www.iras.ucalgary.ca/~volk/sylvia/Magic.htm. Accessed April 17, 2007.
17. Kevin Stuart, "Mountain Gods and Trance Mediums: A Qinghai Tibetan Summer Festival," *Asian Folklore Studies* 54 (1995): 219–37. Available at www.nanzan-u.ac.jp/SHUBUNKEN/publications/afs/pdf/a1072.pdf. Accessed April 17, 2007.
18. Boudewijn Walraven, *Songs of the Shaman: The Ritual Chants of the Korean Mudang* (New York: Columbia University Press, 1994), 6–7.
19. L. Maurizio, "Anthropology and Spirit Possession: A Reconsideration of the Pythia's Role at Delphi." *Journal of Hellenic Studies* 115 (1995): 69–96.
20. "Isabeau Vincent," Musée Virtuel du Protestantisme Français. Available at www.museeprotestant.org/Pages/Notices.php?scatid=136¬iceid=693&lev=1&Lget=FR. Accessed April 18, 2007. (Translation by Kenaz Filan.)
21. Barry Chant, "Undoing Some Myths About Jonathan Edwards." Available at www.pastornet.net.au/renewal/journal14/14c%20Chant.htm. Accessed April 18, 2007.
22. "Catholic Encyclopedia: Paraclete." Available at www.newadvent.org/cathen/11469a.htm. Accessed April 18, 2007.
23. "Catholic Encyclopedia: Montanists." Available at www.newadvent.org/cathen/10521a.htm. Accessed April 18, 2007.
24. Hoyt Edge, "Extraordinary Claims in a Cross-Cultural Context." Available at http://web.rollins.edu/~hedge/ExtraordinaryClaims.html. Accessed April 18, 2007.

25. Francis X. Hezel, S. J. (Society of Jesus), "Distribution of Spirit Possession and Trance in Micronesia" (1996), Micronesia Cultural Seminar. Available at www.micsem.org/pubs/articles/socprobs/frames/distspirfr.htm. Accessed April 18, 2007.
26. Ibid.,"Schizophrenia and Chronic Mental Illness in Micronesia: An Epidemiological Survey" (1992), Micronesia Cultural Seminar. Available at www.micsem.org/pubs/articles/socprobs/frames/schizmentfr.htm.
27. "John Frum," Vanuatu Hotel. Available at www.vanuatu-hotels.vu/country_guides.php. Accessed April 18, 2007.

CHAPTER 3. COSMOLOGIES

1. Margarian Bridger and Stephen Hergest, "Pagan Deism: Three Views," *The Pomegranate: The International Journal of Pagan Studies* 1 (February 1997): 37–42.
2. John Mbiti, "General Manifestations of African Religiosity," Afrikaworld. Available at http://afrikaworld.net/afrel/mbiti.htm. Accessed March 14, 2007.
3. Valdina Pinto, "Candomblé Cosmology and Racism as an Environmental Issue," The Veterans of Hope Project. Available at http://veteransofhope.org/section4_connections/connection_4h.htm.

CHAPTER 6. ON THE NATURE OF SPIRITS

1. Robert J. Wallis, *Shamans/neo-Shamans* (London: Routledge Press, 2003), 88.
2. Francis X. Hezel, S. J., "Distribution of Spirit Possession and Trance in Micronesia," Micronesian Seminar. Available at www.micsem.org/pubs/articles/socprobs/frames/distspirfr.htm. Accessed April 3, 2007.
3. Ibid.
4. Christopher Penczak, *Ascension Magic* (Woodbury, Minn.: Llewellyn Publications, 2007), 47.
5. Leslie Evans, "Spirit Possession Religions and Popular Rituals Flourish in Vietnam," UCLA Center for Southeast Asian Studies. Available at www.international.ucla.edu/cseas/article.asp?parentid=11811. Accessed April 3, 2007.
6. 1 Samuel 28:4–25.
7. David K. Jordan, "A Medium's First Trance." Available at http://weber.ucsd.edu/~dkjordan/scriptorium/firsttrance/FirstTrance.html. Accessed April 3, 2007.
8. Leslie Evans, "Spirit Possession Religions." Accessed April 3, 2007.

CHAPTER 8. HEARING GODS: A GUIDE FOR THE HEAD BLIND

1. Martha S. Rosenthal, "Physiology and Neurochemistry of Sleep." *American Journal of Pharmaceutical Education* 62 (Summer 1998): 204.
2. Cyd C. Ropp, "A Hermeneutic and Rhetoric of Dreams," in *Janus Head Magazine.* Available at www.janushead.org/3-1/cropp.cfm. Accessed December 4, 2006.
3. Erowid Hinduism Vault, *Aitareya Upanishad* (translated by Swami Prabhavananda and Frederick Manchester, © 1957, by The Vedanta Society of Southern California). Available at www.erowid.org/spirit/traditions/hinduism/hinduism_upani_aitareya.shtml. Accessed December 28, 2006.
4. Aristotle, "On Dreams," Internet Classics Archive. Available at http://etext.library.adelaide.edu.au/mirror/classics.mit.edu/Aristotle/dreams.html. Accessed December 4, 2006.
5. Kevin Williams, "Edgar Cayce on Dreams," Near Death Experiences and the Afterlife. Available at www.near-death.com/experiences/cayce14.html. Accessed December 4, 2006.
6. Sigmund Freud, *The Interpretation of Dreams,* chapter 1, section D. Available at www.psywww.com/books/interp/chap01d.htm. Accessed December 4, 2006.
7. Stephen LaBerge, "How to Remember Your Dreams." Available at www.lucidity.com/NL11.DreamRecall.html. Accessed December 4, 2006.
8. From the editors, "Stone and Bamboo Temple in Fujian, China" (January 28, 2003). Available at www.china.org.cn/english/MATERIAL/54660.htm. Accessed December 26, 2006.
9. The Asklepieion, "Temple Cures." Available at www.indiana.edu/~ancmed/curecult.htm. Accessed December 26, 2006.
10. Alan Siegel, "How to Enhance Dream Recall," in *Dream Wisdom: Uncovering Life's Answers in Your Dreams* (Berkeley, Calif.: Celestial Arts, 2003). Available at www.dreamwisdom.info/library/dream_recall.htm. Accessed December 26, 2006.
11. Aleister Crowley, *Magick in Theory and Practice* (Dover, N.H.: Dover Publications, 1976), 59.
12. Ibid., *LIBER Taw-Yod-Shin-Aleph-Resh-Bet (ThIShARB) VIAE MEMORIAE* (CMXIII), 2. Available at www.hermetic.com/crowley/libers/lib913.html. Accessed October 25, 2008.
13. "Schizophrenia Symptoms and Diagnosis." Available at www.schizophrenia.com/diag.php. Accessed November 28, 2006.

CHAPTER 9. SACRED SPACES: PERMANENT AND EPHEMERAL

1. Fred Roe, "Water Witching in the Ozarks," written November 17, 2002. Available at www.tuppenceworth.ie/biglife/dowsing.html. Accessed April 9, 2007.
2. Ibid.
3. The Dalai Lama, "Nechung: the State Oracle of Tibet." Available at www.tibet.com/Buddhism/nechung_hh.html. Accessed April 10, 2007.

CHAPTER 11. THE RIDE: PREPARATION, AFTERCARE, AND HARMFUL POSSESSIONS

1. Aihwa Ong, *Spirits of Resistance and Capitalist Discipline: Factory Women in Malaysia* (Binghamton: State University of New York Press, 1987), x.
2. Michael G. Peletz, *Reason and Passion: Representations of Gender in a Malay Society* (Berkeley: University of California Press, 1996), 177.
3. Randy P. Conner, *Queering Creole Spiritual Traditions: LGBT Participation in African-Inspired Traditions in the Americas* (New York: Haworth Press, 2004), 55–87.
4. Rich, Jewell Grant. "Erika Bourguignon: A Portrait of the Anthropology of Consciousness: Interview." *Anthropology of Consciousness* 10 (2/3) (1999): 50–58.
5. Conner, 9–10.
6. Ibid., 108–9.
7. Ibid., 28.
8. Ibid., 119.
9. Massoume Price, "History of Ancient Medicine in Mesopotamia & Iran," Iran Chamber Society. Available at www.iranchamber.com/history/articles/ancient_medicine_mesopotamia_iran.php. Accessed March 20, 2007.
10. Quoted in T. K. Osterreich, *Possession: Demoniacal and Other*, D. Ibberson, trans. (Secaucus, N.J.: The Citadel Press, 1974), 149–51.
11. Sacred Texts Online, "9. Possession by demons of disease, cured by an amulet of ten kinds of wood," in *Hymns of the Atharva-Veda,* Maurice Bloomfield, trans. Available at www.sacred-texts.com/hin/av/av051.htm. Accessed March 20, 2007.
12. Abu Ameenah Bilal Philips, *The Exorcist Tradition in Islaam* (Dar Al Fatah: Sharjah U.A.E., 1997), appendix.

13. Jeff Belanger, "Dybbuk: Spiritual Possession and Jewish Folklore" (November 29, 2003), Ghost Village. Available at www.ghostvillage.com/legends/2003/legends32_11292003.shtml. Accessed March 22, 2007.
14. Lopön Tenzin Namdak, "The Condensed Meaning of an Explanation of the Teachings of Yungdrung Bon," in *A Collection of Studies on Bon*, 34–35. Available at bon-encyclopedia.wikispaces.com/space/showimage/ACollectionOfStudiesOnBon.pdf. Accessed March 22, 2007.
15. Quoted in Belanger, "Dybbuk." Accessed March 22, 2007.
16. Mohammed Hanif Lakdawala, "The Exorcist!" *Islamic Voice* 17:03/207 (March 2004). Available at www.islamicvoice.com/march.2004/perspectives.htm. Accessed March 23, 2007.
17. Christine D. Worobec, *Possessed: Women, Witches and Demons in Imperial Russia* (DeKalb: Northern Illinois University Press, 2003), 119–22.
18. Moshe Sluhovsky, "The Devil in the Convent," *The American Historical Review* (December 2002). Available at www.historycooperative.org/journals/ahr/107.5/ah0502001379.html. Accessed March 22, 2007.
19. Worobec, *Possessed,* 3–7.

Index